Responsible Governance

Responsible Governance

A Case Study Approach

Steven G. Koven

Routledge
Taylor & Francis Group

LONDON AND NEW YORK

First published 2008 by M.E. Sharpe

Published 2015 by Routledge
2 Park Square, Milton Park, Abingdon, Oxon OX14 4RN
711 Third Avenue, New York, NY 10017, USA

Routledge is an imprint of the Taylor & Francis Group, an informa business

Library of Congress Cataloging-in-Publication Data

Koven, Steven G.
  Responsible governance : a case study approach / Steven G. Koven.
      p. cm.
  Includes bibliographical references and index.
  ISBN 978-0-7656-2059-0 (cloth : alk. paper)
  1. Political ethics—United States. 2. Political ethics—United States—Case studies. 3. Political corruption—United States.
4. Political corruption—United States—Case studies. I. Title.

JK468.E7K68 2008
172.0973—dc22   2007042567

ISBN 13: 9780765620606 (pbk)
ISBN 13: 9780765620590 (hbk)

This book is dedicated to the many people,
both inside and outside of the public sector,
who have supported ethical and responsible behavior.

Contents

Preface

The concepts of responsibility and ethics are ill defined. In the abstract, most Americans would opt to support responsible rather than irresponsible, ethical rather than unethical behavior. In reality, however, responsibility and ethics often come down to individual choices to engage or not to engage in certain types of behavior. These principled decisions can arise from personal convictions of right and wrong. They might also evolve from the ethical climate fostered by organizations.

My experience in the public sector supports the view that the behavior of public sector workers can be placed along a continuum from highly responsible to highly irresponsible behavior. I have gained insight from observing the behavior of colleagues at various universities as well as coworkers at the U.S. Post Office, the U.S. Census Bureau, and the U.S. Department of Health, Education and Welfare. Most significant, as a soldier in the U.S. Army during the Vietnam War, I gained an awareness of the potential for ethical as well as unethical behavior in large, far-reaching organizations. Soldiers develop strong survival instincts and often find themselves in difficult situations, yet at the same time they are representatives of the country whose uniform they wear and should act according to the principles embodied in those uniforms.

This book describes a number of cases in which egregious violations of responsible behavior apparently occurred. The intent of the book is to depict these violations in detail, not in order to castigate the villains, but to identify how organizations can foster more responsible behavior. The type of corrective action and even whether any correction is warranted depend, of course, on the eye of the beholder. I believe, however, that discussion of high-profile cases can shed light on what Americans as a whole think about permissible and impermissible forms of conduct.

As illustrated in this book, history is an important guide to the future. What happened in the past is likely to occur and recur in the present and future. If mistakes are not identified, they are likely to be repeated. Cases involving Boss Tweed, Tom DeLay, Bill Clinton, Hurricane Katrina, My Lai, and Abu Ghraib all raise important questions about American values, behavior, and guiding principles. How American governance evolves in the future, no doubt, will be affected by our current interpretations of behavior and the signals sent today regarding rewards for responsible behavior and punishments for the obverse. A clear, nonpartisan exploration of the concept of responsibility in governance should therefore, I hope, be of great benefit to present as well as future generations.

Responsible Governance

Chapter 1

Responsible Governance

A Case Study Approach

Responsible governance is fundamental to the legitimacy, stability, trust, and credibility of government. Government officials therefore have an obligation to foster responsible actions and deter irresponsible behavior. This is not an easy task since perceptions and definitions of responsibility are often clouded, dependent upon time, place, setting, and situation at hand. Given this ambiguity, it is imperative to define the range of acceptable actions by representatives of the government. Simply stated, government officials should possess a clear idea of what is responsible and what is irresponsible, promoting the responsible and deterring the irresponsible.

This, however, is not as easy a task as it sounds. How are government officials to determine the fuzzy concept of responsibility? This book employs case studies to describe what in retrospect appear to be egregious violations of acceptable behavior. Cases describe both responsible and irresponsible actions in the context of specific times and places. The cases chosen should be familiar to even the most casual observer of American government. These high-profile cases are discussed in detail. Each case concludes with questions that probe the ethical nature of specific actions.

Important to the cases is their resolution in terms of punishment. Ethical lapses can be identified in the abstract or theoretical state. More relevant to

the concept of responsible governance, however, is how public officials address those lapses. Are they severely punished, officially recognized with what amounts to slaps on the wrist, ignored, unofficially encouraged, or officially encouraged?

Penalties imposed reflect prevailing sentiment about how the existing political system interprets ethical violations. Penalties as well as the tone of reproach surrounding behavior convey a sense of acceptable and unacceptable behavior in a given time and place. This knowledge in turn is useful for assessing expectations of public officials and accepted means of chastising transgressions. It is postulated here that perceptions of responsible behavior for public sector workers are not static but fluid and that standards of responsibility are time- and place-sensitive. Responsibility therefore is a moving target, highly dependent upon the prevailing norms and values of given societies. Norms and values are considered in this text as fluid, but still centered in the dominant culture and history of a jurisdiction. Background culture and history are provided in the text in order to lay the foundation from which the concept of responsibility is constructed.

The concept of responsible governance is refined here through case study analysis of specific high-profile controversies. These case studies address not only the usual suspects in ethical lapses (sex and money) but also the issue of responsible behavior in times of war or struggles over political power. The legitimacy of torture as well as the legality of harming unarmed civilians is discussed through the cases of My Lai and Abu Ghraib. The limits of electoral manipulation are addressed in the DeLay controversy. The downside of patronage is observed in the Katrina case. The case studies not only relay the facts surrounding specific incidents, but also uncover the pulling and hauling of antagonistic forces locked in struggle to define acceptable and unacceptable behavior within the American political context.

The book recognizes that actions that define responsibility in governance are ever changing. At the height of the machine era in American politics, the use of inside information to amass wealth was standard operating procedure. The same action today would not be publicly accepted. At the time of the Kennedy administration, marital infidelity was not trumpeted in order to sell newspapers or increase television ratings. During the Mongol invasions of Asia and Eastern Europe, the slaughter of men, women, and children in villages or cities was accepted as a norm. Similarly, in many societies payments to law enforcement officials are condoned and justified as a way to supplement the incomes of poorly paid officers. Paying people to vote or plying them with alcohol as a reward is not unknown in American history. Money and politics always intermix and therefore the rationale for defining improper electoral behavior is not always clear. What is clear is that, at various periods of history, behavior that previously was viewed as morally acceptable becomes unacceptable. In a changing environment, the resolution of ethical conflicts sets new precedents that define the parameters of responsible public sector behavior. Such a "common law" perception sees the concept of responsibility as ever changing, but still grounded in history.

The case studies explored in this book cover a range of issues: sex, money, patronage, torture, murder, and electoral manipulation. All these issues relate to the official abuse of power and the struggles to define the legitimacy of specific actions. Alleged abuses of government officials involve the torture of prisoners (Iraq), general incompetence (New Orleans), electoral manipulation (DeLay machine politics), adultery and lying under oath (Clinton), and murder (My Lai).

Historical parallels can be found for contemporary controversies. Parallels exist between the political behavior of the machine era and more recent efforts by former congressman Tom De-Lay to control the electoral process. Similarities exist between the abuse of enemy noncombatants in prisons in Iraq (Abu Ghraib) and the abuse of civilians in Vietnam (My Lai). The perceived incompetence and patronage appointments of the Federal Emergency Management Administration (FEMA) are matched by experiences of the machine era. Dishonesty and attempts to cover up embarrassing behavior are not unique to the Clinton administration.

Since history is said to repeat itself, exploration of how certain behavior was interpreted at a point in time is useful in identifying perceptions of public sector responsibility. The actions of government officials as well as praise or condemnation of those actions provide a mirror in which to view ethical norms. Responsible governance mandates that the behavior of public officials is consistent with the approved standards of the larger society. If behavior is not consistent with societal norms, then the legal system reverses the imbalance by punishing aberrant behavior. In such a scenario, corrective action establishes the parameters of acceptable behavior for others to follow. Uncertainty is erased through the legal system as well as the court of public opinion. Punishments are set to guide future behavior and to steer norms to a new point of equilibrium. In addition to the legal system, other forces, such as family, peers, churches, schools, and employers, act to influence behavior.

Responsible governance sustains the legitimacy of public institutions. It deters irresponsible actions and promotes positive public sector action. This book focuses on particular instances when the behavior of public officials appeared to go beyond the limits of acceptability, thereby arousing intense criticism. Through investigation of these actions, students will begin to formulate conceptions of ethical public sector behavior and responsible governance.

This chapter describes the basic context in which perceptions of ethics and responsibility have evolved. It is assumed that an understanding of this context is a prerequisite for understanding contemporary behavior as well as assessing the punishment for irresponsible action. First, however, the basic concept of responsible governance is identified.

The Concept of Responsible Governance

Various writers in the fields of political science and public administration have endeavored to identify the concept of responsible governance (Friedrich 1935; Finer 1941; Schubert 1960; Rohr 1989; Cooper 1998; Dobel 1998; Van Wart 1998; Adams and Balfour 1999; Geuras and Garofalo 2005). For political scientists, the quest for responsible governance addresses the distribution of power, an issue as old as political philosophy. Public administrators have also expended much time and energy defining the concept of responsibility. For public administration scholars, responsibility relates to the conduct of public officials within public organizations (Friedrich 1935; Finer 1936).

According to democratic theory, democratic government exists to serve the people (Pateman 1970; D. Thompson 1970; V. Thompson 1975; Gawthrop 1998). The rights of the people and the obligations of the government are laid out in governing documents such as national and state constitutions, in local ordinances, and in legal precedent. In a broad sense, therefore, governance involves aiding the public by promoting its health, welfare, security, freedom, and happiness. Government promotes the public through specific sets of tasks such as treating illnesses at public clinics, assessing who qualifies for public aid, conducting military patrols in foreign countries, driving city buses, arresting law offenders, interpreting the law, and settling child custody disputes.

Implicit in each of these tasks is the understanding that responsible public organizations and representatives of those organizations will act in a manner that upholds the broad goals of aiding the people. Public sector behavior therefore must be consistent with furthering this objective. Public sector behavior in democracies also must be aligned with the nation's law, the mission of the public organization, and higher (natural) law. Identifying violations of any of these mandates, however, is not always easy. The case studies discussed in this book will help to identify violations of the public interest, violations of natural law, and violations of the rule of law.

The cases reviewed describe the killing of civilians in times of war, abuse of prisoners, institutionalized bribery, manipulation of the political system, perjury of high officials, and other forms of irresponsible behavior. Each case describes individual actors who exemplify both responsible and irresponsible action. To place cases in context, a review of settlement patterns and changes in those patterns is instructive. Context helps readers understand perceptions of responsibility since perceptions, values, norms, culture, and expectations of governance are not formed out of thin air.

In a relatively young country such as the United States, it is important to look to settlement patterns in the original colonies, the values of early settlers, the political beliefs of early settlers, the values of immigrants, and the moral controversies that emerged in the nation. In essence, this book argues that the norms of early settlers, efforts to reify early values, efforts to accept new values, and the continuous struggle to define the concept of responsible government shapes current ethical controversies.

The Context of American Governance

Early Settlements

America as we know it today is a composite of the people that settled the new territory as well as later immigrants. It is a cliché to describe the United States as a nation of immigrants; however, a mere 400 years ago indigenous Indians populated what we call America today. The new settlers came to Virginia, Massachusetts, the Delaware Valley, and the Appalachian region for a variety of reasons. Some sought their fortune, some religious freedom, while others were transported in chains. Each group brought with it its values, biases, conceptions of morality, and codes of conduct. Individual groups initially created their own settlements but after the Revolutionary War combined into a greater whole.

The ancestors of modern Americans did not migrate from only one country or continent, but most came from different parts of Western Europe. Early settlers, arriving from Spain, England, Scotland, Wales, Ireland, Holland, Africa, Germany, and Scandinavia, did not share identical religious, political, or social traditions. Later migrants included Poles, Hungarians, Lithuanians, Jews, Russians, Ukrainians, Czechs, Slovaks, Croats, Serbs, Italians, Portuguese, Greeks, Latin Americans, Chinese, and Japanese (Zelinsky 1973, 25). The perspectives of these later groups sometimes clashed and often merged with the views of earlier settlers.

Many historians believe that while the new groups exerted an influence on America's ethical norms, the earliest settlers wielded the strongest sway. This perspective is summarized in what has been termed the Doctrine of First Effect Settlement. Zelinsky (1973, 13) notes that this doctrine is roughly analogous to the psychological principle of imprinting in very young animals. The doctrine posits that whenever an empty territory undergoes settlement or an earlier population is dislodged by invaders, the specific characteristics of the first group able to effect a viable, self-perpetuating society are of crucial significance for the later social and cultural geography of the area, no matter the size of the initial band of settlers. The activities of a relatively small number of initial colonizers can thus have a stronger, more lasting impact on the cultural geography of a place than the contributions of many immigrants a few generations later. The northeastern United States illustrates how early colonial patterns marked the cultural landscape. Applying the Doctrine of First Effect, Zelinsky concludes that the culture of the United States was decisively British; however, three non-British groups (aboriginal Indians, black Africans, and various European ethnic groups) also contributed to America's culture (1973, 14).

Historian David Fischer (1989, 6) traces the creation of what we know as the United States to four large waves of English-speaking migrations. These early settlers came to the New World between 1629 and 1775, each group bringing its own sets of values and moral precepts. According to Fischer, the first wave represents an exodus of Puritans from the east of England to Massachusetts between 1629 and 1640. The second wave is traced to the migration of a small royalist elite and large numbers of indentured servants from the south of England to Virginia between 1642 and 1675. Movement from the North Midlands of England and Wales to the Delaware Valley between 1675 and 1725 represents the third great wave. Fischer identifies the final wave of migration to the new continent in the flow of English-speaking people from the borders of northern Britain and northern Ireland to the Appalachian backcountry between 1718 and 1775.

The four groups possessed many similarities as well as some differences. All these early settlers spoke English, nearly all were British Protestants, most lived under British law, and most were familiar with the concept of British political liberties. Differences between the groups, however, existed with regard to religion, culture, and economic perspectives. Prominent among the early influences on America were immigrants who settled in the Virginia and Massachusetts colonies.

Virginia and Massachusetts Influences

The first permanent English settlement in the United States was established in what is now called the Tidewater section of Virginia. The Tidewater was where the first slaves were transported to British North America, where white men first exercised the right of suffrage, where the first trial by jury was granted, where the first free school was started, and where the first manufacturing began. The Virginian experience, however, represents more than a number of firsts in American history; it represents the beginning of a new life for settlers.

Initially, strict guidelines were laid out for payment to the king of England for gold, silver, or copper that was mined in Virginia. Early times in the Virginia colonies were hard; the Jamestown settlers suffered famine, disease, despair, massacres, and civil war. To complicate matters, few of the original settlers were experienced in rural living, farming, or fishing. Many of the colonists were registered as "gentlemen," a class between nobles and peasants. Some of the new settlers were too proud to work, but too poor to survive without working.

Facing disaster, Captain John Smith put the gentlemen to work, declaring that the sick would not starve but that every colonist should gather as much as he could or be banished. Smith persuaded the settlers to cut timber instead of looking for gold, to trade with Indians for corn, to plant crops, and to tend livestock that had been brought over from Britain (McDougal 2004, 42). Under Smith's leadership, laws were established; wharves, warehouses, stables, churches, blockhouses, and defenses were built.

Early settlers in Virginia planted private lots of maize, beans, potatoes, carrots, and cucumbers. In 1612, a new variety of tobacco was introduced to the Chesapeake area and by 1618 Virginians were shipping 50,000 pounds of tobacco. Proceeds from the tobacco sales were used to buy food and other products. In 1629 the Virginians established a form of home rule and representative government through their House of Burgesses. By 1650 Virginia's population passed 18,000, with many of the new settlers characterized as "distressed Cavaliers"—nobles who lost their land in England when they sided with the aristocracy in the English Civil War (1642–1651).

Extremes in the distribution of wealth characterized the early Virginia colony. A few families possessed large tracts of land that were worked by many indentured servants and slaves. Families such as the Byrds, Carters, Randolphs, and Masons founded great plantations. Many of the owners of the great plantations became eminent orators, soldiers, and statesmen (McDonald 1907, 6). Under the more than thirty-year tenure of Governor Sir William Berkeley (1642–1676), the colony's population increased to 40,000 inhabitants and developed a social order that was very similar to the social order in the south of England in the seventeenth century.

Early Virginian society consisted of a very small and powerful class of landed gentry, a large majority of landless tenants, a small middle class, and in general a high level of poverty. The poor of Virginia—indentured servants, tenant farmers, free laborers who wandered from job to job, and dependent paupers—lived under degrading conditions; the situation of the working poor in the Chesapeake region resembled conditions in southern England (Fischer 1989, 380). Wealth distribution was significantly less equal than in Massachusetts, where middle-class "yeoman" farmers and artisans made up the great majority of the population (376). In Virginia the economic system supported a structure where poor whites and slaves worked to support the gentlemen. The values that shaped Virginia were those of its ruling class of planters. These values were transmitted through social institutions from one generation to the next (382).

In contrast to the royalist settlers of Virginia, migrants to Massachusetts were persecuted for their religious beliefs and came from the economic middle classes. Rather than wealth and adventure, settlers of Massachusetts sought to find religious freedom and "God's regenerative grace" (Dunn 1962, 8–9). The Massachusetts Puritans were committed to establishing the "shining city on the hill" that American politicians such as Ronald Reagan often referred to. In his first sermon in the new world, the Puritan leader John Winthrop encouraged the establishment of a "Company of Christ" bound together in love. He contended that members of the Massachusetts Colony held a covenant with God that must not be broken. The new world would be the place where this covenant could be followed (Koven 1999, 48).

A strict code of business ethics was instituted in the Massachusetts Bay Colony. Boston's minister John Cotton denounced merchants taking advantage of others in business practices. Entrepreneurs who took advantage of others could be fined, denounced from the pulpit, and threatened with excommunication (Ellis 1993, 11). Intolerance

and persecution of wrongdoers also characterize Massachusetts. For example, in 1636 Roger Williams was banished from the colony for preaching in his Salem congregation a message that called for the separation of church and state. Williams and other dissidents established their own settlement in what is now Providence, Rhode Island, where they could practice their own brand of religion. Anne Hutchinson and other colonists were also banished from Massachusetts for disagreeing with official religious dogma.

Many accounts of the trials and tribulations of the Puritans (Bremer 1993; Hammond 2000; Bremer and Botelho 2005; Winship 2005) provide rich detail about one of America's founding cultures. Alexis de Tocqueville, the French chronicler of nineteenth-century America, provides insight into the nature of this culture. Tocqueville ([1836] 1956, 42) notes that adventurers without families founded other colonies; however, Massachusetts's settlers included husbands, wives, and children. They brought with them to the New World their insistence on an ordered morality. Tocqueville claims that the Massachusetts settlers tied to establish a political democracy more perfect than antiquity had dared to dream. In this attempt, Massachusetts Bay Puritans established laws and offices that were intended to promote the general good of the colony.

Major political contributions enacted by the Puritans of Massachusetts included the activism and intervention of the people in public affairs, voting for taxes, the extension of personal liberty, the concept of decentralized governing through townships, and trial by jury. Decentralization of power was evident in the creation of townships that began to spring up in New England as early as 1650. These townships selected their own magistrates, levied their own taxes, discussed affairs of the community, kept their own records, provided for the poor, and maintained public order.

Puritan legislation was guided by the mandate of establishing and maintaining good moral conduct in the community. Monetary fines or whippings were punishment for rape, adultery, and sex between unmarried persons. Legislation also severely punished idleness and drunkenness and prohibited the use of tobacco. Innkeepers were forbidden to furnish more than a certain quantity of liquor to each customer, and simple lying was punishable by a fine or flogging. Attendance at church services was compulsory, and severe punishment (including death) could be inflicted upon any Christian who chose to worship God according to a differing ritual.

Many Puritans sailed back to England between 1642 and 1651 to fight against the royalist supporters of the king in the English Civil War. Puritan victory in the war led to a rapid expansion of the Massachusetts Bay Colony. The population of Massachusetts roughly doubled in every generation from its founding in 1620 for a period of two centuries. Eventually Puritan settlers migrated westward across the United States, to New York, northern Pennsylvania, the upper third of Ohio, the upper Great Lakes, the Mississippi Valley, the Willamette Valley of Oregon and eastern Washington, California, Utah, Kansas, Colorado, and Montana. In the nineteenth century, descendants of the Puritans also moved into Maine, Canada, and the American Northwest. In many respects, what became known as the "Yankee" culture of the early Puritans was diffused throughout the northern portion of the United States (Koven 1999, 51).

Puritan ideals and Yankee values are associated with frugality, industriousness, a strict moral code, self-discipline, and self-denial. Puritans held rigid views of morality and ethics with the goal of establishing a godly state on earth. Both citizens and public officials strove to establish God's kingdom on earth by creating a governmental exemplar, a "shining city on the hill." Concern for ethics and morality was a focal point of people's lives in Massachusetts, with religion and the church exerting control over the establishment of group norms and general public policy.

Both Virginia and Massachusetts exerted tremendous influence on the values and government structure that would later define the United States. Knowledge of Puritan and Cavalier cultures provides insight into how contemporary Americans interpret the concept of responsible governance. The influences of these two colonies do not, however, tell the whole story of the crystallization of American values. Later settlers would also help to define American values as they brought with them their own norms and customs to the new country. Prominent among these later settlers were the Quakers of the Delaware Valley and backcountry settlers of Appalachia. These migrants to America added their own flavor to the Puritan and Cavalier influences. Each group contributed to the American tapestry in bringing to the new world its own sets of religious, political, and economic principles.

The Delaware Valley and Appalachian Backcountry

Notable among the non-Puritan and non-Cavalier settlers were members of the religious group known as the Society of Friends, more commonly known as the Quakers. Quaker settlements in the Americas date to 1682 when twenty-three Quaker ships sailed into Delaware Bay and founded the colony of Pennsylvania. Altogether about 23,000 colonists moved to the Delaware Valley (eastern Pennsylvania, West Jersey, northern Delaware, and northeastern Maryland) between 1675 and 1715. By 1750 Quakers represented the third-largest religious denomination in the British colonies. Quaker numbers, however, fell dramatically relative to other denominations after the mid-eighteenth century (Fischer 1989, 423).

Quaker religious beliefs differed significantly from those of the Puritans of New England and Anglicans of Virginia. Organized religion was much more decentralized for the Society of Friends since the Quakers believed in an "inner light" that brought the means of salvation within the reach of everyone. Quakers repudiated sacraments, ceremonies, churches, official clergy, and tithes, accepting the less formal lay missionaries that they called ministers. Fundamentally rejecting the Puritan (Massachusetts) view of God as a God of Wrath as well as the Anglican (Virginia) view of formal church hierarchy, Quakers wished to follow their own interpretation of the will of God.

Over time the Quakers were associated with openness, an outgoing manner, and hard work. They embraced the ideals of religious freedom, social pluralism, weak government, strong communal groups, strong families, and contempt for higher learning. The Quakers adopted customs that reflected equality of manners, simplicity of taste, self-denial, and sexual modesty (Fischer 1989, 429). Landholdings in the Quaker colony of the Delaware Valley were more egalitarian than in any other region in British America. Quakers viewed virtue as a consequence of actions and character, not a consequence of birth or wealth. This perspective differed most starkly from that of the Virginia Cavaliers, who greatly valued social position based on a family's place within the social hierarchy. Religious freedom, abolishment of capital punishment, and abolition of debtor prisons were all policies advocated by the Quakers.

Quakers of the Delaware Valley discouraged open displays of deference that were required in the Virginia colony. In place of bowing and curtseying, Quakers substituted the handshake. Members of the Quaker community refused to use social titles such as "sir" and "ma'am" and resisted calling gentlemen and high office holders "your honor" and "your excellency." Quakers preferred to address everyone as "Friend" regardless of their high or low distinction. Virtue for the Quakers was exemplified by modesty in dress, self-denial, equal treatment for all, and hard work. These Quaker traits soon began to dominate in the city of Philadelphia and surrounding areas.

Other values were transported by settlers who migrated to the Appalachian region of the Americas. Beginning around 1717, Quaker merchant noticed ships coming from areas of Britain other than London and Bristol as settlers from north Britain (borderlands of the Scottish Highlands, northern England, and northern Ireland) began to arrive. These settlers differed dramatically from the middle-class Quakers of Philadelphia in their economic standing (overwhelmingly poor) and disposition (tempered by generations of warfare in their native regions).

Religion did not play a major role in the decision by these settlers to come to the new colonies. Factors such as high rents, low wages, and heavy taxes in the "old country" played a bigger part in their decisions. A majority of the new migrants to the Appalachian region were farm laborers who owned no land. They worked as tenants to landlords; however, in contrast to Virginia (where 75 percent of immigrants came as indentured servants), very few of the backcountry migrants came in bondage as indentured servants. The characteristics of fierce pride mixed with abject poverty set the new migrants apart from other English-speaking people in the American colonies.

As early as 1717 Quakers complained that the new settlers from northern Britain brought with them their ancient border habit of belligerence toward other ethnic groups. By 1730, Pennsylvania officials were complaining about the "audacious and disorderly" behavior of the new settlers. When the migrants from north Britain landed in Philadelphia, the Quaker leaders encouraged them to move westward—far away from Philadelphia—as rapidly as possible (Fischer 1989, 633). From there the settlers migrated south and west to the mountains of Maryland, Virginia, the Carolinas, and Georgia.

Today's largest concentration of backcountry migrants can be found in southwestern Pennsylvania, western Maryland, western Virginia, North and South Carolina, Georgia, Kentucky, and Tennessee. This area began to take on the dangerous character of the border between England and Scotland, where the rule of law was unknown. The settlers to Appalachia seemed to be more at home than others in an anarchic environment where might made right. Such an environment was well suited to the warrior ethos of the new settlers, their farming economy, their attitudes toward wealth, and their ideas of work (Fischer 1989, 639).

The four settlement patterns (Puritan, Cavalier, Quaker, and Appalachian) described above contributed greatly to the development of contemporary American culture and contemporary American values. The precise impact of early groups, however, is in some dispute. Scholars such as cultural geographer Wilbur Zelinsky (1973) note the importance of the Doctrine of First Effect Settlement. Other research posits that new cultures represent threats to American norms, values, and fundamental ways of life. This research asserts that there is no guarantee that new immigrants will assimilate or adopt the values of the earliest settlers. Instead, faith in assimilation may be replaced with fear that new immigrants will erode core "American" values (Brimelow 1995; Huntington 2004).

Immigration has become a contentious issue as some Americans seek to wall off the nation's borders from the foreign hordes while others covet cheap sources of labor that can increase profits. Critics of both legal and illegal immigration contend that immigration will not only undermine wages but also damage the moral as well as ethical environment of the country. For critics of immigration, the types of people who are coming to America, the countries they are coming from, and their value structure, religious beliefs, work habits, and moral predispositions all have the potential to undermine core "American" values. The issue of immigration therefore is highly relevant in defining norms and values that shape our interpretations of the concept of responsible governance.

Immigrant Influences

From the founder Alexander Hamilton to Secretary of State Henry Kissinger to Governor Arnold Schwarzenegger of California, immigrants have played a large role in shaping norms and values within the United States. There is disagreement, however, in regard to the contribution of different groups and the degree to which new groups should adjust to an established "Anglo" environment.

An "Anglo-conformity" model of how immigrants should adjust is based on the view that immigrants should adopt the morals, norms, and values of the dominant Anglo culture. A second model contends that individuals of all races can blend, as in a "melting pot," into a totally new formulation of a hybrid American. A third model suggests that the United States is no longer a melting pot where immigrants lose their cultural identity but rather resembles a stew or salad in which separate ingredients (cultures) remain intact. In the third model, newcomers keep their own characteristics and add to the vibrancy of the whole in their own unique manner. This stew or salad model contends that the whole is energized when individual differences are able to express themselves and maintain their uniqueness.

Immigration affects perspectives of responsible governance in various ways. In a heterogeneous society such as the United States, perspectives of right and wrong, good and evil compete for acceptance. It is likely that different immigrant groups would have different conceptions of what constitutes ethical or responsible behavior for public servants. Different groups are inculcated to different norms than others, possess different value systems, and hold different ideas about responsible or reprehensible actions. The composition of the population therefore influences the culture and conceptions of responsibility.

Immigration is not a new phenomenon in the United States but ever recurring. All immigrant groups have had to struggle for acceptance. For some, however, the struggle has been greater than for others. The plight of Irish immigrants is one example of the difficulty new groups faced. The Irish faced open hostility and discrimination in the United States when they began to immigrate in large numbers following the potato famine of 1845. Bostonians of the 1840s described the Irish immigrants as dirty, stupid, lazy, alcoholic, quick-tempered, prone to bar brawls, and debauched. Bostonians derisively called potatoes "murphies" and the Irish were labeled "Paddys." Police carts were commonly referred to as "paddy wagons" because they carried off so many Irish troublemakers. Newspaper cartoonists contributed to the negative stereotypes of Irish immigrants by drawing Irishmen as looking like apes with a jutting jaw and sloping forehead. In the 1870s and 1880s cartoonist Thomas Nast portrayed the Irish as bumbling idiots and pugnacious drunks. Job posters and newspaper employment ads specifically stated "No Irish Need Apply." Hotels and restaurants hung signs stating "No Irish Permitted in This Establishment." In 1851–1852, railroad contractors in New York advertised for workers and promised good pay. When mostly Irish applied, the pay was lowered.

The Irish responded to their treatment in various ways. Some changed their accents, their names, and their religion. Others turned to alcohol, crime, or the Catholic Church. Since many Catholic priests and nuns were Irish, the church provided a connection to home and comforted those in need (Baba 2004). Over time politics became a natural outlet for the Irish, particularly in large cities of the East Coast where the Irish Catholics outnumbered Protestant voters. Using their numbers to gain power, they formed the great political machines that dominated large cities in the nineteenth century. These machines helped to transform politics from an idealized, noble calling for the elites to a job designed for personal advantage. Machine politics defined morality and political responsibility as helping your own ethnic group and assuring continued electoral success.

Later immigrant groups such as Italians, Jews, Poles, Asians, Puerto Ricans, Cubans, and Mexicans also influenced American culture (Harrigan and Vogel 2003). By 2000, the U.S. Census Bureau reported a wide diversity of ethnic groups in the United States. Those of German ancestry (15.2 percent) constituted the largest group, followed by Irish (10.8 percent), African-American (8.8 percent), English (7.2 percent), and Mexican (6.5 percent) (U.S. Department of Commerce 2004). The proportion of Hispanic-Americans is estimated to increase substantially by 2040 (Huntington 2004, 224).

Sowell (1981, 4) observes that a mixture of unity and diversity runs through American society. This mix helps to define the cultural filter that interprets vague constructs such as "responsible governance." Conceptions of responsible governance are also influenced by established political beliefs. In the United States no political dogma seems to be more important than the idea of the "American Creed." This ideal includes conceptions of natural rights and freedom. Values of the American Creed are found throughout the U.S. Constitution. They provide a strong frame of reference for interpreting American conceptions of public responsibility.

The American Creed

The American Creed provides insight into the question of "Americanism" and the values that underpin

this ideal. An early American author, J. Hector St. John de Crèvecoeur, attempts to answer the question "What is the American?" in his book *Letters from an American Farmer*, published in 1782. As an early proponent of what would be known as the "melting pot" ideal, Crèvecoeur contends that in America "individuals of all races are melted into a new race of man, whose labors and posterity will one day cause great changes in the world." For Crèvecoeur, the "western pilgrims" of America would create a new society unrestrained by the past biases of the feudal era. Crèvecoeur contends that America was different from Europe since it had no princes for "whom we toil, starve, and bleed." In contrast to the old world of feudal society, in the new world of America people were viewed as free (Crèvecoeur 2004).

Crèvecoeur reflects a prevailing theme of the American Creed, a theme stated by Thomas Jefferson in the Declaration of Independence: all men are created equal. No one in American is anointed by birth; people work for themselves. These ideals are interpreted today as the freedom for people to pick themselves up by their bootstraps and to reap the reward of their efforts.

The American Creed is recognized today as a set of political principles derived from English doctrines such as government by consent of the people. The creed is a coherent mind-set that describes basic American values. These values are underpinned by major influences on America such as the Protestant religion and a distinctive national character that has been termed "Americanism." This national character has been influenced by factors such as the vast spaciousness of the nation, the ease of geographic mobility, independence from others, and the spirit of enterprise.

The American Creed is consistent with the view that Americans are optimistic, individualistic, moralistic, pragmatic, ingenious, resourceful, and always ready to improvise. Americans tend to avoid theories and are willing to experiment with new ideas and ways of doing things (Commager 1950, 29).

Political scientist Rogers M. Smith (1988) identifies a concept he terms "Americanism" that grew into a coherent belief system or "ideology" in the early days of the republic. During this time, many American leaders promoted the notion that Americans had a distinctive character, born of their freedom-loving Anglo-Saxon ancestors and heightened by the conditions of the New World. Liberty, self-government, political awareness, independence, and freedom are all hallmarks of Smith's conception of Americanism.

While conceptions such as Americanism provide a guide to the intellectual orientation of people in the nation, ideals such as responsible governance remain abstract. History and the literature of both political philosophy and public administration provide insight in further refining the concept.

Defining Ethics, Responsibility, and Governance

Historical documents such as the U.S. Constitution encourage checks on unwanted, unethical, and illegal behavior. This is accomplished mainly through the ability of the legal system to control unwanted behavior. The court system is charged with imposing fines, prison sentences, and other penalties on misdeeds. The courts enforce laws passed by the legislative branch of government.

Other checks, such as the internal check (the personal desire to follow moral principles) in contrast to external checks (such as legislative control, administrative control, and codes of ethics), have also been discussed in the literature. In the 1930s alternative views of how to control government officials were formulated by two distinguished scholars. Carl Friedrich (1935, 30) noted that in the past governments have been responsible to God or the church.

Public officials had a responsibility to God for their actions, and Friedrich believed that strong "inner values" of public officials could control wanton abuse. This perspective was more or less retained in Lutheran states such as Sweden and Saxony, while in Calvinist and Puritan nations such as Holland and England, clearly defined secular responsibility became a more realistic check. Friedrich's position became known as the "inner check" since it referred to the personal values of individuals and their desire to remain in good standing with higher, religiously based prescriptions.

In contrast to this religion-based view of responsibility, Herman Finer (1936, 1941) emphasized the need for specific sanctions to counter improper behavior of public officials. Finer claimed that morality was a valuable conception; however, it should not be assigned the same importance as clear external control. Sanctions such as organizational discipline and criminal punishment could send clear messages that certain behavior will be punished. Other controls such as codes of ethics and legislative directives could also work to check unwanted behavior (Cooper 1998).

Codes of ethics are fairly standard for professionals such as lawyers, engineers, physicians, and accountants. Physicians subscribe to the Hippocratic Oath, promising to "do no harm." The American Institute of Certified Public Accountants maintains a detailed code of conduct. One portion of the code states that services must be consistent with acceptable professional behavior for certified public accountants and that the public trust must not be subordinated to personal gain and advantage. Furthermore, members must be free from conflicts of interest in discharging professional responsibilities.

The American Society of Public Administration publishes its own code of ethics in the journal *Public Administration Review.* This code exhorts government workers to serve the public, respect the Constitution and the laws, demonstrate personal integrity, promote ethical organizations, and strive for professional excellence. Others in government pledge to abide by the standards of their profession as they work for the public interest.

Often representatives of the public discover the value of moral and ethical behavior only after they have been convicted of wrongdoing. For example, former Nixon administration official Charles Colson emphasized the value of character long after the disgrace of Watergate, stating that a nation or a culture cannot endure for long unless it is supported by common values such as public-spiritedness, respect for others, and respect for the law. Colson, who discovered the importance of ethics and responsibility following his one-to-three-year prison sentence on Watergate-related charges, noted that societies could not endure unless people who acted on motives superior to their own immediate interest populated them (1989).

Noble motives include respecting human life, loving one's family, fighting to defend national goals, helping the unfortunate, and paying taxes. Virtues such as courage, loyalty, charity, compassion, civility, and duty are needed to accomplish responsible public sector goals. How to identify virtue and responsibility, however, is often problematic. Perhaps, like pornography, we know them when we see them. If this is true, then accounts of historical events should illustrate what Americans as a society have defined as both virtuous and appalling activities. These definitions in retrospect illuminate the ethical landscape at given points in time and the struggles between various interests to establish their interpretation of responsibility and ethics.

The Focus of This Book

The focus of this book is responsible governance. Responsibility is identified through detailed case studies that describe various forms of behavior, both responsible and irresponsible. The actions themselves as well as the systemic response to those actions allow students to assess the ethical state of public affairs at a given point in time. This assessment should lead to evaluation of ethical points of contention and the perceived seriousness of specific violations. Case studies illustrate both historical and contemporary controversies.

Chapter 2 discusses concepts that help to define responsible behavior in a democracy. These include definitions of the public interest, natural law, and the rule of law. It is assumed that responsible government adheres to the interests of the public as well as the interests of the general good. Natural law refers to laws of nature that assist humans as they define right or wrong. Natural laws are not man-made but ever present in nature; they are determined by rationality. Finally, the rule of law is a basic component all modern societies. Law promotes equity, efficiency, justice, and accountability. Organizations or governments run according to laws are viewed as indispensable to modern societies and more efficient than organizations (or societies) run by charismatic or hereditary leaders (Weber [1947] 1964).

Chapter 3 describes the state of ethical, responsible behavior in American elections. The role of money in the electoral process is reviewed as well as two case studies that assess the ethical nature of strategies to gain political power. Case No. 1 describes the historical evolution of machine politics in cities such as New York and Chicago. Case No. 2 discusses the more recent attempts by Congressman Tom DeLay to illegally launder money (raised by national corporations) to be given to U.S. House of Representative races in the state of Texas.

Chapter 4 discusses honesty and competence as they relate to perceptions of proper behavior of American officials. Abuse of power in regard to both honesty and competence has a corrosive effect on the prestige and legitimacy of institutions. This effect and the role of public opinion in democracies are described. Case No. 3 details the events surrounding the impeachment of President Clinton. Case No. 4 discusses the perceived incompetence of the Federal Emergency Management Administration in its response to Hurricane Katrina.

Chapter 5 delineates elements of international law and rules of engagement in warfare. Case No. 5 describes the My Lai massacre and the subsequent trial of one of the participants. Case No. 6 describes the Abu Ghraib prison scandal. Each of these case studies will identify ethical lapses and their implications for responsible governance. Chapter 6 concludes with reference to the linkages between ethics, morality, and responsible governance.

This book is founded on the premise that history can inform the present as well as future. Historical accounts of questionable practices as well as societal interpretations of those actions provide a useful lens to evaluate government. The degree to which government action corresponds to or departs from definitions of responsibility can be assessed from prior behavior. Detailed case studies allow students to speculate about events leading up to certain actions, the condemnation of actions, and whether the punishments fit the transgressions. To a certain extent, the cases reflect a "worst practices" methodology by identifying violations in norms of responsibility. While best practices provide direction for emulation, worst practices are guides for avoidance. Both direct action. Cases are assessed within the framework of the public interest, natural law, and the rule of law. These concepts are used as indicators of responsibility in government.

This concept of responsible governance holds value from an ethical and moral perspective. It is hoped that evaluations of past behavior will further our understanding of the need for ethical behavior. Worst cases described in this book are perceived not as individual aberrations based on personal idiosyncrasies but as actions grounded in environments that created or allowed irresponsible behavior to persist. Fostering responsible governance is not an abstract principle but an essential way to enhance public sector legitimacy, authority, and longevity.

Chapter 2

The Foundations of Responsible Governance

This chapter discusses the broad philosophical base from which the concept of responsible governance is derived. Public interest, natural law, and the rule of law are selected for special consideration due to their relevance to governance in democracies. Public interest relates to the constitutional mandate of government by consent of the people. The principle referred to by Abraham Lincoln in his 1863 Gettysburg Address as a government "of the people, by the people, and for the people" reinforces the ideal of government by consent. Many other politicians have also described the pivotal role assigned to the people in the American democracy. In 1830, for example, New Hampshire senator Daniel Webster denounced the assertion by Senator Robert Hayne of South Carolina that the U.S. government was merely a creature of the states; instead, Webster insisted, the U.S. government was "the people's government made for the people, made by the people, and answerable to the people" (Bartlett and Kaplan 2002, 415). Faith in the people was later reinforced by President Theodore Roosevelt, who stated that the "the majority of the plain people will day in and day out make fewer mistakes in governing themselves than any small body of men will make in trying to govern them" (Schubert 1960, 40).

In light of the above statements, it is reasonable to conclude that for the United States and for any true democracy responsible governance is synonymous with listening to and abiding by the wishes of the people. In democracies, at least in theory, the people are the rulers, exercising their sovereignty through elected representatives. The people retain the power to periodically replace the representatives when they are no longer following the people's desires. Wholesale electoral realignments at various periods of American history have reminded political leaders that the citizens have the option to "throw the bums out" and put new people in power who will, at least for a short time, do better than their predecessors. For example, the election of Abraham Lincoln in 1860 marked the beginning of an era of electoral dominance by the Republican Party. Franklin D. Roosevelt's landslide in 1932 likewise represented a repudiation of the previous Republican policies and a desire to go back to a period of economic prosperity when "happy days" would return. The election of Ronald Reagan in 1980 represented a resurgence of conservative Republican thought consistent with low taxes and low spending, marking a rebuke of Democratic Party policies.

Responsible governance is consistent with the ideal of peaceful changes of power and the ability of the status quo leaders to accept the will of the people. The electoral process is therefore considered a sacred trust due to its link with principles such as the consent of the governed and abiding by the public interest as interpreted by voters. The public interest is defined in American democracy by the broad majority of its citizens; under the rubric of public interest, the many rule and not the few. This is the essence of democracy. If a government is run by the few, for the few most powerful and most wealthy, that government exists in fundamental violation of the principles of democracy and public interest. Responsible governance mandates upholding legal and constitutional directives. Governments that are grounded in principles of representative democracy therefore must be responsive to the wishes of the people. If private as opposed to public interests are followed, it is the responsibility of the people to select new leaders whose actions and policies will be more to their liking.

Natural law is the second component of responsible governance described in this book. The concept of natural law is derived from Western political thought and has been used for millennia to justify right as well as wrong behavior. Natural law analysis is founded on both reason and theology. Natural law theory acknowledges man-made law but asserts that there are also "higher laws" that can be found in nature. The higher natural laws are not to be violated and underpin man-made laws that govern societies. Responsible governance must abide by human understanding of natural law and follow the unwritten, immutable, universal laws that are perceived to be created by God.

The third conceptual leg of the three-legged stool that supports the ideal of responsible governance is the rule of law. The rule of law is based upon the principle that government authority is legitimately exercised only in accordance with written, publicly disclosed laws. This ideal of the rule of law, applied equally to everyone in a society, protects against arbitrary power. Limiting arbitrary power was of great concern to the founders and early settlers. Fear of tyranny or abuse of power exercised by a distant king encouraged the creators of the new

American government to establish the separation of power into distinct branches and limitations on the power of the chief executive. The rule of law implies equal treatment and serves as a consistent guide for behavior. Deviation from the principle of the rule of law would facilitate arbitrary power, threatening both freedom and efficiency. The rule of law, with its universal application to all citizens, supports individual opportunity, open competition, civil protections, and wealth generation. The rule of law protects property from arbitrary confiscation, thereby encouraging work, savings, and economic advancement. In addition to the economic implications, the rule of law also supports democratic principles and individual rights.

Support for the public interest, natural law, and the rule of law helps to establish an environment where proper conceptions of right and wrong, proper and improper, good and evil can be drawn. These conceptions or interpretations of right and wrong in turn influence behavior that will determine the degree to which responsible governance is a reality or a facade. The goal of government should be responsibility, yet responsibility is often difficult to define and irresponsibility all too often becomes the norm. The three concepts (public interest, natural law, rule of law) discussed in this book act as indicators of responsibility. To the extent that facts align with these indicators, governments can be placed along a continuum between full responsibility on one side and total irresponsibility on the other.

The Ideal of the Public Interest

Early Perspectives: Jefferson, Hamilton, and Rousseau

In theory, public sector officials in democracies serve the people or the public interest. In the United States this principle is clearly laid out in foundation documents such as the Declaration of Independence (signed in 1776) and the Bill of Rights (passed in 1791). In the words of the writer of the Declaration of Independence, Thomas Jefferson, governments derive their power from the people and the people have an obligation to oversee the proper functioning of government. The Declaration states, "Governments are instituted among Men, deriving their just powers from the consent of the governed.—That whenever any Form of Government becomes destructive of these ends, it is the Right of the People to alter or to abolish it, and to institute a new Government, laying its foundation on such principles and organizing its powers in such form, as to them shall seem most likely to effect their Safety and Happiness." Similarly, the Tenth Amendment to the U.S. Constitution identifies inherent powers of the people: "The powers not delegated to the United States by the Constitution, nor prohibited by it to the states, are reserved to the states respectively, or to the people."

The Declaration of Independence was not unique in its worldview; its ideas can be traced to Western European philosophy of the seventeenth and eighteenth centuries. European political philosophers such as John Locke, Jean-Jacques Rousseau, and Charles-Louis Montesquieu had previously described the need for leaders to serve the public interest rather than their own interest. In *The Social Contract*, Rousseau states that the people are sovereign and that each person enters into a contract with each other. Each puts his or her power in common trust under the direction of the "general will." Under Rousseau's concept of the general will, the people take on an active rather than passive role in governance: "only the general will can direct the powers of the state in accordance with the purpose for which it was instituted, which is the common good" (Rousseau [1762] 1994, 63). The common good remains at the core of the ideal of the public interest. They become interchange-

able since leaders automatically pursue the public interest when they pursue the common good.

According to Rousseau, the will of the state should take priority over all other types of will, such as the will of the individual (which focuses on the private advantage of individuals) or the will common to members of government (which focuses on attaining personal advantages for members of the ruling body). Rousseau concludes: "the individual or particular will should count for nothing, the corporate will pertaining to the government for very little, and consequently the general or sovereign will should always dominate and be the rule that uniquely determines the others" (97).

In an age of monarchy and feudalism, the question of what role the people should play in governance was highly controversial. Defenders of representative democracy and individual rights such as Thomas Jefferson advanced Rousseau's notion that the people were sovereign. The signers of the Declaration of Independence risked their lives in signing on to what was a radical proposition for its time. Jefferson believed that the guiding governance principle for a political leader should be to direct the affairs of the people "with a single eye to their good, and not to build up fortunes for himself and family." Jefferson stated, "the will of the people . . . is the only legitimate foundation of government, and to protect its free expression should be our first objective." This perspective is further reinforced in Jefferson's statement that "I subscribe to the principle that the will of the majority honestly expressed should give law." The will of the majority and the people's ability to freely express their views provide stability in government. For Jefferson, rulers ignore the people at their own peril: "If this avenue [the expression of the voice of the people] be shut to the call of sufferance it will make itself heard through that of force, and we shall go on as other nations are doing in the endless circle of oppression, rebellion, reformation; and oppression, rebellion, reformation again; and so on forever" (Jeffersonian Cyclopedia n.d.; Thomas Jefferson on Politics & Government n.d.). True democracy offers a solution that would break this endless cycle.

Jefferson's faith in the people as shepherds of good governance was not universally shared. For example, Alexander Hamilton, New York's delegate to the 1787 Constitutional Convention and secretary of the treasury in the new government, argued that a House of Lords would be needed to check the unsteadiness of the masses. Hamilton cautioned, "the voice of people has been said to be the voice of God; and however generally this maxim has been quoted and believed, it is not true in fact." For Hamilton, "the people are turbulent and changing; they seldom judge or determine right." In a political debate with Jefferson, Hamilton stated, "Your people sir, is nothing but a great beast" (Schubert 1960, 2–3).

Citizenship and Elitist Democratic Theory

Over time, the disparate views of Hamilton and Jefferson were distilled into two competing perspectives. Citizenship theorists who exalt the capacities of the people embrace Jefferson's perspective. On the other hand, elite democratic theorists view the people with great suspicion. These two perspectives represent latter-day versions of the Hamiltonian and Jeffersonian disputes at the time of America's founding.

Political theorists such as Dennis Thompson (1970, 10) posit that citizenship theory relies upon two essential presuppositions: the autonomy of citizens and the improvability of citizens. The presupposition of autonomy is based on the view that citizens are the best judges of their own interests. Improvability rests on the notion that citizens should be treated as capable of showing better political and social judgment over time.

According to Thompson, these two suppositions are essential elements of citizenship. Citizenship calls for the political involvement of ordinary citizens and places great faith in the ability of average citizens to make good electoral decisions over the long run.

The nineteenth-century English political theorist Graham Wallas also emphasizes the need for active participation in the political process. He stresses that a chief goal of politics is to increase the political strength of the individual citizen (D. Thompson 1970). Wallas advances the notion that the environment can instill proper values in citizens. He claims that a healthy environment can provide the average citizen with "proper moral and intellectual ideals necessary for democracy" (D. Thompson 1970, 21).

Scottish political philosopher A.D. Lindsay was a strong defender of the value of autonomy. Lindsay argues that the opinions of ordinary citizens must be treated with the utmost respect, reasoning that their claims to share in governance are justified because the average citizen knows "where the shoe pinches." In other words, Lindsay assumes that the common people know their own best interests and know when things are not going well. Lindsay acknowledges that ordinary voters have only vague ideas as to what legislative or administrative reform can stop the shoe's pain. Nevertheless, Lindsay asserts, "only he, the ordinary man, can tell whether the shoes pinch and where; and without that knowledge the wisest statesman cannot make good law" (Lindsay [1943] 1962, 270; D. Thompson 1970, 17). The free expression of people who know their own best interest is viewed as a check on arbitrary power and a check on leaders whose policies are antagonistic to the interests of the people.

The concept of improvability is closely linked to autonomy. Citizenship theorists believe that treating citizens as if they are the best judges of their own interests (autonomy) is the best way to improve their competence in the future (improv-ability). Thompson (1970, 19) observes that "un-less citizens' competence can be assumed to be improvable, citizen theorists would be less likely to look favorably on the political behavior which citizens exhibit at present." This view holds that citizens may not always make optimum decisions but over time people will learn from their mistakes and improve upon their previous miscalculations. Education is the key to improvement.

Some citizenship theorists, such as the phi-losopher John Dewey, believe that asking people what they want, not telling them what they need or what is good for them, is an essential component of the democratic idea. Participation therefore is essential for democracy. Dewey contends that it is not sufficient for government to produce the highest social good. All citizens must share in se-lecting governors and determining policies. Dewey claims that democracy is not perfect, but restricting public input is not the way to improve democ-racy. He stated that, on the contrary, the "cure for the ailments of democracy is more democracy." Dewey pleads for the cultivation of critical and inquiring minds in average people. Such a critical mind would lead to sounder electoral decisions and greater awareness of the behavior of leaders (D. Thompson 1970, 21).

In contrast to the optimistic view of the aver-age citizen expressed by citizenship theorists, elite democratic theorists are disillusioned by the failure of average citizens to engage actively and responsibly in politics. They accept some features of democracy in that they do not view the leader-ship structure as entirely closed or unified. They also maintain that elites are subject to some elec-toral control. Elite democratic theorists, however, do not accept presuppositions of autonomy and improvability. A prominent elite theorist, Walter Lippmann, deeply distrusted citizens' desires and judgments. Lippmann, a prominent author and

journalist of his time, portrays the average citizen as "a deaf spectator in the back row, who ought to keep his mind on the mystery off there, but cannot quite manage to keep awake." Citizens are affected by "rules and regulations continually, taxes annu-ally and wars occasionally"; however, Lippmann views citizens as spectators who are swept up by "great drifts of circumstance":

> [Private citizens] are for the most part invisible. They are managed, if they are managed at all, at distant centers, behind the scenes, by unnamed powers. As a private person he does not know for certain what is going on, or who is doing it, or where he is being carried. No newspaper reports his environment so he can grasp it; no school has taught him how to imagine it; his ideals often do not fit with it; listening to speeches, altering opinions and voting do not, he finds, enable him to govern it. He lives in a world which he cannot see, he does not understand and is unable to direct. In the cold light of experience he knows that his sovereignty is a fiction. He reigns in theory, but in fact he does not govern. ([1927] 1993, 3–4)

Lippmann further contends that the judgment of private citizens is distorted because the images inside their heads do not correspond with the world outside their immediate environment. In short, they do not have an accurate picture of the larger world; political matters are simply not familiar to the average citizen. Lippmann believes that only a few people have the time and ability to interpret a remote and complex reality. Furthermore, he contends that the elite few do not have to be very sensitive to popular demand and that citizens should intervene only when the political process is out of adjustment. Citizens could from time to time fundamentally alter the course of politics, but Lippmann does not believe average citizens should deal with everyday public policy. For Lippmann, statesmen do not have to give people what they want but can teach them what to want (D. Thomp-son 1970, 23).

The view that leaders do not have to directly follow constituent desires but can act as they wish in accord with their interpretation of the best course of action has been termed the trustee model of democracy. In the trustee model, representatives vote their conscience and try to convince constituents about the wisdom of their action. In contrast, the delegate model of democracy stipulates that the job of elected representatives is to follow the wishes of the people who place them in office. If the representatives do not abide by the desires of their constituency, they should be replaced by others who will.

Another prominent elite theorist was Joseph Schumpeter, an Austrian economist who immigrated to the United States and became a prominent professor at Harvard University. Schumpeter categorically rejects the existence of Rousseau's "common good" that can be identified by the force of rationality. According to Schumpeter, no such common good could exist because different people and different groups are not able to agree on what it means. In place of a vague conception of a common good that directs all action, Schumpeter prefers the conception of democracy as "a competitive struggle for the people's votes" ([1943] 1981, 269). Under his version of democracy, people have an opportunity to accept or refuse their rulers. Once voters elect a government, they should not exert pressure until the next election. Elite democratic theories contend that direct citizen input other than voting does not greatly improve governance. These theorists are more concerned with the quality of leadership than the ability of the average citizen to provide input. In contrast to this elitist vision of democracy, citizen theorists advocate the active participation of citizens since, as Dewey states, the cure for the problems of democracy is not less democracy but more.

The variety of views regarding the role of the people in governance shapes our perceptions of the "public interest." In general, the public interest refers to the notion that the people should exert strong influence on public policy. Scholars, however, do not agree about how to define the interests of the people and who should be involved in defining those interests. Some theorists accept variants of Rousseau's ideas of the general will and common good. Other theorists are reluctant to assign such an important role to the common people. They prefer to identify the public interest in metaphysical and religious terms. These theorists rely upon natural law or higher law that is unwritten, universal, and sensed in an individual's heart. Finally, still other theorists look to the resolution of conflicts between interest groups in order to define the public interest. These alternative views of how to define the public interest are described in greater detail below.

Alternative Conceptions of the Public Interest

Political scientists have long debated the meaning of the term "public interest"; however, a consensus definition is still lacking. In general, the public interest reflects behavior that benefits the many, not the few. Glendon Schubert (1960) further refines "public interest" by placing public interest theories into three separate groups: rationalist theories, idealist theories, and realist theories.

Rationalist Theories of the Public Interest

Rationalist theories of the public interest adopt a hierarchical model of authority with the public on top of the hierarchy. In this model, the people elect representatives, political parties help to define the public's will, the elected legislators translate the public will into law, the president oversees the execution of the law by administrators, and judges enforce the law. As in the representative model of democracy, the job of administrators is to translate the people's desires into specific rules. Under this rationalist model, the public interest is served because delegates of the people actualize the public will. The public interest is promoted when discretion of public officials is minimized or eliminated. Rationalist theorists contend that responsibility lies in behavior that automatically abides by the will of the people. For the rationalist theorists, discretion promotes arbitrariness and can lead to abuse of power. Automatic, directed behavior helps to guarantee a direct link between the popular will (wishes of the people) and the actions of government.

Rationalists rely upon the common good or general interest. According to Schubert (1960, 31), rationalists define the general interest "as being either those values which (it is assumed) all citizens necessarily share, or it is viewed as the lowest common denominator of values prevalent in American society." Numerous political scientists have supported the rationalist public interest perspective. For example, E.E. Schattschneider (1952, 22) discusses a political situation in which "private and special interest conflicts are strongly subordinated to a dominant concern for the preservation of the great common interests of the nation." Echoing the views of the philosopher Jean-Jacques Rousseau, Schattschneider observes that the public interest is more than the sum of special interests. He also notes that the only satisfactory political base for policies that address the public interest is a majority. Schattschneider cautions that leaders should be careful to make sure they govern for the general good rather than for the purpose of lining their own pockets. This is a popular theme that helps define our understanding of public interest.

Political scientist V.O. Key lends further support to the rationalist view of the public interest in his discussion of political parties. Key and Schattschneider both consider individual interest and the interests of the powerful as enemies of the common interest. Identifying the two-party system as the chosen instrument for implementing the will of the majority, Key and Schattschneider both view political parties as organizations that could transcend the narrow demands of special interests (Schubert 1960, 33–34).

Schubert (1962, 165) differentiates between two types of rational public interest theorists: party rationalists and popular rationalists. Party rationalists defend a strong two-party system as a means for expressing the public will. Popular rationalists, on the other hand, promote public opinion polls in order to discover the will of the people. Both are considered to be public interest rationalists in the sense of following the will of the people. Party rationalists urge elected representatives to follow the wishes of their party leaders. Popular rationalists believe that elected representatives do not need the intervening body of party leadership but should carry out the wishes of their constituents directly. In this respect the views of popular rationalists are consistent with the delegate model of democracy.

Idealist Theories of the Public Interest

Idealist theorists of the public interest are linked to ancient theories of natural law. In contrast to the rationalists who identify the public interest in the majority of people or majority of voters, idealists, by themselves, interpret the "true interests of the public." These "true interests" may not coincide with the majority but are to be discovered in identification of "higher law" or "natural law." Idealist public interest theorists view the public interest as separate from and independent of the political process. According to Schubert, under the idealist perspective public officials must find the true meaning of the public interest through their own thoughts and perceptions. The public interest in essence becomes whatever the consciences and minds of officials believe it to be (Schubert 1962, 166).

Since public officials themselves are charged

with the responsibility of interpreting the public interest, political parties and interest groups are perceived as being irrelevant or even dangerous. According to the idealist perspective, elected legislators are not responsible to either political parties or constituents but have a higher obligation to God and their own consciences. Public officials are to refer to an inner voice that should guide their actions. This inner voice relies upon the forces of reason in making assessments. Neither political parties nor interest groups should be able to mandate policy, according to idealist theorists, since individuals should follow their inner voice in interpreting God's laws.

A suspicion of both political parties and interest groups is not unusual and has a long tradition in the United States. James Madison in the *Federalist* No. 10 (published in the newspaper *New York Packet* in 1787) castigates both political parties and interest groups as determinants of a public interest. Madison is suspicious of majority rule, which he believes is dangerous. He believes that the ruling passion of the masses might sacrifice the interests of both the public good and the rights of other individual citizens (Schubert 1960, 81–82). Madison's views in this regard are similar to those of elite theorists such as Hamilton, who fears the "tyranny of the majority" and "mob rule." These political theorists worry about the potential for "demagogues" who would stir up mass passions. Madison prefers a governance process that puts less power directly in the hands of the people and is replete with various checks and balances. Leaders should have discretion to discover the "true" laws for governance.

Public interest idealists are also associated with social engineering and the belief that the consciences of public representatives should guide laws. Implicit in this perspective is the view that laws made by humans who are guided by popular sentiment may be inadequate since they may be in conflict with the higher natural law. In contrast to public interest rationalist theorists, idealist theorists seek to maximize or expand the scope of official autonomy and discretion. Officials would use their own judgment and their own consciences in interpreting what is best for the people. Because of the great discretion idealist theorists give to public representatives, their views are similar to those expressed by ancient Greeks such as Aristotle (Schubert 1960, 80).

Realist Theories of the Public Interest

The realist view of the public interest is best described in what political scientists have labeled group theory. Public interest realist theories see the government as the mediator of disputes between various groups in society. Noted group theorists such as Arthur Bentley and David Truman have developed a theory that defines the public interest as an equilibrium point defined by competing interest groups. Bentley views society as nothing more than the groups that compose it. He believes that all politics could be explained by conflicts and compromises between groups that compete with each other for influence and material advantage. Public officials automatically take into consideration the power of various groups and act accordingly. Ultimately, official actions reflect the equilibrium position of the various groups that are vying with each other for advantage (Bentley [1909] 1949).

Truman restates Bentley's basic view of the public interest as the result of group influences. Truman denies the existence of some inclusive "national" or "public interest" that is universal and stands apart from and superior to the interests of the various groups included within the jurisdiction. In contrast to this universalistic view, Truman views government as simply a mediator between both visible and well-established groups as well as "unorganized" or "potential" groups that compete for influence. Potential groups are not always involved in decision-making but defend the concept of fair play and can be activated by behavior that they feel goes beyond the boundaries of acceptance. Potential groups are believed to be so well entrenched that their positions do not require organized expression. They are activated when their notions of fair play are "flagrantly violated or when they are in the process of alteration." Major government leaders in the legislative, executive, and judicial branches constitute some of the unorganized groups. If officials fail to represent the unorganized group interests adequately, alternative leaders inside or outside of government will arise to better express those interests (Truman 1951, 448–449).

Contemporary Views on the Public Interest

Contemporary scholars have recently revisited the concept of public interest. For some of these scholars, the public interest is found in empowering administrators to be more responsive, accountable, competitive, customer-driven, enterprising, anticipatory, efficient, and results-oriented (Osborne and Gaebler 1992; Gore 1993). According to this perspective, the public is served when governments know what citizens desire, deliver services effectively, prevent problems from occurring, and pursue a clear mission. Rejecting the hierarchical model of bureaucracy, this perspective contends that public officials should have more discretion to seek out opportunities (be entrepreneurial) and to look for new ways to deliver services (increase privatization). For other theorists, the public interest is identified in administrators who are virtuous and good citizens. It is believed that these individuals are more likely to faithfully support the interests of the public. The virtuous administrator will be less susceptible to corruption and more likely to

set a good example for others to follow (Cooper 1991; Box and Sagen 1998; King and Stivers 1998; Timney 1998; Cooper 2004).

Attention to the idea of citizenship has focused interest on citizen discontent and the need for public managers to be sensitive to the people. A flaw in contemporary governance that is identified by citizen theorists is the perceived gap in perceptions between public workers and citizens (King and Stivers 1998, 17–18). Box and Sagen (1998, 158–159) are critical of barriers that prevent more citizen self-government. They contend that citizens feel a sense of separation from their government, citizens are skeptical of governmental action, citizens resist providing money for programs, and they are convinced that elected officials and public professionals are inept, corrupt or both. As a solution to these dilemmas, these authors advocate creating a more open and welcoming environment for citizens who wish to govern themselves. Two barriers, however, exist to making government more welcoming: (1) the policy process is controlled by community elites, and (2) policy implementation is controlled by public sector professionals.

Box and Sagan support promoting decentralized structures that enhance citizen responsiveness. An overall better quality of life is thought to be possible through (1) policies that emphasize the local community as a place where citizens can get involved in solving local problems, (2) policies that emphasize smaller and more responsive government, and (3) policies that support practitioners who help citizens achieve their collective goals. The objective of an overall better quality of life for citizens is not necessarily congruent with the bureaucratic end of advancing the careers of professionals who work for the government.

Timney discusses a new model of public administration as a means to better serve the public. She calls for administrators to become facilitators and partners with citizens rather than the sole expert in policy decisions. She recommends that professional administrators use their expertise in the service of the people to enable citizens to develop their own solutions. From her perspective, this model of behavior would more truly represent "government by the people." According to Timney, truly effective long-term solutions to vexing problems of our day will only arise "from an open, inclusive process where administrators welcome citizen participation as essential to their work rather than as a challenge to their own expertise" (1998, 100–101).

Public administration scholar James Svara also develops a model of administrative ethics that places duty to the people at the center. Duty is defined as a commitment to serve the public and the obligation to put the interests of the public above one's self-interest. In addition, Svara believes that duty holds special importance for people in public and nonprofit organizations. These individuals have a duty to serve the public, fulfill the obligations of public office, and act as a trustee of public resources (2007, 68). Svara notes that the duties of the public servant also include working actively to establish goals (11). These public servants have the opportunity to pursue the public interest. According to Svara, public administrators should (1) serve the public in their one-on-one interactions with individuals and in their commitment to service over self, (2) advance the public interest following basic precepts of public administration, including fairness, consistency, impartiality, neutrality, and equity, and (3) seek to create the greatest good for the greatest number over the long term while protecting the rights of minorities. Svara summarizes his views on ethics and commitment to the public interest in the following statement:

> Without ethics public administration is merely an instrument and administrators are simply the tools of their political masters. The founders of public administration would never have accepted these characterizations nor should we now. Without a

dedication from public administrators to advance the public interest, the public loses the benefits of the distinctive expertise and values that administrators bring to the political process. When administrators have a dedication to duty and an independent ethical standard, government and nonprofit organizations are better able to serve the public. (159)

Svara concludes that administrators act on their duty to protect the public interest by seeking to balance the three philosophical concepts of virtue, principle, and good consequences. The idea of virtue helps define what a good person is. The virtuous individual has qualities such as integrity, tolerance, civility, self-restraint, impartiality, caring, and citizenship. In contrast to the concept of virtue, a principles-based guide to action relies upon the application of fundamental truths and principles such as honesty, justice, and constitutional rights. The principles-based approach relies heavily on the writing of the German philosopher Immanuel Kant (1724–1804), who held that principles are universal and invariable. From the Kantian perspective, one should never deviate from principles regardless of the consequence. Finally, the concept of a consequences-based approach emphasizes the ends, purposes, and goals that result from actions. Under this perspective, a good end may justify deviation from given principles (Svara 2007, 49–59).

Cooper contends that public administrators have ethical obligations to citizens and should view the citizen as the focus of their loyalty. Public administrators conduct the public's business since they have the time, technical training, and resources. The administrator should encourage civic virtues and maintain concern for the common good. Cooper reminds his readers that the essence of public interest is obligation to the broad, shared interests of society rather than to private interests. He contends that the concept of public interest could serve as a moral compass for administrators by orienting them to their obligations to the people. The concept of public interest can also help recalibrate governmental processes that have gone awry. Cooper notes that the ideal of public interest is often raised retrospectively—when things go wrong: "when confronted with scandal and gross misconduct, the idea of public interest provides an intuitive navigational beacon that points in the right direction" (2004, 399).

This book accepts Cooper's view that the concept of public interest can act as a navigational beacon to help public administrators recalibrate direction and alter course when appropriate. Allegiance to the public interest can help them censure misconduct and set a course of prescribed action intended to prevent future abuses. The case studies in the following chapters identify instances when the public was ill served by government representatives whose misconduct egregiously violated their responsibilities and abused the public trust. The case studies provide examples of the ship of state veering dangerously off course and in need of some redirection.

At least one theory helps to explain government officials' disregard for the broad public. Public choice theorists contend that those on the public payroll may not be responsive to a vague conception of what is in the public interest. Rather, public choice theorists contend that like any manager, public sector bureaucrats wish to maximize their budget, increase their salaries, and expand the number of perks of office. In order to increase their power and enhance their freedom from oversight, they strive to make their departments independent bureaucratic fiefdoms. For elected officials, such independence will reduce their accountability to the people who elected them (Niskanen 1971; Stein 1991). In essence, the public choice perspective is consistent with the model in which public servants become autonomous and unaccountable in an effort to secure more individual discretion, power, and perquisites of office. The ideal of public service is lost in this model, replaced by the goal of accumulating power, prestige, and other benefits.

Summary of the Concept-Public Interest

There is little agreement about the concept of the public interest. Some political theorists, such as Rousseau, subscribe to the view that the people are always right; others, such as Hamilton and Lippmann, hold deep distrust of the masses while still others such as Wallas and Lindsay place their faith in complying with the wishes of the people. Contemporary citizenship theorists call for greater participation of average citizens in governance. Natural law theorists, however, reject this perspective and embrace the "inner voice" of conscience as a guide to proper action. This inner voice responds to a "higher authority" that governs behavior. Various perspectives on the concept of public interest are described in Table 2.1.

It is evident from Table 2.1 that there are not one but many different perspectives that define the public interest. A few dominant themes, however, can be observed. These include the belief in the ultimate wisdom of the people, belief in the wisdom of a higher authority, and belief that group conflict ultimately will produce a common good. The first theme recognizes that all classes of people need to be heard; the second theme focuses upon an unseen hand of "higher law," while the third theme places its faith in group struggle.

Each of these perspectives recognizes that the public may not be all knowing but in the end hold some degree of collective wisdom. In the words of Abraham Lincoln, "It is true that you may be able to fool all of the people some of the time, you can even fool some of the people all of the time; but can't fool all of the people all of the time" (Bartlett and Kaplan 2002, 477). When the people can no longer be fooled by the tired nostrums of political demagogues, they will demand change. Respon-

Table 2.1

Conceptions of the Public Interest

1. Belief that the people know their own interests and can check abusive power

2. Belief that representatives of the government must act in the interests of the people

3. Belief that the autonomy and improvability of the common man can lead to a good society with concern for the public interest

4. Belief in a common good or commonweal that directs public officials to faithfully execute the will of the people (Rationalist View)

5. Belief in a higher natural law that guides public officials through a voice of conscience that may be revealed to each official (Idealist View)

6. Belief in the public interest defined as a resolution of conflicting claims of interest groups (Realist View)

7. Belief that the public interest is enhanced through active citizenship

Sources: Schubert 1960; Thompson 1970; King and Stivers 1998.

sible governance facilitates such shifts in power when the public is fed up with the status quo and demands fresh thinking. Public interest mandates that the people will be allowed to reject their current leaders ("throw the bums out") and turn to others who promise to deliver more responsible governance.

The Ideal of Natural Law

Ancient Greek Conceptions of Natural Law

Natural law is difficult to define. Many scholars have expended a great deal of time and energy in trying to identify the concept. The ancient Greeks introduced the idea of eternal and immutable laws directing the actions of all rational beings. The Greeks also made a clear distinction between man-made law (positive law) and laws that are found "in nature" (natural laws) or laws that are created by a superhuman force. In the Declaration of Independence, Jefferson identified the natural law rights of life, liberty, and the pursuit of happiness. These commonly recognized words argue that some rights are divinely granted and are not subject to repeal by any human power. In the 1776 document these rights are inalienable; they constitute recognition of universally held rights as well as recognition of a divine power greater than that of any government.

Natural law is perceived to influence man-made law since humans strive to discover "true justice," which is found only in an understanding of the natural laws. Natural law theory recognizes that human laws can be deeply flawed, departing grossly from the true natural law. Human laws, however, may at time also approximate the true law. Time, place, and the disposition of the rulers will influence how closely human law is in agreement with the natural law. Natural law theory maintains that it is for humans and rulers to discover the natural law (law that is universal and unalterable) and then to live in accordance with the unchanging rules.

The ideas that support natural law date back to the earliest accounts of Western thought. The Sophists of ancient Greece developed ideas about nature, life, and the need to live in accord with nature. For the Sophists, state law or the laws of government were imperfect and antithetical to natural law. The Sophists made many contributions to our understanding of natural law by distinguishing between what is merely legal and what is naturally and morally just. They furthered the concepts of freedom, equality, and universal rights (Crowe 1977, 10).

By the end of the fifth century BC, however, the Sophists acquired the reputation of being more interested in persuasion than in truth. They traveled extensively and became known as professional teachers who provided the kind of training that was required for those who wished to enter into public life. They were known for their oratory and speech-making skills rather than as seekers of truth and justice. The ancient Greek philosopher Plato (427 BC–347 BC) viewed the Sophists as mere pests who had a corrupting influence on everyone who had anything to do with them. He knew them as word spinners and conscious deceivers who presented the appearance of truth by juggling words. Their corollary is found in the modern "spin doctors" and speech writers of contemporary political campaigns. Aristotle (384 BC–322 BC) also shared Plato's disdain for Sophists, stating that they dealt in pseudo-science (Crowe 1977, 8). This negative perception of the Sophists remains today; for example, the *Random House Dictionary* defines sophism as a clever but specious argument and a sophist as a clever but specious reasoner.

The negative image of Sophists is countered by a view of Sophists as providers of *sophia* or wisdom, based on understanding of natural law. An early Sophist, Heracleitus of Ephesus (540 BC–475 BC), believed in a fundamental unity in the world and divine reason (Rommen 1948, 5; Crowe 1977, 3). He contended that human law was nourished by divine law which was superior to man-made law, Divine law was also believed to be universal, enduring, and unchanging (Crowe 1977, 4).

Sophist philosophers were well aware of the distinction between what was naturally right and what was legally right. The laws of the city-state could reflect the changing personal wishes of rulers, yet the unwritten natural laws were perceived to be eternal and unalterable. These laws did not come from human design but sprang from a higher source. Eventually three main ideas were generated from the body of Sophist philosophy. The first idea was that man-made laws were artificial constructions likely to serve the interests of rulers. In contrast to man-made laws, natural laws reflected only what is naturally right. The second idea of the Sophists was that all people were by nature fellow citizens and therefore all people had natural rights. The laws of nature applied to everyone, not just the few who possessed power. The third idea of the Sophists revolved around the precept that organized political entities originate from contracts between humans. These contracts are preceded by a fundamental state of nature in which natural law is more powerful. Sophists maintained that the state of nature, since it came from a higher source, could not be altered or abrogated by human governments (Rommen 1948, 10).

The ideal of natural law as an unwritten law was also promoted by popular playwrights of ancient times, such as Sophocles (490 BC–405 BC). In his play *Antigone*, Sophocles describes a character that is recognized today as an eternal heroine of God's laws. In the play, Antigone defies the decree of her uncle, King Creon, by burying her brother Polyneices. The reason Antigone gives for disobeying her uncle's law is that her act of disobedience is "just by nature." Through the words of Antigone, Sophocles makes the case for a universal law that takes precedence over King Creon's man-made law. In pleading her case before the king, Antigone declares:

> That order [Creon's order not to bury Polyneices] did not come from God. Justice, that dwells with the gods below, knows no such law. I did not think your edicts strong enough to overrule the unwritten unalterable laws of God and heaven, you only being a man. They [unwritten laws] are not of yesterday or today, but everlasting, though where they came from, none of us can tell. Guilty of their transgression before God I cannot be. (Sophocles [442 BC] 1970, 138)

Sophocles also discusses the concept of natural law in other plays. For example, *Oedipus the King* (written around 420 BC and also called *Oedipus Tyrannos* or *Oedipus Rex*) is regarded as an expression of the power of the unchanging laws of nature. Sophocles refers to laws that bind mortals but "whose parent was no race of mortal men" (Crowe 1977, 6). Throughout the play, Sophocles stresses the idea of an eternal law and a "fate" that cannot be avoided.

In *Oedipus the King*, Laius, the king of Thebes, is told by an oracle that he will have a son who will kill his father and marry his mother. In order to avoid fulfillment of the prophecy, Laius gives his newborn baby to a slave to be left to die on a nearby mountain. Taking pity on the baby, the slave disobeys the king's order and gives the boy to a shepherd who in turn gives the baby to the childless king of Corinth. Eighteen years later the boy, Oedipus, travels to consult the oracle of Apollo, who informs him that his fate is to kill his father and sleep with his mother. Leaving the site of the oracle, Oedipus quarrels with a man at an intersection and slays him, not knowing that the man is his father, King Laius.

Oedipus proceeds to the city-state of Thebes, where he encounters the Sphinx, a monster who kills anyone who cannot answer her riddle, "What is that which is four-footed, three-footed, and two-footed?" Oedipus successfully answers the riddle with the response "man," who as a child crawls on four feet, as an old man uses a cane, as an adult walks on two legs. Oedipus is then welcomed by the people of Thebes as their savior. When King Laius fails to return, the people of Thebes make Oedipus their king, and, following the custom of the times, Oedipus marries his mother, and wife of his father, the widowed queen, Jocasta. A plague descends upon the city and an oracle announces that the plague will leave Thebes when the unknown murderer of King Laius departs. Oedipus lays a bitter curse on the king's murderer, whose crime has put Thebes in such misery. An old high priest commanded by Oedipus to reveal the name of the murderer names Oedipus. Finally understanding that the man he killed at the crossroad was the former king, Oedipus realizes he is the slayer of his father and the husband of his mother. Jocasta hangs herself; Oedipus plunges pins from Jocasta's dress into his eyes, blinding himself. The blind Oedipus is ordered by the new king to go into his house to await the disposition of the gods. He complies but insists that he should be left to die on the mountain as Laius had instructed and as originally intended by the gods. Eventually Oedipus leaves Thebes as an exile (A. Wilson 2006). This Greek drama served to reinforce the inevitability of one's fate and the certainty of God's will.

By the time of Aristotle, the conception of an unwritten, eternal, immutable law had gained widespread acceptance. Aristotle, known as the "father of the natural law," provided the doctrine with a solid foundation and helped to popularize it (Rommen 1948, 16). For Aristotle, some actions correspond to nature and are naturally good while others are repugnant to nature and naturally bad. Following the Sophists, Aristotle distinguishes between legal justice and natural justice. He contends that since legal justice originates in the will of the lawmaker, it can vary with different people at different times. Natural justice, however, is grounded in nature, is naturally just, and is unalterable. Legal justice and man-made (positive) laws are viewed as attempts—that may or may not be successful—to realize natural law.

Aristotle, as well as his teacher, Plato, developed a doctrine of natural law that defended the status quo of the city-state. Contending that the man-made laws of the Greek city-states were striving to realize the natural law, both Aristotle and Plato promoted the idea of achieving perfection as good citizens of a city-state. They contended that the city-state by establishing guides for proper action was the ultimate teacher. Aristotle's overall philosophy paved the way for the clearer conception of natural law that is found in Stoic and Roman thought.

Stoic and Roman Conceptions of Natural Law

The Stoics occupy a crucial place in the development of natural law thinking (Rommen 1948, 21; Simon 1965, 31). Stoics were disciples of Zeno of Citium (333 BC–264 BC), whose students gathered around stoas or colonnades built outside temples, houses, and marketplaces. The Stoic school of thought originated in Greece but was transported to Rome, where it was popularized by figures such as Cicero (106 BC–43 BC), Seneca (AD 3–65), Epictetus (AD 60–100), and Marcus Aurelius (AD 161–180). Stoic thought was then passed on to the medieval world mainly through the writings of Cicero.

Zeno's written works did not survive; however, his disciples passed on his teachings. Stoics such as Zeno taught self-control, fortitude, and detachment from emotions (also interpreted as indifference to pleasure and pain). These attributes would allow one to become a clear thinker, levelheaded and unbiased. The Stoics contended that by mastering passions and emotions, people could overcome the discord of the outside world and find inner peace. Stoics placed living a virtuous life and obtaining happiness of mind through the true, the good, and the beautiful above sensuality, pursuit of wealth, and pride of life. The Stoics sought virtue in "right reason"; one pursued a life in harmony with oneself and tried to live in accord with one's rational nature (Rommen 1948, 21; Wikipedia 2006a).

Stoic thought is characterized by the idea of human unity and the notion that human affairs are governed by universal rules. The Stoics thought of themselves as citizens of the world. They believed that certain propositions were not based upon time and place but were immutable, unchanging, and true for all parts of the world (Simon 1965, 30). For the Stoics, law is based in nature, man has inborn notions of right and wrong, and law in its very essence rests not upon the arbitrary will of the ruler or the will of the majority but upon nature.

The Roman philosopher Cicero became the dominant interpreter and transmitter of the Stoic doctrine of natural law. For Cicero, there was a true law that was agreeable to nature, known to all humans, constant and eternal. He states that there is not "one law at Rome and another at Athens, one thing now and another afterwards; but the same law, unchanging and eternal [that] binds all races of men and all times; and there is one common, as it were, master and ruler—God, the author, promulgator and mover of this law" (Crowe 1977, 38). Cicero defined true law as right reason that was in agreement with nature. He stated that it was a sin to try to alter nature's law, repeal any part of it, or abolish it (d'Entréves 1961, 20).

Another Roman expounder of natural law, Epictetus, taught that the test of whether or not a law is in accordance with nature is found in its agreement or nonagreement with reason. Like others, Epictetus noted differences in man-made laws that prevailed at various times among different peoples. He and other Romans, such as Seneca, renounced slavery and supported the dignity of human beings. According to these philosophers, natural law formed a basis for freedom and equality. These ideas, however, were not embraced by the majority, many of whom willingly accepted slavery, gladiator combat, and entertainments featuring the killing of human beings by beasts. Eventually, however, Romans accepted the ideal of a higher law that could be discovered through reason.

Through the efforts of Cicero, Romans began to accept the Stoic idea of an eternal law that ordered the universe. The natural law was adopted as a template by which Roman jurists replaced ancient law with the concept of an "inner voice" that directed and provided meaning to man-made law. Roman law maintained that natural law must prevail in cases of conflict with civil law. In Anglo-Saxon lands, it was believed that a royal judge possessed and understood the natural law "in the shrine of his breast." In Anglo-Saxon common law, the act of handing down a decision set a precedent and was thought to be validated by God through the concept of natural law. To the Roman jurists, the law involved knowledge of things both divine and human; it was the science of what is just and unjust (Rommen 1948, 29). The Romans passed on the idea of natural law to the Christian era and the age of scholastic philosophy. Under the interpretation of the scholastic philosophers, natural law became firmly established in eternal philosophical truths.

Christian Conceptions of Natural Law

Natural law developed coherence, force, and clarity under early Christians and later canonist lawyers of the Christian church. St. Paul preached that since the pagans did not have the benefit of Revelation (the laws of Moses), they should not be castigated for not having observed the law. Instead, he contended that they had another law, which taught them the difference between right and wrong, good and evil. This natural law was thought to be inscribed in the hearts of the heathens and made known to them through their conscience (Rommen 1948, 35; Crowe 1977, 53).

Early Christians adopted Stoic ideas of natural law in proclaiming the doctrine of a personal Creator-God who was author of the eternal, natural, moral law. Natural law was identified in the inner voice of conscience and reason. Among the great Christian theologians who helped define the concept of natural law were St. Augustine of Hippo (AD 354–430) and St. Thomas Aquinas (AD 1225–1274). St. Augustine refers to the idea of natural law as the Will of God, the Divine Wisdom, or the Supreme Reason. This eternal law is immutable and universal, ruling all that is preserved or ordered. Augustine believes that the

rules of conduct are clear enough to enable even the wicked to judge how a man ought to live. According to Augustine, the rules of the universe are the source of every just law and are impressed upon the heart of every person, just as the image of a ring can be impressed on wax (Crowe 1977, 64).

Two passages that reappear in later scholastic writings summarize Augustine's views on natural law. These include Augustine's definition of sin as "any saying, deed or desire against the eternal law" and his definition of the eternal law as "the divine reason or the will of God commanding that the natural order be preserved and forbidding its disturbance." Augustine summarizes his conception of natural law in three short maxims: it is written in the hearts of people, it consists fundamentally in the precept of doing to others what one would have them do to you, and it had to be supplemented by the Mosaic law (Crowe 1977, 66–67).

St. Thomas Aquinas is considered by many as the most systematic thinker of the Middle Ages. His philosophy was at first bitterly opposed, but remains the most authoritative expression of the Catholic view of life (d'Entréves 1961, 39). His theory of natural law is closely linked to the idea of an eternal divine order on which the whole of creation rests.

Aquinas believes that natural law is an expression of the dignity and power of humans. Alone among created beings, humans (due to their rational nature) are called upon to participate in the rational ordering of the universe. Reason is the essence of human life, the divine spark that determines human greatness. The "light of natural reason" enables people to "discern good from evil." This light of natural reason is closely associated with the notion of the law of nature. Natural law becomes the foundation of morality and all political institutions, the paramount standard by which all institutions could be judged.

St. Thomas relies heavily on reason to interpret

right action and justice: "in human affairs a thing is said to be just when it accords with the rule of reason: and, as we have already seen, the first rule of reason is the Natural law." He suggests that allegiance to the state or the governmental entity can be only conditional because unjust laws are not proper laws: "Man is bound to obey secular rulers to the extent that the order of justice requires. For this reason if such rulers have no just title to power but have usurped it, or if they command things to be done which are unjust, their subjects are not obliged to obey them" (d'Entréves 1961, 39).

Aquinas's contribution to our understanding of natural law is considerable. He develops a doctrine of free will that distinguishes humans from other earthly creatures. Aquinas contends that the natural law is a norm that "ought" to be obeyed, not a law that must be blindly followed. A basic norm of natural law is to act in conformity with one's rational nature. The eternal law reflects God's wisdom so far as it directs and governs the world in accordance with God's wisdom. For St. Thomas Aquinas, the supreme commandment of the natural moral law is that good should be done (Rommen 1948, 48).

Summary of the Concept-Natural Law

Natural law remains a difficult concept to grasp. A few dominant features, however, can be identified from the readings of the ancient, scholastic, and early Christian periods. Table 2.2 describes these features.

The most vital elements of natural law include its superhuman features, its immutable nature, its universality, its unspoken character, and its presence in the hearts of humans. Natural law supersedes laws created by men and women and is discovered through what ancient philosophers called "right reason." Under the theory of natural law, laws made by humans attempt to replicate

Table 2.2

Features of Natural Law

1. Natural law is not made by human beings
2. Natural law is the same for all human beings
3. Natural law at all times is an unchanging rule or pattern for humans to discover
4. Natural law is inscribed in the hearts and consciences of humans
5. Natural law is superior to laws made by humans
6. Natural law orders all things and is discovered through right reason
7. Natural law can be found in laws made by humans

Sources: d'Entréves 1961; Crowe 1977.

laws found in nature. Man-made law can either approximate or differ starkly from natural law, depending upon the makers of the human laws. Natural law provides a guide for assessing man-made law. According to the precepts of natural law, men and women innately can sense whether they are in compliance or variance with natural law. This sixth sense can also help citizens assess the degree to which their government leaders act in a responsible manner.

Right and wrong are also difficult concepts to define. Natural law provides one means of measuring concepts such as good and evil, right and wrong, justice and injustice. How do people know right from wrong? One school of thought holds that interpretation of natural law is intuitive and innate: "You feel it. You believe that you have a sense of what is right. . . . You sense that something is not right. If matters were otherwise, then you would have a sense of well-being" (Bloch 1986, 1).

Natural law includes a wide variety of interpretations. All natural law theories, however, have something in common, namely the view that there is some standard independent and above the laws made by humans. Some philosophers see the laws of nature in the physical world; others see natural law as coming directly from God; still others see natural law as the consequence of reason or in the general nature of humans. All these theories, however, support the view that there exist unchanging, universal, everlasting, and unspoken principles that distinguish right action from wrong.

In general, natural law theorists contend that the law reflects and should reflect "natural" tendencies, whether coming from God or from the inherent nature of people (Chambliss and Seidman 1982, 66). These theorists differ from legal positivists who argue that law may be valid while still violating standards of morality. Positivists recognize that laws may not always have a sound moral content but are still passed by legislators. Natural law theorists, in contrast, argue for a necessary connection between law and sound morality. They hold that one cannot make law without relying on morality (Dyzenhaus 2003, 25).

The Ideal of the Rule of Law

Greek and Roman Contributions to the Rule of Law

The idea of the rule of law did not spring out of thin air. It has deep historical roots going back to ancient Greek and Roman times. At the height of its glory in the fifth century BC, the city-state of Athens took great pride in being a democracy directed by its citizens. Every male citizen over the age of thirty was eligible to serve on juries, serve as a magistrate, and participate in legislative assemblies. These positions were filled by lot and all male citizens had an obligation to serve.

For the citizens of the city-state of Athens, democracy was synonymous with the rule of law and the law was revered as a means to protect citizens against populist tyrants. Courts and assemblies

acted as guardians of the law and laws passed during the time of Solon, (638 BC–558 BC) were venerated. The law was an instrument of stability. In the days of ancient Athens, proponents of new laws had to demonstrate the inadequacy of existing law as a condition for passage of the new legislation. All decrees of assemblies were examined for consistency with preexisting law (Tamanaha 2004, 7–8).

Not surprisingly, the ancient philosophers Plato and Aristotle contributed greatly to the development of the concept of the rule of law. Plato insists that the law must serve all and that without law that answered to the collective society (rather than the individual) the collapse of the state was not far off. Plato's student Aristotle, agreeing with the views of his teacher, states, "The rule of law is preferable to that of any individual." Aristotle reasons that when individuals govern they have to be guardians of the law. God and reason rather than passion should guide those who defend the law. Aristotle explains that those who follow the rule of law do the bidding of God and reason. He contends that desire and passion pervert the minds of rulers (even the best of rulers) and that the law of reason should prevail (Tamanaha 2004, 9).

Aristotle raises a number of issues that have surrounded the concept of rule of law throughout time. He believes in the subjection of government officials to the law, the identification of law with reason, and self-rule. Both Plato and Aristotle believe that the law should further the good of the community and enhance the moral development of all citizens. Both recognize the possibility that the law might be co-opted to serve the interests of elites. Both caution against the rule of "the mob"—the uneducated and untalented. Both philosophers also believe that the masses are susceptible to seduction by demagogues. Aristotle and Plato both believe that people have unequal talents and that those who are superior should rule and deserve more rewards. At the height of Athenian democracy under the rule of law, free Athenians achieved a degree of liberty and autonomy from the government.

Early Romans borrowed from the Greeks; however, over time their attitude toward the rule of law departed fundamentally from the Athenians' view. The Roman orator Cicero condemns the king who does not abide by the law. Cicero emphasizes that the law, not the individual magistrate, should rule and that the status of laws hinges upon their consistency with natural law defined through reason. Reason mandates that law should be for the good of the community, should be just, and should preserve the happiness and safety of citizens. Latter-day Romans, however, denounced the idea that laws should be consistently applied to everyone. For example, under Roman law it was understood that the king or emperor held a position that was superior to others.

When Justinian became emperor of the Roman Empire in AD 527, he began to codify Roman law. What came to be known as the Justinian Code largely consisted of existing customs, rules, decisions, and commentaries of jurists. The Justinian Code also established the notion of absolute monarchs who could operate above the law: "What has pleased the prince has the force of law"; "the prince is not bound by the law." The edicts of the Justinian Code, however, were generally ignored in the western Roman Empire (outside the eastern empire that was centered in Constantinople) until the twelfth century (Tamanaha 2004, 13).

Medieval Contributions to the Rule of Law

In the first few centuries after the fall of Rome, conflict emerged over who held authority for rule making. Kings and popes both claimed ultimate authority over behavior and the ability to make or change rules. During coronation ceremonies of the medieval period, kings committed themselves to upholding both ecclesiastical and other laws. Although the church performed these ceremonies, they incorporated the secular German idea that the king's chief duty was to be guardian of the community's laws. This Germanic "customary law," which posited the supremacy of law over all individuals, including kings, was in fundamental disagreement with the early Roman view of absolute rule by the emperor. The Germanic tradition, which reduced the discretionary powers of individuals, was based on universal principles that applied to all, regardless of social class, rank, or position.

The general populace of the Germanic tribes abided by and gave their support to the customary law. Eventually the customary law prioritizing equal treatment was reconciled with Roman law, which gave more authority to the supreme ruler. This reconciliation was accomplished through an understanding that monarchs absorbed the law in their will. The monarch was perceived to exist within the law and the law was oriented toward the interest of the community. This perspective linked the law to justice, morality, and an obligation to serve the people fairly.

According to Germanic tradition, the law took supremacy over the monarch, and the people could abandon any king who breached the law. A "right to resistance" underscored obligations that monarchs owed to the people. People who felt misused by the monarch maintained a right to resist. The law was to be supreme, preserved by both the king and the people from infringement and corruption (Tamanaha 2004, 19–25).

Perhaps the most famous example of the rule of law principle in the medieval period is the Magna Carta, which was signed in 1215. The Magna Carta or Great Charter is widely exalted for its attempt to restrict the arbitrary power of the king of England. For example, Clause 39 states that no free man shall be taken or imprisoned or outlawed or exiled or in any way ruined "except by the lawful judgment of his peers or by the law of the land." The Magna Carta originally applied only to great barons and church leaders of England. Over the centuries, however, it was transformed into a legal document. This document became revered as the basis for protecting personal liberties of average citizens (Reid 2004, 14). The idea of trial by a jury of one's peers, so fundamental to American democracy, was adopted by America's founders from the Magna Carta.

The Magna Carta also promoted the ideal of constitutionalism—legally structuring the relationship between a government and its people—and the notion of due process of the law. While the words "due process of law" are not directly found in the Great Charter, they appeared in a 1354 statute that traced its roots to the charter. This English statute identified legal protections that were to be made available to the king's subjects. Procedures that provided these legal protections included a fair hearing and the opportunity to be heard before a neutral decision maker. The Great Charter also added courts and juries of peers to the existing legal system. These two features of the law provided greater consistency and supplemented abstract declarations about natural law and laws according to custom.

A few decades after the Magna Carta was signed, an English judge, Henry of Bracton (AD 1210–1268) began to document the development of English rule of law. His writings captured much of the sentiment expressed in the charter, stressing three propositions: (1) the law made the king or the government, not the other way around; (2) the law was not power but restraint on power; and (3) the rulers must rule by rule of law. Bracton called the law "the bridle of power" and stated, "Nothing is more fitting for a sovereign than to live by the laws, nor is there any greater sovereignty than to govern

according to law, and he ought properly to yield to the law what the law has bestowed upon him, for the law makes him king" (Reid 2004, 11).

The English traditions regarding the sanctity and supremacy of the law were carried over to the New World, particularly in the British settlements of North America. These ideas of the law were quickly adopted and became the basis for the American legal tradition.

Early American Contributions to the Rule of Law

The earliest settlers in British North America did not come with empty minds, but brought with them the values and precepts they acquired in England. One of these values was a demand for the rule of law that as a principle stood in sharp contrast to expectations of arbitrariness often associated with monarchs of the time. A number of documents point to the respect the earliest settlers gave to the principle of rule of law. Even before landing at Plymouth, Massachusetts, the colonists signed the Mayflower Compact. This landmark legal document pledged to promulgate and publish "just and equal laws," as well as promising "all due submission and obedience" to those laws. The first colony of New Plymouth (later to become the province of Massachusetts Bay) had laws that were collected in a code. This code contained a rule of law section mandating that no person shall suffer damage of life, limb, liberty, or good name without being able to seek a just resolution for the harm by the process of the law. Although quite vague, this provision marked a beginning of efforts to articulate the rule of law in colonial New England (Reid 2004, 34).

In the early days of the Massachusetts Colony, controversy surrounded the issue of discretionary sentencing under the law. The colonists of Massachusetts were fearful of judicial arbitrariness since they had previously (as persecuted Puritans) been subject to discretionary and unpredictable decisions of English tribunals. In England the colonists had opposed the arbitrary authority of the aristocracy. In the Massachusetts Colony, it seemed to some of the colonists that their new magistrates were violating the principle of the rule of law. For example, in what some considered an arbitrary decision, in 1631 a colonist was sentenced to a whipping and loss of both ears for making seditious speech against the government and church. Colonists such as Roger Williams and Anne Hutchinson were banished from the colony for their outspoken comments. These rulings struck many colonists as both arbitrary and harsh.

People in England noted that the colonies were beginning to acquire a reputation for severity of punishment that could discourage migration. Severity of punishment, however, became less of an issue to early settlers than the problem of arbitrary rule. The people of Massachusetts wished to have a clear delineation of their rights and to codify their rights in published sets of rules. This is the essence of the rule of law. At first, the governor of the colony, John Winthrop, resisted the calls to establish a set of laws but by 1641 he bowed to popular pressure.

In 1641 a code titled the Body of Liberties, consisting of almost one hundred sections, was created that enunciated rights of the Massachusetts colonists. Civil guarantees identified in the Body of Liberties included the right to migrate freely from the colony, the privilege against double jeopardy, the principle of trial by jury, one-year statutes of limitation for noncapital crimes, the prohibition against compulsory self-incrimination, and the prohibition against cruel and barbarous torture (Reid 2004, 38). The creation of the Body of Liberties constituted an initial step in establishing the rule of law but did not go far enough to satisfy all the colonists. Through their representatives, the people expressed a desire for published laws linked to defined, known punishments. This demand led to the formulation of the General Lawes and Libertyes, also called the Code of 1648. In this code of laws, many of the punishments (particularly the punishment of death) were taken directly from the Old Testament. For example, the section in the Bible (Deuteronomy 21:18–21) concerning the death penalty for stubborn or rebellious sons was copied directly into the Code of 1648. The code also mandated the death penalty for adultery and for any man or woman who was a witch or consulted with spirits. The prohibition against witchcraft was taken from Exodus 22:18, Leviticus 20:27, and Deuteronomy 18:10–11. In each of the fourteen laws linked to the death penalty, the Code of 1648 cited the biblical passage on which the law relied, printing the citation as part of the legislation.

Settlers of Massachusetts Bay clearly wanted to be governed by known rules, not by the discretion of magistrates. The principle that they sought was that no person could be damaged except by virtue of an express law. Legal scholar John Reid summarizes the importance of the rule of law in governance in colonial Massachusetts:

> The rule-of-law demanded by the Massachusetts settlers is perhaps the purest expression of rule-of-law to be found in Anglo-American history. . . . It did not ask that law be just, good, or humane. The settlers did not seek to be governed by rules in order to promote social policy or promote economic well being. They wanted rules because, if followed rules would eliminate administrative and judicial arbitrariness. . . . the settlers were indifferent to the reality that fixed penalties determined prior to the adjudication of fact could lead to heavier retribution than might be just. They were saying that to be under the rule-of-law of harsh or unfair sanctions was preferable to rulelessness. . . . For the first colonists of Massachusetts Bay, law was supreme and no official or institution should be above it. That was what they meant by rule-of-law. It freed citizens from arbitrary power. (2004, 50–51)

In 1780 John Adams drafted the constitution of the Commonwealth of Massachusetts, the most famous example of the application of the rule of law to America. He carefully defined the purpose of the constitution: "to the end it may be a government of laws and not men." This phrasing of the ideal of a government of laws and not men has been quoted by the U.S. Supreme Court as well as every state supreme court in the United States. Thomas Paine also promoted the ideal of the rule of law in the 1776 pamphlet *Common Sense.* Paine noted that "in America THE LAW IS KING." Such a perspective is antithetical to practices of absolute governments where "the king is law." Paine concluded, "in free countries the law OUGHT to be King; and there ought to be no other" (Wikipedia 2006b).

The rule of law is still valued in contemporary American society. Upon taking office as president in September 1974, Gerald Ford stated, "Our constitution works. Our great republic is a government of laws and not men. Here the people rule" (Ford 1974). Ford's adherence to the rule of law was a source of great comfort in a time of turmoil following the resignation of President Nixon.

Five Views of the Rule of Law

A general conception of the rule of law principle views the law as a set of rules, norms, and institutionalized processes that creates known standards. These standards, in term, limit the discretion of government officials and facilitate impartiality. Various authors have further refined the concept of rule of law. Prominent among these authors and philosophers are Albert Dicey, Friedrich Hayek, John Rawls, Joseph Raz, and Ronald Dworkin.

In his 1885 classic, *Introduction to the Study of the Law and Constitution,* British jurist and constitutional theorist, Albert Venn Dicey identifies three principles that established the rule of law in England: (1) the absolute supremacy or predominance of law in contrast to the influence of arbitrary power; (2) equality before the law or the equal subjection of all classes of people to the law; and (3) rights that are derived from everyday legal decisions of ordinary criminal and civil law (precedent), not from a central constitutional document.

Dicey identified allegiance to the ideal of rule of law as a particular English phenomenon of those descended from English tradition. He observed that in reality rule of law is "peculiar to England, or to those countries which, like the United States of America, have inherited English traditions." Rule of law traditions are not common to continental Europe and serves to protect individuals from the arbitrary exercise of power. Dicey states, "In almost every continental community the executive exercises far wider discretionary authority in the matter of arrest, of temporary imprisonment, of expulsion from its territory, and the like, than is either legally claimed or in fact exerted by the government in England; and a study of European politics now and again reminds English readers that wherever there is discretion there is room for arbitrariness, and that in a republic no less than under a monarchy discretionary authority on the part of the government must mean insecurity for legal freedom on the part of its subjects" (Dicey 1885, Parts II, IV).

Dicey fostered a clearer enunciation of English based rule of law principles. These include the idea that no one may be punished except in accordance with the laws, no one is above the law, and rights evolve according to everyday decisions issued in the legal system (Neumann 2002, 2). Dicey's rule of law is consistent with the principle that government authority is legitimately exercised only in accordance with written, publicly disclosed laws that have been adopted and enforced in accordance with established procedure.

Friedrich Hayek (1899–1992) contributed significantly to our present understanding of the concept of rule of law. He was one of the most important economists and political philosophers of the twentieth century, sharing the 1974 Nobel Prize in Economics for his analysis of the interdependence of economic and social phenomenon. As a critic of both socialism and Nazi Germany, Hayek stressed the importance of limiting government authority, which could be accomplished by tying government authority to fixed and known rules. According to Hayek, rules would limit arbitrary use of power, enable individuals to plan ahead and spur economic growth. Hayek believed that allowing individuals to know the rules of the game alleviates fears of arbitrary confiscation of property, thus encouraging work, savings, investment, and wealth creation.

Hayek was known as a champion of individual freedom and free market capitalism. He believed that the coercive power of the state must at all times be limited and that the rule of law distinguishes free countries from others. The rule of law allows people to plan their lives according to the laws of the land. They should expect impartial treatment and freedom from state coercion as long as they abide by the rules. Hayek stated, "Stripped of all technicalities this means that government in all its actions is bound by rules fixed and announced beforehand—rules which make it possible to foresee with fair certainty how the authority will use its coercive powers in given circumstances and to plan one's individual affairs on the basis of this knowledge" (Hayek 1944, 54).

In general, Hayek was associated with advocacy of personal freedom and fear of big government. In his view, the rule of law allows private individuals to operate independently, while government intervention builds a road to serfdom. In the preface to the 1956 edition of the classic *Road to Serfdom*, Hayek identifies the rule of law as the cornerstone of liberty. He argues that a connection exists between "the growth of a measure of arbitrary administrative coercion and the progressive destruction of the cherished foundation of British liberty, the Rule of Law" (Tamanaha 2004, 65). State intervention for Hayek is consistent with dependency, paternalism, and weakness of character. Freedom is consistent with independence, self-sufficiency, and prosperity. These views were later enunciated by Nobel laureate Milton Friedman.

Hayek lays out three attributes of the rule of law: the law must be general, the law must be equal, and the law must be certain. The attribute of generality requires that law be set out in broad, abstract terms that are not aimed at specific individuals. The law then must be applied to all subjects of the state as a whole. Hayek contends that the separation of powers between the legislative and judicial branches of government is necessary because it mandates the passage of general laws before the laws are applied to individuals. Equality refers to laws that apply to everyone without arbitrary distinctions. Hayek's third attribute of rule of law requires that those who are subject to law should be able to predict reliably what rules govern their conduct. This predictability and certainty facilitates freedom of action (Tamanaha 2004, 66).

Hayek is recognized as one of the most prominent champions of individual freedom. In his book *Law, Liberty, and Legislation: Rules and Order*, he contends that the law is a prerequisite rather than a determinant of success. For Hayek, the law should be viewed as a condition for the successful pursuit of people's desires. The law envisions no particular outcome but only the freedom of people to pursue their own objectives (Richman 2001). A major insight of Hayek is his belief that individual freedom operating under the rule of law leads to economic prosperity while big government leads to serfdom.

John Rawls (1921–2002) provides further insight into the rule of law. As a professor of philosophy at Harvard Universitry, beginning in 1964 and continuing for almost forty years, Rawls trained many of the contemporary figures in moral and political philosophy. Rawls defines the rule of law as a regular, impartial, and fair administration of public rules. Such an administration of rules would include the following:

1. Possibility of compliance (rules that can be followed): This refers to the expectation that individuals are able to comply with the rules. Rawls believes that those who enact the laws should make sure that required action can be met reasonably. The legal system should recognize that performance may be impossible and that the impossibility of performance can serve as a defense or mitigating circumstance.
2. Regularity (similar cases should be treated similarly): Judges should make distinctions based on relevant legal principles, not on whim or the importance of the defendants. All rules should be applied consistently.
3. Publicity: Laws should be known and clearly defined.
4. Generality: Rules should not be aimed at particular individuals to give them unfair advantage over others.
5. Due process: The legal system should provide fair and orderly procedures. The system should facilitate orderly public trials and hearings. It should contain rules that provide a reasonable process to discover the truth. Due process also provides that judges should be independent and impartial; no person should judge his or her own case. (Rawl 1999, 206–213; Legal Theory Blog 2006)

In his analysis, Rawls focuses upon the uniform, fair application of rules, stressing that procedures must be fair, open, impartial, designed to find the truth, and consistent. For Rawls, the legal system is a means of regulating conduct and providing a framework of cooperation. The rule of law implies impartiality and fair enforcement of standards but does not ensure the passage of just laws (Neumann 2002, 8). Unjust laws may be passed and impartially applied under the banner of rule of law.

A professor of philosophy of law at Oxford University, Joseph Raz further defines the concept of the rule of law. Raz was born in 1939, received a Magister Juris degree in 1963 from Hebrew University, and a Doctor of Philosophy degree in 1967 from Oxford University. He has attracted numerous scholars to Balliol College, Oxford University to study under him. Raz developed the following eight principles of law:

1. All laws should be prospective, open, and clear.
2. Laws should be relatively stable.
3. The making of particular laws (particularly legal orders) should be guided by open, stable, clear, and general rules.
4. The independence of the judiciary must be guaranteed.
5. The principles of natural justice must be observed.
6. The courts should have review powers.
7. The courts should be easily accessible.
8. The discretion of the crime-preventing agencies should not be allowed to pervert the law. (Raz 1979, 210–232)

The eight rule of law principles identified by Raz draws widely upon previous scholarship. They reinforce the thinking of Puritans in the early Massachusetts Colony. The desire for clear, stable, and openly known rules is viewed by both the early Puritans and Raz as a bulwark against the potentially abusive practice of arbitrary discretion.

Ronald Dworkin, American legal philosopher and former professor at Oxford University, also adds to our understanding of the rule of law. Dworkin describes two different conceptions of the rule of law. In what Dworkin terms the "rule book" conception, the rule of law insists that the power of the state, so far as possible, should never be exercised against individual citizens except in accordance with rules that are explicitly set out in a public rule book available to all. Both the government and ordinary citizens must play by the public rules until they are changed.

In contrast to the "rule book" conception, a second and more expansive conception of the rule of law is described by Dworkin as the "rights" conception. This perspective assumes that citizens have moral rights and duties with respect to one another as well as political rights with respect to the state as a whole. Dworkin's "rights" conception insists that moral and political rights must be recognized in the law. The rule of law under this "rights" perspective requires that moral rights be enforced. The "rule book" view is narrower in the sense that it does not consider the content of the rules, but only requires that rules must be followed until changed. In contrast, the broader "rights" conception contends that rules must also reflect moral rights.

Dworkin claims that the principle of the rule of law may at times be violated and the government periodically may simply not follow its own rules. For example, police may not follow regulations in arresting or failing to arrest individuals. Dworkin cites three types of "rights" oriented violations. First, government might limit the scope of individual rights it enforces. Second, governments might decline to enforce individual rights. Finally, governments might not accurately recognize rights (Dworkin 1985, 12–13).

Summary of the Concept-Rule of Law

The rule of law is credited with helping to make America what we know it is today. It predates the founding of the United States, tracing its ancestry to the earliest colonies. Puritan fears of arbitrary and unjust power came to the North American shore on the *Mayflower* and affirmed a desire for consistent, known, and equally applied sets of rules. According to Friedrich Hayek, the rule of law fostered liberty, economic growth, and free market competition, which was facilitated when free individuals could assess with reasonable certainty how the government would use or not use its coercive power.

Another benefit of the rule of law is its contribution to justice. Equal treatment under the law and other concepts that we take for granted today were not always accepted. For example, in colonial Virginia, poor convicted felons were often sent to the gallows while literate felons could escape with a branding on the thumb, and gentleman felons sometimes were branded with a cold iron that would not leave a mark. Violence was often condoned if it involved gentlemen against common folks; however, the violent acts of common folk against gentle folk were severely punished (Koven 1999, 53).

Equality before the law, knowledge of what is permitted and not permitted, acceptance of human rights, and protection against the arbitrary action of the government are all hallmarks of the rule of law. These features and others are described in Table 2.3.

The concept of the rule of law in concert with the ideals of natural law and the public interest

Table 2.3

Features of Rule of Law

1. Consistent application of rules
2. Equality of treatment for all under the rules
3. Predictability of environment assists free enterprise
4. Facilitates security, liberty and freedom
5. Changes in law respond to popular sentiment
6. Allows people to pursue their own objectives
7. Serves as a bulwark against tyranny, chaos, and injustice
8. Affords protection of fundamental human rights
9. Accessible and understandable to the common people
10. Protects people against arbitrary power of rulers

Sources: Hayek 1994; Reid 2004; Tamanaha 2004.

contributes to our understanding of responsible governance. Responsibility is grounded on following constitutional mandates such as support for the common people. It is assumed that in democracies rulers represent the people as a whole and that leaders serve the people's interest, not their own or only the interests of the wealthy. It is further assumed that the public can act as a check on irresponsible governance by throwing out incumbents and electing new sets of representatives. This is the ultimate check on leaders who lose touch with their constituents and fail to provide for the common good.

Natural law represents a second input into responsible governance. The concept of natural law implies that average citizens instinctively (by their gut instinct or by the hidden hand of God) know right from wrong, good from evil. Governance is consistent with natural law in the sense that it acts in accordance with the rules of nature. Representatives of government have an obligation to follow what seems naturally good and reject what seems to be naturally repugnant. Following the logic of St. Augustine, responsible governance would act in accord with the Will of God, Divine Wisdom, or Supreme Reason. Following the views of St. Thomas Aquinas, responsible governance would encourage leaders to respond to reason, the divine spark within people. By following the "light of natural reason," leaders would govern responsibly and instinctively reject actions that fail to accord with the laws of nature.

The rule of law contributes to responsible governance by limiting arbitrary action of government officials and providing a consistent playing field where citizens can predict the actions of government. The rule of law lends itself to responsible governance since it provides equal treatment before the law, establishes rights for citizens, and clearly identifies permissible and impermissible actions. Inputs that help to define responsible governance are described in Figure 2.1.

The concept of responsible governance remains somewhat subjective. The degree of responsibility or irresponsibility of any given governmental entity is, to a certain extent, in the eye of the beholder. The ideal of responsible governance, however, is not a blank slate waiting for anyone to inscribe his or her own definitions. Responsibility can be assessed by objective indicators such as degree of responsiveness to the people, alignment with natural law principles, and judicial fairness. All these contribute to the concept of responsible governance. Readers can assess for themselves the degree to which certain actions aligned or misaligned with the concept of responsible governance. Chapter 3 discusses this concept through the lens of American elections.

Figure 2.1 **Influences of Responsible Government**

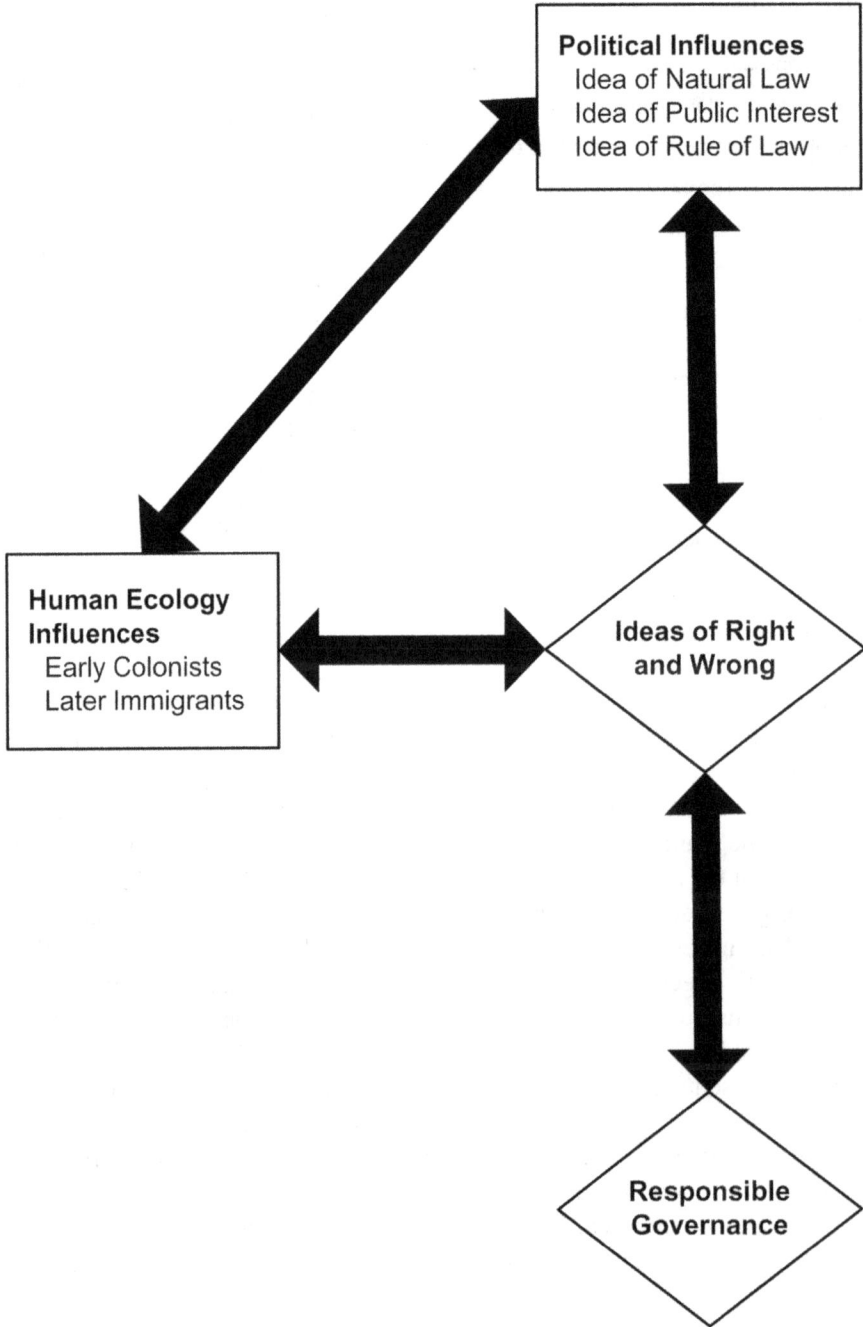

Chapter 3

The Influence of Money on Elections

Even a casual observer of American history recognizes that while the Declaration of Independence and other government documents enumerate noble ideals (all men are created equal, all people have inalienable rights, all government derives its powers from the consent of the governed), there is often a disconnect between the ideals and the reality. In the United States, responsible governance requires compliance with the basic precepts of democracy, including relatively open elections, the ability of the people to have their voices heard in the selection of candidates, fair counting of ballots, and the ability to transition peacefully from one administration to another. Responsible governance strives to be responsive to the general populace. Such behavior promotes legitimacy and accountability. In contrast, electoral behavior such as bribing, deceiving, intimidating, misrepresenting, and miscounting votes represents irresponsible governance. It is incumbent upon leaders to eliminate or mitigate such behavior.

This chapter will discuss the role of money in American politics. The corruption of the ideal of democracy is not new. The ideal of democracy exists when citizens are free to clearly identify their best interests, to vote in accordance with their interests, and to provide other forms of input (such as contact with representatives, contributions to interest groups, membership in organizations)

into the political process. Although citizens may strive to live up to the principles of pure democracy, in reality various factors intervene to tarnish the ideal. In the past, money, personal connections, and coercion have altered the electoral playing field to the advantage of the wealthy, the well connected, and the powerful. The two case studies in this chapter describe deviations from the pure ideal of democracy, as well as the efforts made by responsible administrators to bring behavior back in line with the noble ideals of democracy.

Case No. 1 describes the rise of political machines in the mid to late nineteenth century and the electoral abuses associated with some of the most powerful machines. This case illustrates the degree to which reality departed from the democratic ideal. The case also describes "good-government" advocates who worked to limit electoral abuses emanating from political machines. Case No. 2 discusses the misuse of money by Texas congressman Tom DeLay in 2002 as well as his illegal plan to capture the U.S. House of Representatives for the Republican Party. The case study shows that efforts to manipulate elections are not merely matters of ancient history. The case contends that illegal electoral activities erode confidence in the government and denigrate the overall process of electing leaders.

The ideal of free and fair elections is a hallmark of American society. A paradox, however, exists. While Americans travel to distant lands to supervise other people's elections, many American citizens talk about "President Gore" and allege that the 2004 presidential election was stolen. Accounts of broken polling machines, confusing ballots, excessively long lines in certain precincts, and "hanging chads" being examined under magnifying glasses continue to remind Americans about the imperfect nature of the voting process. While American soldiers go overseas allegedly to spread democracy, the American record of free and fair elections is far from unsullied.

Early elections in the United States were far from representative of the entire population. When the U.S. Constitution was written in 1787, voting was limited to white, male landowners; U.S. senators were elected by state legislators, not by plain citizens. In the machine era, of New York's Boss Tweed (1823–1878) to the latter day Chicago boss Richard Daley (1902–1976), ballots were regularly stuffed, dumped, miscounted, or ironed together to look like they were one ballot. Repeat voters showed up at the polls; others were driven away by armed thugs. Names of voters for hire were taken from gravestones in cemeteries. In the late nineteenth century, many of the grossest violations were reformed and the system was periodically purged of its excesses. However, the case studies identify an ongoing tension between forces supporting honest elections and those seeking power through guile or fraud.

More Americans have the ability to vote and to shape public policy today than at the time of the nation's founding. Some people, however, still have greater ability to influence elections than others. Money plays an undeniable role. Corporate and individual givers have access to leaders that others do not have. The demands of modern campaigns force political candidates to raise great amounts of money, obligating them (knowingly or subconsciously) to the wealthy few rather than the many. Money today is a prerequisite for electoral success because it purchases media advertisements, pollsters, strategists, campaign staff, and other necessities of political campaigning. Corporations and wealthy individuals are able to extract rewards from politicians, often to the detriment of the population as a whole. People who are not independently wealthy and are not currying favor with well-financed interest groups are effectively excluded from the process.

While it is easy to criticize current flaws in American elections, historical perspective is important. This perspective is provided in the machine politics case study and the discussion of the influence of money in early American elections. The objective of the discussion is to identify violations of responsible governance and society's reaction to those violations, thus providing insight into the values of the times as well as the continuous struggle to define acceptable and unacceptable behavior. The concept of responsible governance is defined in behavior. Actions that mitigate violations of ethical election behavior are viewed as responsible; the opposite is the case for actions that encourage or implicitly accept violations.

A tight connection between money and elections infringes upon principles of democracy. If elections can be bought, then the principle of "one man—one vote" is violated. Not all citizens have similar influences since those with means can use their money to perpetuate advantages. The use of money to purchase power, however, is not new, as the following section illustrates.

Elections and Money in Historical Perspective

Early Influences of Money on Politics

From the earliest times in the American colonies, wealth was associated with privilege. In colonial

Virginia, punishment, dress, housing, political power, and civil rights were differentiated by social class. Planters who held large tracts of land ruled and became members of Virginia's governing body, the House of Burgesses. This pattern was also the case in other colonies. For example, in the Massachusetts Colony, those with the largest landholdings tended to sit on the governing bodies.

Wealth became synonymous with political power and elections were virtually bought by those with the means to do so. In Virginia it was common practice for candidates to throw lavish parties (called treats), invite local property owners, and convince them of the candidate's qualifications through a display of hospitality. Many ambitious colonists engaged in "treating," sparing no expense in their pursuit of public office. While treating was common, there were some accepted rules and at various times colonists were accused of excessive extravagance. For example, in 1757 George Washington was charged with campaign irregularities in his race for a seat in the House of Burgesses. Historians note that Washington's campaign managers dispensed twenty-eight gallons of rum, fifty gallons of rum punch, thirty-four gallons of wine, forty-six gallons of beer, and two gallons of cider in his election campaign. This was considered exorbitant since there were only 391 individuals in the district who were eligible to vote. Despite his absence from Virginia (he was away serving in the British army), Washington was elected in a landslide, receiving 78 percent of the vote (Lammers 1982, 3; Green 2002, 28).

In the early days of the American republic, money and land were directly tied to political power. In Maryland around 1776, a person was required to own at least 5,000 British pounds' worth of property to run for governor and at least 1,000 British pounds' worth of property to run for the state senate. Such a linkage between money and political office is common throughout history.

During the times of the ancient Greeks, vote buying and bribery were widely accepted. Candidates for office in ancient Rome entertained voters with gladiator contests, games, and acts of conspicuous generosity. English elections in the seventeenth and eighteenth centuries were also corrupted. "Rotten boroughs" in England of the early nineteenth century were controlled by a patron who exercised undue and unrepresentative influence. The purchase of well-paid jobs with little or no responsibility was also a common practice (Thayer 1973, 26; Green 2002, 27).

Early Influence of Money at the National Level

Initially, elections in the United States were dominated by the wellborn and economically influential. Beginning in 1828, however, common folks gained power as average citizens helped to elect the "backwoodsman" Andrew Jackson to the presidency. Jackson used his office to consolidate political power, hire his friends, and generate revenue, instituting what became known as the spoils system in American government. According to Thayer (1973, 28), Jackson replaced about 40 percent of the entire national bureaucracy with his own appointees, soon after he became president. These appointees were expected to "kick back" or contribute 6 percent of their weekly pay to the Democratic Party. Jackson's Democratic Party grew in power and influence after these practices were instituted (Thayer 1973, 27–29).

The use of elected office to extract money and offer benefits was not unique to the Jackson presidency. Patronage was widely utilized at all levels of government in an effort to build loyalty, generate revenue, and continue to win elections. Political parties became depositories of money extracted from jobholders. Those contributing to political parties included business owners seeking government contracts and the heads of criminal enterprises seeking protection from the law. Money from these sources was pumped back into elections in which candidates spent lavishly in efforts to secure votes.

Beginning with the administration of Ulysses S. Grant, the Republican Party began to dominate national elections and became associated with wealthy industrialists and bankers. These individuals strongly supported Republican policies such as laissez-faire economics, low taxes, few regulations placed on business by government, and unfettered free-market competition. By 1896 the linkage between money and politics was firmly established by a wealthy Ohio businessman and chair of the Republican National Committee, Mark Hanna.

Hanna initially contributed his own money in the contest to nominate Republican William McKinley in 1896. After McKinley was nominated, Hanna implemented "businesslike methods" for collecting money from corporations in support of McKinley. As head of the Republican National Committee, Hanna levied regular assessments on all businesses throughout the country according to each company's "stake in the general prosperity" and special interest in a region. Banks were assessed one-quarter of one percent of their capital. The massive corporation Standard Oil contributed about one-quarter of one million dollars; large insurance companies contributed slightly less. If a company sent a check to Hanna that he believed was too small, it was returned; if a company paid too much, a refund was issued. According to historian George Thayer (1973, 50), Hanna used techniques of fund-raising that already existed. Hanna's innovation was that he formally institutionalized and legitimized the link between money and electoral control.

Hanna is recognized as a forerunner of the modern campaign manager since he crafted the message, raised the money, and vigorously sold the party line to the uninformed public. As the party's campaign manager, he did not use campaign money for personal gain and promised personal arrangements in return for money. "True" machine politicians considered him "naive" for failing to fully understand the personal advantages derived from political power. Companies paid their assessments willingly because they understood that their contributions supported the type of leaders that would facilitate their prosperity. Payments were also made as a means to buy safety from public criticism or government antitrust action. Businesses had an overall understanding that Republicans would conduct the affairs of government to their benefit (Thayer 1973, 50).

Hanna and McKinley delivered in their support of policies that favored business. These policies included opposition to free coinage of silver (which businesses perceived as inflationary and fiscally destabilizing), support for protective tariffs (to help domestic businesses and maintain economic prosperity), and general distrust of labor (since businesses considered unionized workers un-American or even socialist). From the perspective of business, McKinley, a former businessman himself, was a trusted "protectionist" who would shield domestic businesses from foreign competition.

The effect of Hanna's "taxes" on business was clearly visible. McKinley's campaign was the most expensive campaign of its time, with Republicans from Wall Street raising a large proportion of the money. The money was used to plaster McKinley's face on millions of posters, billboards, pamphlets, and buttons. The campaign was carefully planned and coordinated. Hanna sent 1,400 trained speakers across the country to support McKinley and each week delivered short statements or what is now termed "talking points" to local newspapers. Over 300 million campaign documents, including some in German, French, Spanish, Italian, Swedish, Danish, Dutch, and Yiddish, were sent out by the Republican National Committee (Thayer 1973, 50).

Early Influence of Money at the State and Local Level

The link between money and political power was also strong at the state and local levels. As early as 1790, Aaron Burr, then leader of New York's Tammany Hall, recognized that most workers in New York City did not own land and therefore were unable to vote. In order to expand the power of his political party, he managed to have the State Assembly establish a bank that would make loans to known Democrats so they could purchase property. In 1828, Tammany Hall adopted the spoils practices of the Jackson administration, requiring New York City employees to contribute 6 percent of their weekly pay to the Democratic political organization. With money coming in from political appointees, vote buying became common. For example, in 1832 the price for an uncommitted vote approximated five dollars. This represented two or three days' wages for an ordinary laborer. By 1838 both major parties in New York City (Whigs and Democrats) commonly paid "floaters" (nonresidents) to vote early and often. The Whigs paid $22 for the first vote of a floater and $18 for each additional vote (Thayer 1973, 29).

Corruption in elections intensified following the Civil War, a period recognized as the most politically corrupt time in American history (Green 2002, 35). In what has been called the "golden age of boodle," no office was viewed as too high to purchase, no man too pure to bribe, no principle too sacred to destroy, and no law too fundamental to break. Thayer states, "The old Anglo-Saxon belief that public duty required certain personal and financial sacrifices was giving way to the conviction among certain men that politics, at least in part, was a lucrative source of personal enrichment" (1973, 37). New York and Pennsylvania were particularly notorious for their corrupt political machines; however, blatant bribery occurred elsewhere.

In the 1860s in New York, William Marcy Tweed, the notorious Boss Tweed of the Democratic Party's organization Tammany Hall, ran the "Black Horse Cavalry," a group of state legislators in Albany who sold their votes for cash. Vote selling became a highly lucrative venture, depending upon the issue at stake. During a battle over which financier, Jay Gould or Cornelius Vanderbilt, would control the Erie Railroad, state votes were sold for as much as $5,000 each.

Anticipating Mark Hanna's practice, by the 1870s and 1880s local politicians were systematically using their political power to extract large amounts of money from those who wanted specific legislation passed or killed. Boss Tweed's successor at Tammany Hall, "Honest John" Kelly, instituted a procedure whereby all candidates contributed a fixed sum to the Democratic campaign committee and officeholders were assessed a percentage of their salaries. Kelly then justified the large salaries for New York City employees on the grounds that they were required to make hefty political contributions. Such schemes to raise money for one's political party were not unique to New York, and requiring government workers to contribute part of their salaries became an accepted practice. An example of this practice is illustrated in the 1882 letter delivered to every employee of the state of Pennsylvania: "Two percent of your salary is _____. Please remit promptly. At the close of the campaign we shall place a list of those who have not paid in the hands of the head of the department you are in" (Thayer 1973, 38). In the city of Philadelphia assessments were even higher. Payments from Philadelphia employees by the turn of the century ranged from 3 percent for salaries of $600 to $1,200 to 12 percent for salaries of $10,000 and above. Other states also followed the practice of forcing employees to remit part of their salaries. In Louisiana, state employees contributed a flat 10 percent to the ruling party's campaign chest.

While extortion of government workers was a sure way to generate revenue for political parties, eventually the practice was banned. With the assassination of President James Garfield in 1881 by a disappointed office seeker, the practice of political appointment came under severe criticism. The result was the passage of the Pendleton Act of 1883. The Pendleton Act banned all political contributions from civil servants. Undeterred by this ban, however, politicians simply shifted their tactics and began to look for new sources of revenue. They again turned to business for campaign contributions. In a refinement of this practice of pressuring business owners, politicians in both New York and Pennsylvania introduced what became known as "squeeze bills"—legislation that was particularly hostile to business. In order to kill the hostile bills, businesses were forced to make significant political contributions. In essence, large and small businesses were "squeezed" into making payments that went to the majority political party. If the contributions were made, the bills were allowed to die in committee. This money-raising strategy was also known as "frying the fat" since it put the heat on wealthy businesses and fried away their money—their excess fat. In Pennsylvania, public utilities and heavy industry companies (such as steel and locomotive companies) made large contributions to the Republican Party to prevent enactment of hostile legislation. In New York, similar practices were employed for the benefit of the majority Democratic Party.

Major industrialists such as Andrew Carnegie and Henry Frick were large contributors to the Republican Party in Pennsylvania. One expert in "frying the fat," Pennsylvania politician Bois Penrose, successfully ran for the U.S. Senate in 1896 after spending half a million dollars in contributions to members of the Pennsylvania legislature. He is quoted as stating, "I'll take money from any man. You can't run a party on nothing and when

you need money the place to get it is from them that have it." According to his biographer, Penrose was particularly effective in getting money from business corporations, extorting "millions for party support any time he asked them to give." Pennsylvania policies initiated by Penrose also "made billions in profits for his clients, the corporations" (Thayer 1973, 47).

Another source of local funding was groups seeking to obtain or retain licenses and those seeking to obtain implicit permission to run illegal establishments. Representatives of utilities, racetracks, saloons, houses of prostitution, gambling houses, and streetcar companies all contributed to political campaigns, seeking lucrative government contracts or protection from prosecution. Those who were prospering under the status quo contributed to political campaigns in order to be allowed to continue doing what they were doing. Money raised by the political parties was then spent on publishing and distributing partisan literature, speaking tours, ox roasts, bean feeds, dances, rallies, and other events (Thayer 1973, 41).

Money and politics peacefully coexisted at the turn of the twentieth century. Paying members of state legislatures for votes to obtain a U.S. Senate seat became so widespread that the Senate became known as the "millionaire's club." Novelist Mark Twain sarcastically commented that legislatures in the United States brought higher prices than anywhere else in the world. According to a popular saying of the times, "It is harder for a poor man to enter the United States Senate than for a rich man to enter Heaven" (Green 2002, 36).

Modern Influences of Money on Politics

Not a great deal seems to have changed in regard to the influence of money on American elections. Money still is essential; however, the strategies by which money is raised and funneled to elections are different. Various campaign practices that were the norm in an earlier time are illegal today. As election laws are passed, however, clever politicians figure out new ways to bypass them. Influence peddling still occurs; however, it is a bit less overt. Political action committees and independent groups have become new sources of revenue, replacing squeeze bills and assessments on wages. Instead of plying voters with rum punch and paying floater for votes political candidates today use money to buy airtime on radio and television, hire pollsters, pay consultants, and seek advice from an assortment of image shapers.

Large corporations and interest groups contribute to campaigns today to purchase access and to gain special privileges. Money is parceled out by well-paid lobbyists who are adept at seeing that those who pay their bills are protected from unwanted legislation and/or benefit from favorable legislation. The influence of lobbyists forces elected officials to cater to special interests rather than the general interests of their constituents. This by definition is a direct contradiction of the principle of public interest.

Political Action Committees

Political action committees (PACs) are voluntary associations of like-minded people who pool their resources to maximize their political clout. PACs arose after reforms were enacted in 1974 to limit the amount of money individuals can contribute to candidates. To circumvent the new restrictions on individual giving, PACs replaced "fat cats" (wealthy individual contributors); large contributions were made in the name of entire committees. Normally, PACs consisted of business, labor, agrarian, ideological, or issue groups. These groups raised money from employees, stockholders, or like-minded individuals for the purpose of combining numerous small contribu-

tions into large amounts. These large amounts were then contributed to candidates or political party committees.

PACs aid fund-raising because (1) they have access to large numbers of individual contributors (such as company employees or mailing lists of like-minded citizens), and (2) they have an internal means of communication (through memos to employees or mailings to those of similar ideological bent). Following passage of the 1974 reforms, PACs grew significantly. In 1996, PAC money made up 41 percent of the money raised by incumbents for U.S. House of Representatives races and 20 percent of the money raised by U.S. Senate incumbents (Alexander 1992, 58; Green 2002, 61; Gordon 2005, 2).

PACs have grown due to their ability to circumvent campaign finance legislation. They exist within the letter of the law yet their goal is to violate the spirit of the law. They act as a means of funneling money to those who hold power. According to Philip Stern in *Still the Best Congress Money Can Buy* (1992, 5), PACs enable money-power to replace people-power as the driving force in American politics. The aim of PACs is relatively straightforward—to further their own group's special interest by either killing or promoting legislation in Congress. PACs have helped a variety of individuals and interest groups, such as specific families, dairy farmers, and auto manufacturers, in the past.

The Influence of PAC Money on Legislation

A few examples illustrate the tremendous return on investment of well-placed campaign contributions. Stern provides telling examples of how PAC money ends up serving interest groups or individuals rather than the general population (1992, 55–56). In one example, the political generosity of Ernest and Julio Gallo (bottlers of one-fourth of the wine sold in the United States) played a role in the approval of a special tax provision tailored to them. The tax provision came to be known as the "Gallo amendment" since it seemed to apply only to their extended family.

Over an eight-year period the Gallo brothers generously contributed an estimated $325,000 to parties and candidates, divided about equally between Democrats and Republicans. In 1986, the two Gallo brothers plus their wives made the maximum legal contribution of $5,000 each to Senator Robert Dole's political action committee. Dole, as ranking Republican member of the Senate Finance Committee, shepherded the Gallo amendment through the legislative process until it ultimately was signed into law.

The Gallo amendment in essence allowed the two Gallo brothers to pass along roughly $80 million to their grandchildren without paying the customary 33 percent estate tax. The amendment was estimated to be worth about $27 million in tax savings.

In another example of the influence of individuals on legislation, international media mogul Rupert Murdoch was confronted with opposition in the U.S. Congress to the growing concentration of media power. In 2003, Congress was on the verge of limiting any company from owning local television stations that reached more than 35 percent of American homes. The Murdoch-owned Fox television stations, however, reached nearly 39 percent of American homes. If the contemplated legislation were passed, Murdoch would be forced to sell some of his American media empire.

In order to kill the intended legislation, Murdoch used the influence of Political Action Committees and lobbyists that were controlled by his media company, News Corporation. The News Corporation groups then joined with interests from other media companies to oppose legislative controls. With the backing of the Bush administration,

Murdoch and other media interests were able to get congressional leaders to raise the limit in the proposed legislation to 39 percent.

An early leader of the congressional movement to limit the concentration of media in the United States, Trent Lott, initially supported the 35 percent ownership limit but later backed the rise to 39 percent. Months before the agreement to raise the limits, HarperCollins, another Murdoch-owned company, signed a $250,000 book deal to publish Lott's memoir. Following the example of the Gallo brothers and others, Murdoch has spread his campaign donations to both Republicans and Democrats, nurturing relationships with Bill and Hillary Clinton. As a consequence of his direct contributions and fundraising for Hillary Clinton's presidential campaign, Murdoch hoped to gain access to future American leaders. In 2007, Murdoch's holding company (a company that owns part, all, or a majority of another company's stock but does not produce goods or services itself) offered $5 billion to buy the parent company of the *Wall Street Journal* (Becker 2007)

Many Americans viewed the growing influence of Murdoch, a native of Australia, with alarm. The takeover of the *Wall Street Journal*, which was finalized in December 2007, ended a century of control by Boston's Bancroft family. The deal further concentrated media power in the hands of a single individual. In addition to the *Wall Street Journal*, Murdoch's News Corporation also owns the Fox broadcast network, Twentieth Century Fox, Fox News Channel, satellite TV businesses in Europe and Asia, MySpace, the *New York Post*, and groups of newspapers in Australia. Congressional advocates of limiting Murdoch's influence in the United States argued that greater diversity in ownership (particularly pertaining to businesses involved in shaping citizen attitudes) was healthy for American democracy. Murdoch surrendered his Australian citizenship and became an American citizen in 1985 in order to further his business interests in the United States.

Other legislation has also been very costly to taxpayers and consumers. In 1986, for example, the House of Representatives considered whether to maintain a subsidy to the dairy industry at a higher level (as desired by the approximately 200,000 dairy farmers in the United States) or at a lower level (as desired by a coalition of consumer and labor groups). At an estimated cost to taxpayers of $2.77 billion in direct payments and $11.52 billion in higher prices to consumers, the dairy interests secured their costly subsidies through Congress. The $3.3 million collected, in 1984, by three large dairy PACs and the distribution of this money to members of Congress appeared to have influenced voting behavior.

Much of the dairy lobby money was distributed to big-city members of Congress who had, at most, a few dairy cows in their district. Voting statistics reveal that 100 percent of the congressional representatives who received more than $30,000 from the dairy lobby between 1979 and 1986 voted for the higher dairy subsidies. Ninety-seven percent of the representatives who received between $20,000 and $30,000 from the dairy lobby voted for the higher subsidies. In contrast, only 23 percent of representatives who did not receive any campaign contributions and 33 percent of representatives who received between $1 and $2,500 voted for the higher subsidy (Stern 1992, 166). In retrospect, the money raised by the dairy lobby seems to have been very well spent, yielding a return many times in excess of the outlay.

Contributions made on behalf of the auto industry appear to be even more costly (at an estimated annual cost of $38 billion) to American consumers. For example, in 1990, Nevada Democratic senator Richard Bryan proposed a bill to require automakers to increase fuel efficiency by 20 percent by 1995 and by 40 percent by 2001. Auto industry advocates, however, mounted a concerted campaign to kill the bill. They first attempted a filibuster. Ending the filibuster required sixty votes in the Senate; sixty-eight senators voted to cut off debate. Following this vote, auto industry supporters (with the backing of the Bush administration) intensified their efforts to continue the filibuster and were successful. In a few short days, eleven senators switched their votes and sided with the auto industry. Sixty-four percent of the senators who received more than $20,000 from the auto industry between 1985 and 1990 voted with the auto industry to kill the bill by sustaining the filibuster. Only 15 percent of senators who received between zero and $11,999 voted to end the filibuster (Stern 1992, 174).

The Influence of PAC Money on Principles of Representation

Large sums of money are required today in order to compete for high political office. PACs give large amounts of money to politicians, particularly incumbents who are likely to be reelected. These incumbents in turn often remember their friends and reward them in a number of ways. Methods of repayment include passing favorable legislation, defeating costly legislation, changing the wording of legislation to negate its impact, and letting potentially damaging legislation die in committee. Changing one or two words in bills that representatives have no direct interest in can produce millions or even billions of dollars in added costs to consumers and added profits to special interest groups. The process allows well-placed campaign contributions to yield tremendous rewards for the contributors.

Political candidates today are under great pressure to raise money that is needed for successful elections. Candidates use the money to attack opponents and create positive images of themselves.

The need for money has created a "subway" system in which contributors donate money in order to gain access to the candidate. Johnny Chung, the reputed front man for at least $400,000 in illegal foreign campaign donations to the Democratic Party, stated in an interview with the *Los Angeles Times* that in Bill Clinton's White House it was understood that there was a price for admission: "I see the White House is like a subway—you have to put coins in to open the gate."

In return for Chung's 400 contributions to the Democratic Party, he received forty-nine visits to the White House. While President Clinton was in office, Chung's picture was placed not only in the Oval Office but also in the White House private dining room, the president's movie theater, and the White House bowling alley. Chung admitted that he contributed $50,000 to Hillary Clinton's chief of staff in 1995 to help defray the cost of a Christmas reception. Following allegations of influence peddling, the Democratic National Committee returned $366,000 to Chung. Although Chung's financial contributions generated a great deal of negative publicity, they were not found to be illegal. The Justice Department conducted an investigation of Chung's activities in 1997 and concluded that there was insufficient evident to suggest criminal wrongdoing on the part of officials in the Clinton administration (amarillo.com 2007; Wertheimer 2007).

Philip Stern (1999, 32) notes that money and PACs are fundamental threats to a sense of fairness, since PACs, with their capacity to pool money, have the power to command congressional attention far more than ordinary, unorganized citizens. Only about 10 percent of ordinary citizens are thought to contribute any amount of money to political candidates. Perhaps more important, Stern notes that PAC contributions to incumbents limit the selection process and inhibit fresh candidates from emerging:

Suppose, for example, that Abraham Lincoln were alive today and aspired to a seat in the House in a congressional district represented by a powerful committee chairman. Chances are that, whatever his personal merits or the quality of his ideas, most PACs and, for that matter, most individual givers would greet the candidate Lincoln with, at best, polite snickers and send him away empty handed. Since Lincoln's committee-chairman opponent could raise almost unlimited funds from special interest groups, Lincoln's candidacy would be snuffed out, purely for want of money. What a price to pay! What a way to ration candidates! (Stern 1992, 38)

In the sense that PACs limit the choice of good candidates, their influence is detrimental to the public interest. PAC contributions correspond to ever-rising costs for political campaigns. For example, between January 1, 2003, and June 30, 2004, PACs raised $629 million, a 27 percent increase in receipts when compared with 2002. Increases in PAC collections accelerated in 2004 when compared to the pattern of growth in earlier elections.

In the 2007–2008 election cycle, total expenditures of the top five PACs (EMILY's List, [both a PAC and 527 organization], Act Blue, Service Employees International Union, International Brotherhood of Electrical Workers and the American Federation of State, County, and Municipal Employees) were greater than $38 million. The largest contributors to individual federal candidates were the Operating Engineers Union, International Brotherhood of Electrical Workers, American Bankers Association, Machinists/Aerospace Workers Union and AT&T Inc. These contributions approximated $5.5 million (Opensecrets.org 2007).

PACs represent a serious but not the only contemporary concern regarding the influence of money on elections. Independent tax-exempt groups (527 groups) are illustrative of a more recent strategy aimed at influencing elections. Independent group money is quite effective in bypassing strict campaign finance rules. The influence of these new groups is described below.

527 Groups

A 527 group, named after Section 527 of the U.S. tax code, is a type of tax-exempt organization created primarily to influence the nomination, election, appointment, or defeat of candidates for public office. The Federal Election Commission and state election commissions do not regulate these organizations because they do not make expenditures that directly advocate the election or defeat of any candidate for federal elective office. Many of the 527 organizations, however, have the express goal of influencing elections, and the line between issue advocacy and candidate advocacy is ambiguous. Most issue advocacy seems to have electoral implications.

The fundamental question about 527s is similar to that about PACs, namely whether well-placed monetary contributions distort the truth, misinform the public, and manipulate the wishes of the people. Independent 527s played a prominent role in the 2004 presidential election as questions arose regarding the veracity and objectivity of various 527 television spots. Some claim that 527s impugn the integrity of an opponent while allowing candidates to distance themselves from ads. Ads may also be misleading or loose with the facts. Apologies for the ads can be made and the ads pulled off the airwaves once the damage has been effectively done.

Although 527 organizations existed prior to 2002, the passage of the Bipartisan Campaign Reform Act of 2002 (BCRA, also known as the McCain-Feingold Act) spurred their growth. The sharp growth in the new campaign tactic coincided with the ruling that organizations formed under Section 527 of the tax code could avoid the Federal Election Campaign Act (FECA) defini-

tion of "political committee." Because 527s were not defined as political committees, they were not subject to the same limitations as PACs. Independent 527s claim that their primary purpose is not to influence any specific election but to advocate for specific issues.

Most of the 527 groups, however, are closely aligned with political parties and have a direct interest in helping or destroying specific candidates. In 2004, groups such as America Coming Together and the Media Fund supported Democratic candidates, while groups such as Progress for America and Swift Boat Veterans and POWs for the Truth supported Republicans. Some 527 groups, such as EMILY's List, backed pro-choice (pro-abortion) Democratic women candidates. Other groups, such as the Club for Growth, assisted free-market Republicans. The League of Conservative Voters attempted to accomplish its objectives through both PAC and 527 organizations. In theory, PACs influence elections by contributing directly to congressional candidates while the 527 groups use their money for issue advocacy. Some 527 groups adopt innocuous names in order to conceal the identities of their financial backers. For example, the 527 group United Seniors Association is financed by the pharmaceutical industry (Herrnson 2006, 173).

While the McCain-Feingold Bipartisan Campaign Reform Act of 2002 tried to limit the amount of money contributed to elections, the bill did not succeed in its overall objective. In 2004, the amount of money raised and spent by groups in presidential elections was greater than in any previous election. Groups effectively evaded the BCRA limitations on "soft money" (money not regulated by federal election laws) through their contributions to political parties. Soft money contributions were initially permitted in order to encourage state and local party-building activities such as voter registration, get-out-the-vote drives, and distributing bumper stickers. Before long, however, soft money emerged as the political parties' primary means of raising cash from wealthy contributors. BCRA closed the soft money loophole by limiting such contributions, but the independent group 527s provided a new means to funnel large amounts of money to candidates.

One of the advantages of 527 groups is that there is no limit to how much donors can contribute. In addition, gift taxes are not applied to 527 donors. The U.S. Tax Code established provisions for setting up 527 committees since 1974, yet only recently have groups representing interests such as banking, labor, and women taken full advantage of the legislation. Political scientist, Allan Cigler concludes that "the huge expansion of 527 fundraising and spending so prominent in the 2004 elections was the direct result of the new campaign finance law. It was BCRA's banning of soft money contributions to the national party committees that proved to be the catalyst for expanded soft money activity among interest groups, particularly for individuals and groups supportive of Democrats" (2006, 223).

In the 2004 presidential election campaign, President George W. Bush ran against Democratic senator John Kerry of Massachusetts. Many large contributors to 527 committees were hostile to Bush. The list of large 527 contributors included Democratic-leaning unions as well as wealthy individuals committed to progressive causes. Individuals who contributed heavily to anti-Bush 527s included billionaire financial entrepreneur George Soros ($24 million) and the chair of a large insurance firm Peter Lewis ($24 million). Unions such as the Service Employees International Union (SEIU) contributed more than $53 million. A 527 (Joint Victory Campaign) organized by prominent Democratic leaders and interest group allies were the top contributor in 2004 at more than $56 million. Republicans began to refer to the new 527s

as the "shadow Democratic Party" (Cigler 2006, 225).

Initially arguing that raising money through 527s violated the McCain-Feingold BCRA, Republicans filed a complaint with the Federal Election Commission (FEC) accusing the Kerry campaign of violating the BCRA. The Republican National Committee charged that the 527s were engaged in an unprecedented conspiracy and an illegal campaign finance scheme. After their appeal was rejected by the FEC, however, Republican quickly began to create their own 527s.

Republicans began to attack Kerry's character once they recognized the potential power of 527 campaigns. One anti-Kerry 527 group (the Progress for America Voter Fund) had a particularly close connection with the Republican Party and the Bush campaign official Karl Rove. Another 527 committee (Swift Boat Veterans and POWs for Truth) ran anti-Kerry ads, largely funded by Texas oilman T. Boone Pickens. The top ten 527 committees, by receipts for the 2004 election cycle, are described in Table 3.1.

It is evident from Table 3.1 that more of the 527 money was raised in the presidential cycle of 2003–2004 than in the nonpresidential 2005–2006 election cycle. Some of the organizations, such as America Coming Together, Joint Victory Campaign 2004, Media Fund, Swift Boat Veterans and POWs for Truth, were created in 2004 strictly for the presidential election. Contributions from these groups were drastically reduced in the 2006 nonpresidential election year. Organizations that remained consistent contributors to 527s included unions and EMILY's List.

In another blow to the viability of BCRA, the Supreme Court ruled on June 25, 2007, that a portion of the McCain-Feingold campaign finance law was unconstitutional. In a 5–4 ruling, the court determined that restrictions on television advertising (paid for by corporate or union money) in

Table 3.1

Top Ten 527 Committees, by Receipt, 2004 and 2006 Election Cycle

2004 Election cycle

Rank	Committee	Total receipts (in millions of dollars)
1	America Coming Together	79.8
2	Joint Victory Campaign 2004	71.8
3	Media Fund	59.4
4	Service Employees International Union	48.4
5	Progress America	44.9
6	AFSCME	25.5
7	Swift Boat Veterans for the Truth	17.0
8	MoveOn.org	13.0
9	College Republican National Committee	12.8
10	New Democratic Network	12.7

2006 Election cycle

Rank	Committee	Total receipts (in millions of dollars)
1	Service Employees International Union	24.6
2	AFSCME	20.7
3	America Votes	13.1
4	EMILY's List	11.8
5	Club for Growth	7.2
6	Progress for America	6.2
7	International Brotherhood of Electrical Workers	5.5
8	September Fund	5.2
9	Economic Freedom Fund	5.1
10	America Coming Together	4.5

Source: Center for Responsive Politics, "527 Committee Activity," www.opensecrets.org/527s527cmtes.asp (January 22, 2007).

the weeks before an election represented censorship of political speech unless the advertisements explicitly urged a vote for or against a specific candidate. The decision held that a Wisconsin group had a constitutional right to run commercials in 2004 that specifically criticized Senator Russ Feingold even though the commercials were run in the so-called thirty-day blackout period before the primary. Writing for the majority, Chief Justice John Roberts stated that discussion of issues cannot be suppressed simply because the issues may also be pertinent in an election, and "where the First Amendment is implicated the tie goes to the speaker, not the censor." Some election experts claimed that the decision would negate a major portion of the McCain-Feingold law regarding limits

on soft money. The four Supreme Court dissenters in the decision (Souter, Stevens, Ginsburg, and Breyer) believed that the decision would invite easy circumvention of McCain-Feingold. Some legal experts said the ruling represented a swing away from a tight regulation of political contributions. Others, however, viewed the ruling as a victory for free political advocacy (Greenhouse and Kirkpatrick 2007; Will 2007).

527 Ads: The Swift Boat Controversy

In 2004, some 200 Vietnam swift boat veterans founded a 527 group called Swift Boat Veterans and POWs for the Truth (SBVT), formerly known as the Swift Boat Veterans for Truth. Swift boats were officially termed Fast Patrol Craft (PCF) and were used toward the end of 1968 to block Vietcong supply routes through the Mekong Delta. This assignment was significantly more dangerous than the task of coastal patrol that was previously assigned to the PCF. In 1968, Kerry found himself commanding one of the 50-foot long, aluminum vessels that patrolled inland rivers and canals (Dobbs 2004).

The members of SBVT were united in their anger against Democratic presidential candidate John Kerry, a decorated Vietnam veteran, for his participation in antiwar protests after he returned from Vietnam in 1969 and for his antiwar testimony before Congress in 1971. Funded by a few wealthy individuals, SBVT ranked seventh in the amount of money raised in 2004 (Cigler 2006, 233). Most of this money was collected after the group ran four devastating anti-Kerry ads on television. The success of the ads indicated that a well-placed message could be as important or more important than the sheer amount of money spent.

During the period between the Democratic and Republican national conventions (August 5–31, 2004), the SBVT ads received widespread national attention. The first ad showed a videotape of Kerry's vice presidential running mate, Senator John Edwards, praising Kerry's war record, followed by comments of swift boat veterans who accused Kerry of "lying" and betraying his shipmates. The veterans in the ad stated that Kerry was dishonest, unreliable, and unfit to lead because he had dishonored his country and his fellow veterans.

A second ad displayed videotape footage of Kerry testifying before the U.S. Senate Foreign Relations Committee on behalf of Vietnam Veterans Against the War (VVAW). In his testimony Kerry relayed information collected by the VVAW about atrocities committed by U.S. troops in Vietnam. The ad included charges by Vietnam veterans that Kerry's accusations had demoralized and

"betrayed" soldiers serving in Vietnam. A third ad attacked Kerry's assertion that he was in Cambodia during Christmas 1968. A fourth and final ad showed Kerry in a 1971 television interview saying that he had given back several of his Purple Hearts in a symbolic gesture. The ad asked whether a man who "renounces his country's symbols now can be trusted."

The four SBVT ads, which cost less than $2 million, gained immediate notoriety, and Kerry's standing in the polls started to sink soon after the ads aired. Campaign professionals have concluded that the ads, combined with the lack of a credible response from the Kerry camp, might have been the defining moment in the election. Some individuals, however, criticized the ads as so misleading that they approached slander (Cigler 2006, 234; Wikipedia 2007a). The popularity and effectiveness of the SBVT ads eventually led to the coining of the term "swiftboating" to refer to ad hominem attacks against a public figure that are coordinated by an independent or pseudo-independent group.

Swiftboating messages employ "viral marketing" techniques that use preexisting social networks to increase brand awareness (Wikipedia 2007b). The main strength of viral marketing is its ability to attract the attention of large number of interested people at a low cost. Viral marketing attempts to create buzz around certain phrases, quotes, or images. The SBVT ads were quite successful in creating negative images of Kerry, despite his distinguished war record, producing a portrayal of Kerry as anti-American and unpatriotic.

Controversy arose almost immediately after the SBVT ads were aired. Many major media outlets were skeptical about the ads' allegations. A *New York Times* article concluded, "On close examination, the accounts of Swift Boat Veterans for Truth prove to be riddled with inconsistencies." The *Times* article further noted that in many cases, official U.S. Navy records undercut material offered as proof by Swift Boat Veterans. Several of the men who declared Kerry "unfit" in the television spot had been praising him only one year before the creation of the ads. In 1969, Kerry's written performance evaluations included the phrases "unsurpassed," "beyond reproach," and "the acknowledged leader in his peer group" (Zernike and Rutenberg 2004).

The strategy of the SBVT group was to portray Kerry as a "baby killer" and the fabricator of malicious stories. The SBVT organization applied the same political advertising agency that was used by George W. Bush's father in 1988 when it created the "tank advertisement" that mocked his opponent in that presidential race, Senator Michael Dukakis. Kerry denounced SBVT as a "front for the Bush campaign" (Zernike and Rutenberg 2004).

In a *Wall Street Journal* editorial, columnist Albert Hunt questioned the attention on Kerry's war record. He claimed that attacks by SBVT were orchestrated by a few wealthy backers of George W. Bush. Hunt claimed that the ads were "significantly funded and directed by Texas fat cats and political operatives who have more than a passing relationship with Bush political guru Karl Rove." The backers of the swift boat ads were identified as "some of the same people who surreptitiously smeared John McCain in the last election." Hunt noted that ten of the eleven men who served on Kerry's two swift boats supported Kerry. He stated, "every serious journalist that has examined the record" supported Kerry's version of events (Hunt 2007).

As a direct response to the SBVT ads, an alternative group, Texans for Truth (TfT), was created by Democrats to oppose the reelection of George W. Bush. This 527 group focused its advertisements on Bush's National Guard record and was supported financially by the 20,000-member Texas group DriveDemocracy as well as the roughly 2-million–member online group MoveOn.org. A number of

TfT ads implied that Bush's service in the Texas National Guard was negligent, inattentive, soft, or the consequence of favoritism. For example, one of the ads posed the question, "Was George W. Bush AWOL in Alabama?" The ad featured a former National Guard member stating that he had served in the 187th Air National Guard, Bush's unit, but did not remember seeing Bush there. A final graphic stated, "George Bush has some explaining to do" (Annenberg Political Fact Check 2007).

A second television ad sponsored by TfT reiterated charges that George W. Bush did not adequately fulfill his military service requirements. The ad accused George W. Bush's father, George H.W. Bush, of using his influence to get his son into the Texas Air National Guard where it was very unlikely that he would be sent into combat in Vietnam. In 1968 when George W. Bush joined the Texas Air National Guard his father George H.W. Bush was a Republican congressman. A former speaker of the Texas House of Representatives and former Texas lieutenant governor, Ben Barnes, issued a statement, in 1999, saying that he had helped Bush get into the Guard at the request of a Bush family friend, Houston oilman Sidney Adger. In the statement Barnes, asserted that neither then Congressman Bush nor any other member of the Bush family had contacted him directly.

In a CBS, *60 Minutes* interview that aired in September 8, 2004, Barnes described placement into the National Guard as "preferential treatment" since there were "hundreds of names on the list" and "chances are they would not have to go to Vietnam." At a rally for John Kerry (his choice for president) Barnes stated, "I got a young man named George W. Bush in the National Guard when I was Lieutenant Governor of Texas, and I'm not necessarily proud of that, but I did it. And I got a lot of other people in the National Guard because I thought that was what people should do when in office; you helped a lot of rich people." In response to the TfT ads, the Bush campaign labeled the TfT organization as a smear group launching baseless attacks on behalf of John Kerry's campaign that will be rejected by the American people. The Bush team contended, "the president served honorably in the National Guard, fulfilled his duties and was honorably discharged" (Annenberg Political Fact Check 2007; Wikipedia 2007c).

In retrospect, it appears that the SBVT anti-Kerry attack ads were more effective in casting doubt on Kerry than the TfT ads were in undermining Bush's support. Both sets of ads sought to circumvent election law by spending above the mandated expenditure limits. Both sets of ads sought to sway voters with emotional appeals and character assassination. Though the ads claimed to be merely providing useful information to help voters make up their minds, the ads actually denigrated opponents. The choice of information to relay to the public was well thought out and aimed to have maximum effect at a time when foreign policy was a central concern. Although the truthfulness of both sets of ads was questioned, neither group retracted its assertions. The basic messages remained that John Kerry abandoned his fellow troops when he criticized the Vietnam War and that George W. Bush was a no-show when it came time for his military obligation.

Even if it had been "proved" that Kerry was unfaithful to his fellow soldiers or that Bush was at best a summertime patriot, their actions did not differ significantly from those of many others who criticized the Vietnam War or served in the National Guard to avoid going to Vietnam. The salient issue in terms of responsible governance relates to the content and legality of 527 ads. For example, *Wall Street Journal* columnist Albert Hunt questioned whether certain campaign tactics of the candidates went "beyond the pale" (2007). Responsible governance must establish acceptable boundaries of discourse, balancing the desirabil-

ity of open, vigorous debate protected under the umbrella of free speech with the desirability for honesty and fair play.

Dishonest manipulation of public opinion obviously is dangerous to democracy. Images molded by modern-day illusionists through deceit and distortion have the potential to undermine the spirit of elections as much as the machine-era habit of allowing the dead to vote. Crossing ill-defined boundaries of electoral fair play can lead to the rise to power of well-financed demagogues who suppress rights and ignore the public interest. The rule of law must be employed to allow candidates to reasonably compete in the free marketplace of ideas while at the same time eliminating false attacks.

Once statements of questionable veracity are aired by groups that are at best marginally linked to specific candidates, the candidates can distance themselves from the group. In essence, the rise of independent groups and 527 ads allows much of the dirty work of elections to be off-loaded to third parties. After the damage is done to opponents, the candidates can take the high road by questioning or even criticizing the tactics of their supporters. The general strategy of 527 ads is to lay the seeds of doubt in the voter's mind and set the stage for voter conversion. Modern campaign tactics carefully target swing voters who in the end have to choose between differing sets of emotional appeals.

Responsibility in governance means maintaining some level of truthfulness and integrity in the electoral process. The level of oversight remains controversial as advocates of unethical electoral competition are pitted against others who want to play by more gentle rules. Some degree of truthfulness is necessary in order to maintain the principles of public interest and democracy.

Efforts to clean up the electoral system have periodically been successful in making changes and eliminating the worst abuses. The rules of the electoral game have been altered at various times. These alterations have in turn forced changes in campaign tactics, but the reforms did not eliminate the influence of money on elections. Reform of the system of campaign financing remains an issue. The following section describes various attempts made in the United States to limit the impact of money on elections. As described in this chapter, money has always played a role in attaining political power. The issue to be considered is what kinds of action responsible government should take to maintain free and fair elections.

Attempts to Limit the Impact of Money on Elections

Early Reforms

As previously stated, the influence of money on politics can be traced to the nation's earliest elections. Since the middle of the nineteenth century efforts have been made to limit the importance of money on elections. Often these attempts have been fruitless. Invariably, reform legislation is passed, then the legislation is circumvented, and finally new reforms are sought to eliminate the current abuses. This circular pattern of electoral abuse, reform of the system, new electoral abuse, and new reform indicates that, despite the best efforts of reformers, they cannot eliminate the influence of money on elections or congressional votes.

A review of attempts to identify and correct campaign abuses is instructive. Attempts to clean up questionable electoral practices in the United States date to the middle of the nineteenth century. The first law to regulate campaign financing at the federal level is traced to the Naval Appropriations Bill of 1867. This act stated that no officer or employee of the government could require or request any worker in any navy yard to contribute money for political purposes and that no workers could be

discharged for their political opinions; any government employee who violated this provision would be dismissed from government service. The intent of these reforms was to cut off a lucrative source of political funding. In 1868 it was estimated that at least 75 percent of the money raised by the Republican Congressional Committee was given to the Republican Party by federal government officeholders (Lammers 1982, 3).

A similar motivation to limit mandatory campaign contributions led to passage of the Civil Service Reform Act (Pendleton Act) of 1883. The Pendleton Act authorized establishment of civil service rules similar to those placed in the 1867 Naval Appropriations Bill. It also mandated that no person in public service was under any obligation to contribute to any political fund and that no employee would be removed from office for refusing to contribute.

The Pendleton Act made it more difficult and risky to shake down government officials in order to finance political campaigns. As a consequence, campaign financing shifted to large corporations, with politicians such as Mark Hanna establishing new ground rules for collecting large campaign contributions. The growing influence of large corporate contributions in turn spurred legislation such as the Tillman Act of 1907, which made it unlawful for a corporation or national bank to make a monetary contribution to federal candidates, and the Federal Corrupt Practices Act of 1910. The 1910 legislation established disclosure requirements for candidates running for election to the U.S. House of Representatives. Political committees were also required to file with the clerk of the House of Representatives the names and addresses of contributors.

The Federal Corrupt Practices Act of 1925 regulated campaign spending and disclosure of receipts by both House and Senate candidates. This law provided the basis for campaign finance oversight until 1971. It incorporated existing regulations (such as prohibitions on corporate or bank contributions, bans on contributions from federal employees, requirements of campaign finance reports) and set new limits for campaign expenditures. The 1925 legislation limited the amount that candidates could legally spend to $10,000 for a Senate race and $2,500 for a House race. Spending limits could also equal three cents for each vote cast in the last election, but could not total more than $25,000 for a Senate race and $5,000 for a House race. Despite the Federal Corrupt Practices Act, however, candidates were able to evade spending limits by channeling most of their expenditures through separate committees. From a practical point of view, therefore, the federal spending limits became meaningless. This law was a relatively early example of campaign financing legislation that had the best intentions, but ultimately was unsuccessful in achieving its goal of limiting spending.

Another significant piece of campaign finance legislation was the Hatch Clean Politics Act of 1939 and its 1940 amendments. The Hatch Act of 1939 is a federal law whose main provision is to prohibit federal employees (civil servants) from engaging in partisan political activity. The Hatch Act amendments contributed three significant additions: (1) they forbade those working under contract for the federal government from contributing to a political committee or candidate, (2) they gave Congress the right to regulate federal primaries, and (3) they made it unlawful for anyone to contribute more than $5,000 to a federal candidate or political committee in a single year.

Reforms After the 1970s

Campaign finance did not become a major concern for politicians again until the 1970s. By the early 1970s it had become evident that existing laws were not limiting the influence of money on politics and were not cleaning up politics. Richard Nixon's 1968 presidential campaign produced numerous assertions of foul play, dirty tricks, and corruption. A number of congressional representatives elected in 1968 were concerned about the tenor of status quo politics and, along with good-government watchdog groups such as Common Cause, spearheaded the drive for campaign finance reform. The intent of the Federal Election Campaign Act (FECA) of 1971 was to reduce or eliminate existing abuses and the ever-present influence of money on politics. FECA had three major provisions that worked to (1) significantly tighten disclosure and reporting requirements for candidates for federal office, (2) limit the amount of money that candidates could spend on media advertising, and (3) limit the amount that candidates and their immediate family could contribute to the campaign.

Three years later, amendments were added to FECA in an attempt to fundamentally alter the electoral landscape. The 1974 amendments represented a comprehensive overhaul of the election system. They were motivated by the Watergate scandal and the exposure of widespread abuses in the 1972 presidential campaign. After Nixon's 1972 landslide, it was revealed that his administration was basically reproducing the strategy employed by Mark Hanna in 1896. In the 1972 election, Nixon's campaign managers had established a system that assessed corporations 0.5 percent of their net worth. A secret campaign fund was established, smaller cash accounts were held in safes, millions of dollars were laundered through foreign countries, and hundreds of thousands of dollars were deposited into accounts of political committees that did not exist (Green 2002, 52). Leading contributors to Nixon's campaign were the dairy industry; insurance executive W. Clement Stone; Richard Scaife, heir to the Mellon banking and oil interests; and the eccentric millionaire Howard

Hughes (Lammers 1982, 10). In 1974, President Nixon's lawyer, Herbert Kalmbach, pleaded guilty to illegal campaign operations and was sentenced to six to eighteen months in prison. Revelations of these as well as other abuses led directly to passage of FECA amendments of 1974.

The 1974 law is viewed as the most sweeping campaign finance reform ever enacted (Alexander 1992, 32). The bill signed two months after Nixon's resignation by his successor, President Gerald Ford, on October 15, 1974, contained a variety of controversial features, such as public funding for presidential elections, matching funds for private donations of $250 or less, money given to political parties in order to support nominating conventions, grants to party nominees, the establishment of a federal election commission, and a curtailment of the role of "fat cat" contributors. Major features of the 1971 act as well as the 1974 amendments are described in Table 3.2.

Not unexpectedly, the 1974 bill was challenged in the courts almost immediately. In a 1976 Supreme Court case (*Buckley v. Valeo*, 424 U.S. 1), the court struck down limits on campaign spending, limits on independent expenditures, and limits on contributions by a candidate to his or her own campaign. The Court ruled that spending limits violated the First Amendment, reasoning that restricting the amount of money a person or group can spend on political communication reduces the quantity of expression, restricts the number of issues raised, limits the size of the audience reached, and constrains the depth of explanation. The Supreme Court upheld disclosure requirements, public financing, and limits on contributions from individuals, PACs, and political parties (Malbin 1984a, 8). A ceiling remained on spending for presidential candidates who accepted federal matching funds.

Both supporters of reform and supporters of the status quo favored some aspects of the Supreme

Table 3.2

Major Features of the 1971 Act and 1974 Amendments

1. Required candidates to disclose sources of campaign contributions

2. Required candidates to disclose campaign expenditures

3. Created Federal Election Commission

4. Public funding made available for presidential primaries and general elections

5. Set a legal limit on campaign contributions by individuals and organizations

6. Prohibited campaign contributions directly from corporations, labor unions, national banks, government contractors, foreign nationals, and contributions in the name of another

Source: Malbin 1984b.

Court decision. Reformers praised the limitations on individual contributions. Those advocating unlimited spending applauded the court's action that struck down as unconstitutional the limits on campaign expenditures.

The Bipartisan Campaign Reform Act (BCRA) of 2002, also known as the McCain-Feingold Act, represents the next major piece of campaign finance legislation. This law is illustrative of continued efforts by reformers to fix problems that had evolved since the last reform. A main focus of McCain-Feingold was to limit the amount of "soft money" used in campaigns. Such money was not subject to limits and was mostly used for issue advertisements. These ads in theory did not expressly advocate the election of one candidate or another, yet their intent was to influence the public's perceptions of candidates (Malbin 2003, 5).

The aim of BCRA was to restore balance to political campaigns following allegations of questionable money-raising practices in the 1996 election.

The most infamous of these practices were forcing visitors to pay for the privilege of overnight stays at the White House and donations from representatives of foreign countries. In reaction to these abuses, reformers sought to (1) prohibit soft money contributions to national political parties, (2) prohibit soft money expenditures by national political parties, (3) prohibit soft money contributions and expenditures to state and local political parties, (4) prohibit federal candidates and officeholders from accepting or spending soft money, and (5) ban supposedly nonpartisan issue ads funded by soft money from corporations and labor unions.

While its intent was clear, BCRA did not eliminate the influence of money on elections. Similar to the experience of the past, BCRA merely shifted the means of raising and spending money. BCRA led to the rise of the 527 organizations, which do not directly advocate the election or defeat of a candidate yet seek to destroy the images of opponents. Unregulated by the Federal Elections Commission, 527 organizations such as SBVT are the latest method of circumventing the letter of campaign finance legislation.

The Implications of Money for Democracy

The corrupting influence of money is a fundamental problem for all democratic regimes. Democratic theory is based upon the idea that the people can identify and vote their interests. Democratic theory in turn supports the ideal of rule of the many rather than rule of the few. The principles of democracy, however, are undercut when candidate choice is limited, citizens' perceptions are manipulated, debate is constrained, wealth becomes a prerequisite for office, and voters cannot find candidates who will support their interests.

Philosopher John Rawls suggests that money distorts the goals of democracy and limits the opportunity for everyone to hold public office. Rawls contends that political liberty for all citizens, whatever their social or economic position, must be approximately equal (1993, 326). Political theorist Dennis Thompson agrees with Rawls's basic posture about the preeminence of elections for democracy:

> Elections can occur without democracy, but democracy cannot endure without elections. They are not the only method of maintaining popular control of government, but they are the essential one. They directly serve what the framers of the U.S. Constitution saw as the chief aims of any respectable constitution: to obtain rulers who possess the "most wisdom" and "virtue to pursue the common good," and to keep the rulers virtuous while "they continue to hold their public trust." Expressed in less noble language, these remain the central purposes of elections today. (D. Thompson 2002, 1)

Thompson contends that money impairs free electoral choice and therefore advocates moderating that influence. He notes that money prevents voters from being exposed to a reasonable balance of influences. Thompson advocates reforms that would allow for a wider variety of influences rather than "the plutocracy of pressures that currently reigns in the electoral process" (D. Thompson 2002, 190).

Other critics have also observed that money corrupts elections, which should be one of the basic pillars of democracy. For example, political scientist Theodore Lowi contends that corruption can erode fundamental constitutional values. He distinguishes between Big Corruption, or Big C, defined as corruption that contributes to the decomposition, dissolution, or disorientation of the Constitution, and Little Corruption, or Little C, which reflects or contributes to individual moral depravity. The influence of money represents Big C in that it erodes the fundamental constitutional principle of free and fair elections as well as government by the true consent of the governed. Because acts of Big C put the state itself at risk, Big C is much more pernicious than Little C, which Lowi recognizes as scandal involving acts such as embezzlement, tax evasion, or use of special privileges of office (deLeon 1993, 25; Lowi 1981, 2–3). Little C can lead to disaster for individuals who are caught in the act, but it does not rise to the level of threatening the legitimacy of the system.

The influence of money undermines principles of equality that underline the theory of democracy. Its pernicious impact also weakens cherished constitutional ideals such as the ideal of equality of influence in elections and equality of input into elections. In the extreme, the influence of money can lead to governance of the wealthy few, by the wealthy few, and for the wealthy few, turning Lincoln's Gettysburg Address ("government of the people, by the people, for the people") on its head. Nonwealthy individuals may at times attain public office, yet they are likely to be obligated to the wealthy few who give them money through campaign contributions. Responsible governance therefore should work to limit money's influence even if it recognizes that the electoral playing field will never be perfectly equal.

Conclusions

While money and power have always been linked, there is evidence that money's influence on elections has eroded public confidence. For example, a 1997 *New York Times* survey revealed that 89 percent of people questioned contended that significant and fundamental change is needed in the campaign finance system. In 2000, a national study by National Public Radio, the Kaiser Foundation, and Harvard University's Kennedy School of Government found that 89 percent of those surveyed believed that government corruption was a very important or somewhat important problem (Gordon 2005, 3).

Corruption, particularly when it relates to the electoral process, degrades the stock of goodwill that supports the governing structure. Corruption of elections increases cynicism, disgust, distrust, and disregard for the system. In contrast, responsible governance buttresses the political system by limiting abuse and establishing norms of acceptable behavior. This in turn enhances the legitimacy of the state as the populace witnesses the punishment of wrongdoers and the rewarding of those who work to preserve the integrity of the electoral process. Periodic punishment alone, however, does not guarantee responsible governance. The norms of acceptable behavior have to be inculcated into the people over an extended period of time. Legislation helps to establish parameters of acceptance, but legislation by itself is insufficient. Legislative rules have to be enforceable and not circumvented. Too often, campaign finance reforms have been skirted, leading to newer forms of corruption.

Former senator William Proxmire, a Democrat from Wisconsin, tells the following story to illustrate corruption and its potential to arouse the public. The scene is Yankee Stadium during the seventh and deciding game of the World Series. The pitcher completes his warm-ups, walks to the plate, and in plain view of more than 57,000 people, reaches into his pocket and proceeds to methodically count out and place into the umpire's outstretched palm 100 new hundred-dollar bills. The umpire pockets the $10,000, takes his position behind the plate, and says, "Play ball."

It is conceivable that the umpire's judgment will be unaffected by the pitcher's money, but none of the fans believe so. They proceed to throw everything they can lay their hands on at the umpire and the pitcher who gave the money. Then, in protest, the fans empty the stands. Later, in a well-attended press conference, the umpire emphatically denies that his judgment has been in any way affected by the pitcher's gift. However, not a single baseball fan believes him (Stern 1992, xix).

Proxmire's story indicates that in any environment a point is reached when the prevailing structure is simply no longer credible. It may be difficult to discern when that point is close to being reached, but the extent of trust or distrust can be assessed along a continuum ranging from total trust to total distrust. Where a society stands along this continuum is a matter of speculation, roughly indicated by public opinion polls of trust or distrust, systemic support or systemic rejection. Electoral corruption of a particularly egregious nature would tend to move the society toward rejection of systemic values, while legislation such as electoral reform moves the society toward enhanced support. Responsible governance works to minimize action that encourages rejection of the system and to reinforce action that supports the system. Proxmire's story describes a contest that has been totally corrupted, identified as corrupt, and rejected by those who previously supported the system.

Elections in the United States may not have reached the point of rejection described above; however, the objective of responsible governance is to ensure that the game of politics is played upon a reasonable playing field with impartial umpires and does not reach the point described in Proxmire's tale. There may never be a totally level field for elections, but the principles of democracy demand that influence is not bought or sold in full view of the population. As in Proxmire's story, the people may figuratively empty the stands in protest through apathy, nonvoting, and extreme cynicism. Despite statements from politicians (as the denial of the umpire) that they are totally objective, it stretches credibility to believe that some citizens or groups will not get better treatment than others because of their campaign contributions and that politicians are completely impartial in their treatment of citizens. Secretly acquired influence may not arouse the populace, however, covert influence is still antithetical to the core principles of democracy. It is even more insidious to principles of democracy since its actions are out of the public eye and unavailable for public scrutiny.

This chapter has shown that in the United States money has always been strongly interrelated with politics and power. This was true yesterday, it is true today, and it probably will be true tomorrow. Candidates who can raise money or can use their own money have a large advantage over others. Well-funded special interest groups often benefit from their ability to generously support candidates. When reformers attempt to correct election abuses through legislation, drawing new lines regarding permissible and impermissible behavior, seekers and holders of power all too often cross these lines of acceptability and figure out new ways to gain or hold power. Ethical behavior and responsible governance require mitigation of electoral abuse and adherence to principles of free and fair elections. Such adherence should enhance the legitimacy, long-term survival, popularity, and credibility of the state.

The following two case studies provide a historical account of electoral abuse (Case No. 1) and a contemporary example of electoral misconduct (Case No. 2). These cases illustrate the potential for corruption in the American political system and the necessity for eternal vigilance. Examining these cases can help readers identify previous transgressions and recognize the limits of permissible action in a given time and place. Case studies identify historical abuses while also recognizing the ability of the system to engage in self-correction. Corrective action helps to restore faith in responsible governance.

Case No. 1: Machine Politics

The Philosophy of Machine Politics

Political machines are not a new phenomenon, and despite the numerous accounts of their death, they will exist as long as ambitious men and women plot to gain, expand, and retain political power. Predating the creation of the American republic, machines are organizations built to obtain political power. They provide some system-wide stability by providing an avenue of advancement for those who were previously excluded from the halls of power. Machines also act as a lubricant to ease the friction between rigid laws and people trying to survive in unfamiliar environments.

In 1893 the Englishman Lord James Bryce, after visiting America, made a number of insightful comments about political machines in the United States. According to Bryce, "city rings" effectively controlled politics in many large American cities. Members of these rings met every year or two to discuss appointments ranging from messenger and doorkeeper to state legislator and member of the U.S. Congress. An election slate (list of candidates) was drawn up by the machine and supported by the party at the polls. Slates could be modified if members of the ring complained that they or their friends had been slighted.

Discipline in machines was strict, with members of the machine holding to their own moral code. This code did not forbid lying, ballot stuffing, or repeat voting, but it denounced apathy, disobedience, and, above all, disloyalty to the party. Unquestioned allegiance to the party, unity of heart, and unity of effort were the expected norms of machine members. Members who set their own course became known as "kickers" or "bolters" and were severely punished. Punishments included exclusion from conventions, blocked promotion within the political party, and dismissals from

office. Machine lore even included talk of the mysterious disappearances of men who dared to testify against the ring.

Lord Bryce noted that in urban machines the bond between the party chief and followers was seldom broken. The relationship was equated with that between clients and patrons in ancient Rome and that between vassals and lords in the Middle Ages. Bryce stated that workers rendered services and were repaid with the gift of a livelihood. The machine worker, like the vassal, kept his post only by the favor of the lord or the boss. Patronage therefore lay at the heart of the political machine:

> The aim of a Boss is not so much fame as power, and power not so much over the conduct of affairs as over persons. Patronage is what he chiefly seeks, patronage understood in the largest sense in which it covers the disposal of lucrative contracts and other modes of enrichment as well as salaried places. The dependents who surround him desire wealth, or at least a livelihood; his business is to find this for them, and in doing so he strengthens his own position. It is as the bestower of riches that he holds his position. ([1893] 1972, 8)

Bryce pointed out that, aside from patronage, a primary asset of the boss was his knowledge of human nature, which taught him when to bully, when to cajole, whom to attract by the hope of gain, and whom to attract by appeals to party loyalty. The boss, like any leader of a large organization, had to recognize how to keep power and how much to reward his supporters. Those who could deliver large numbers of votes or large amounts of money understandably would get larger rewards. A certain type of individual was attracted to machine politics and rose in the organization.

Bryce contended that the boss could not be fastidious in his tastes; he should be fond of drink, jovial in manners, and ready to oblige even a humble friend. This type of individual thrived in the urban politics of the nineteenth century, when large numbers of impoverished immigrants were arriving from Europe. Bosses and rings aided these poor immigrants in return for their loyalty. Machines therefore introduced new arrivals to the ways of America, helping them to survive. In return, machine politicians gained great riches and power.

According to Bryce, certain conditions were highly favorable to the rise of political machines: (1) the existence of a spoils system or the presence of offices that can be freely given or taken away at the discretion of political party officials, (2) opportunities for illicit gains arising out of the possession of office, (3) the presence of a mass of ignorant and pliable voters, and (4) the insufficient participation in politics of "good citizens." These conditions were most fully met in large cities such as New York, Philadelphia, Chicago, St. Louis, Cincinnati, San Francisco, Baltimore, and New Orleans. In these cities the majority was seen as easily led since the "best citizens" were engrossed in business and less concerned with politics (Bryce [1898] 1972, 9–10).

In Bryce's day and later, a few specific elements characterized, in general, the philosophy of the machine. These are summarized in Table 3.3.

As noted in Table 3.3, machine politicians are basically nonideological and motivated by political survival. They are fundamentally interested in material gain. They believe that voters should be manipulated and used in order to gain power for party officials. Once political power is attained, it is used to hand out jobs to supporters (patronage), to help those in need through favors or food baskets if necessary, and to personally enrich oneself. Rakove (1975, 9) notes that machine politicians are pragmatic and hardheaded, rejecting romanticized notions of a public interest. Machines thrive on attention to the day-to-day gut-level issues of individuals. Machine politicians, realizing that future support depends upon fulfilling the private self-interests of

Table 3.3

Philosophy of Political Machines

1. Believes that men in politics are greedy, emotional, and passionate

2. Believes that people are not governed by reason, morality or concern for their fellow men

3. Believes that men can be co-opted, bought, persuaded or frightened into subservience to cooperate with the machine

4. Believes that every man has his price and the job of the machine is to find out what the price is and whether it is worth paying

5. Like Machiavelli, morality is separated from politics; they are able to conduct their private lives in accordance with their moral beliefs, and their public lives in accordance with practical political realities

6. Machine leaders have little use for ideology or philosophy

7. If they hold any ideology machine leaders are always willing to subordinate those beliefs to practical political necessity

Source: Rakove 1975.

constituents. They parcel out favors in return for promises of loyalty that are later redeemed in order to maintain and expand political power.

The machine boss is careful not to offend constituents, recognizing that voters will not forget personal slights. As a consequence, machine politicians avoid embarrassing potential voters and shun emotional issues where clear winners and losers emerge. Machines avoid philosophy and abstract ideals, which only tend to arouse constituent emotions. Ideals are not glorified because it is not believed that they help to build the party as an effective organization. Well-run machines in the past all have focused on material matters. Trimming the trees, repairing the curbs, getting the children summer jobs, and lowering property taxes are the kinds of private interests that machine politicians are likely to focus upon. Machines believe that constituents will return politicians to office or reject them on the basis of how well they have served their constituency's private interests (Rakove 1975, 9–10).

Machine bosses share many common characteristics in regard to the type of people that become bosses, the strategies of bosses, and their relationship with their constituents. However, clear differences exist between the reign of one boss and another. For example, the personal avarice of Boss Tweed contrasts with Richard J. Daley's concern for political power and his disregard of personal wealth. Machines emerged from both political parties, Democratic and Republican. They arose in all regions of the nation, not just the Northeast. People of various ethnic groups controlled machines, dispelling the image of machines as predominantly the tool of the Irish.

The First Boss: William Marcy Tweed

William Marcy Tweed (1823–1878) is recognized as the first major urban boss who seized power as the undisputed head of the New York political organization, Tammany Hall. Tweed's background, his rise to power as head of the "Tweed Ring," and his fall provide a great deal of insight into the rough electoral politics of the times.

Tweed was born in 1823 to a middle-class, Scottish, Protestant family in New York. His father was a furniture maker and William was the last of the family's five children. In his prime Tweed stood well over six feet tall with a weight of 270 pounds. His size and strength marked him as a leader from the time he was a boy and head of his own youth gang.

When Tweed was still a young man growing up in New York City, rival Whig and Democratic parties vied for power. The two parties openly recruited gangsters to keep opposition voters from the polls. During elections, convicts were let out

of prison, housed in city hotels, and often allowed to escape after they cast their votes for the party in power. Young Tweed quickly learned the ways of New York politics, including the sale and purchase of votes, repeat voting, and miscounting. In the 1844 presidential election, he observed that the combined city vote for the two presidential candidates, James K. Polk and Henry Clay, was 10,000 votes higher that the total number of qualified voters in the city (Cook 1973, 13).

Anxious to be a part of an organized group, in 1848 Tweed joined a neighborhood fire company, the Americus Engine Company No. 6. Due in large part to his size and force of character, he was elected assistant foreman in 1849 and foreman of the fire company in 1850. During this time volunteer firefighters formed an effective voting bloc, and Tweed capitalized on this association to run as a Democrat for political office. Before long, he was elected to the powerful position of New York City alderman.

As alderman, Tweed became a member of a governing body that came to be known as the Forty Thieves. The twenty aldermen and twenty assistant aldermen had great power, including the power to appoint police officers, to grant saloon licenses within their districts, and to award franchises for bus lines, streetcar lines, and ferries for the city. The forty members of the Common Council also could pick grand juries and rule on a variety of legal issues. From the beginning, Tweed sought to take the existing levels of plunder to new heights. He then used his wealth to gain a seat in the U.S. House of Representatives in 1852.

Tweed did not like Washington and preferred to return to New York, where he had greater opportunity to personally enrich himself. He would accomplish this goal by the 1860s. In 1855, Tweed was elected to the minor city office of school commissioner. In 1857 he was elected to the powerful New York City Board of Supervisors. Within a year he placed three of his cronies in important city government positions. By the age of thirty-five he was becoming known as "The Boss" (Cook 1973, 21).

Tweed held a variety of positions that he used to his advantage as he climbed the ladder of political power. As street cleaning commissioner, he controlled thousands of jobs. He was also a member of the New York state senate. This position allowed him to influence financial decisions for the entire state. Tweed also served as commissioner of public works, an envied position as a rich source of patronage (Allswang 1977, 43). In 1861 Tweed became chair of the New York County Democratic Central Committee and two years later chair of the General Committee of Tammany Hall. With these appointments he was recognized as the first "one-man" boss of the New York Democrats.

The power of Tweed and his associates grew immensely in the 1860s. In 1863 Tweed had himself proclaimed a lawyer, although he had no formal legal training—a practice that was legal at the time. He then used his status as a lawyer to extract huge payments for "legal advice." By 1870 Tweed openly bragged that he was worth $20 million.

The demise of Boss Tweed came relatively quickly, spurred by a crusading press and disgruntled associates. William Marcy Tweed was indicted in December 1871 on charges of felony, forgery, grand larceny, false pretenses, and conspiracy to defraud. Released on bail, he was first tried in January 1873. The jury could not reach a verdict and Tweed was tried again in November. Eventually the jury found Tweed guilty of fifty-one of the fifty-five charges brought against him and he was sentenced to twelve years in prison. In 1875 Tweed escaped but was captured in Spain and returned to New York City in 1876. He died in a New York City jail in 1878 at the age of fifty-four (Callow 1966, 297).

The New Jersey Machine and Boss Hague

A powerful political machine that operated between the time of the first great boss, William Marcy Tweed, and the last great boss, Richard J. Daley of Chicago, was the New Jersey political machine of Frank Hague. Author Fred Cook (1973, 105) states that no other political machine endured so long and wielded so much statewide influence as Hague's Democratic organization in Hudson County in northern New Jersey. This organization, operating from a power base in Jersey City (New Jersey's second-largest city), helped to establish New Jersey's reputation as the most boss-ridden state in the nation between 1917 and 1972. At the peak of his power, Hague determined the fate of gubernatorial aspirants, sent his hand-picked choices to the U.S. Senate, and decided how many times names on gravestones would be voted in order to carry the state of New Jersey for Democratic presidential candidates.

Hague's background had similarities to as well as differences from that of Tweed. Hague was born in 1876 in the Jersey City Irish slum known as the Horseshoe. He was the third of eight children born to his Irish parents. Hague's father worked as a blacksmith for the Erie Railroad until he was appointed a bank guard through the influence of the local Democratic leader. As a child, Hague did not like school or work and preferred life on the streets. In later years he described his first day at school: he stayed for just ten minutes, then climbed out a basement window and ran away. In 1889, when he was thirteen, he was labeled as an incorrigible and expelled from school. He then became a drifter, roaming the streets and spending most of his time at the local gymnasium, where he learned how to box. Eventually, he became the manager of a Brooklyn prizefighter (Cook 1973, 109).

Hague's first opportunity in politics arose in

1896 when the proprietor of a local saloon asked him to run for the position of constable. Although this position did not pay a salary, it allowed Hauge to develop political contacts with other Jersey City politicians, advancing his career. He was appointed precinct leader in 1901, ward leader in 1906, and custodian of City Hall in 1908, and in 1911, after the death of Jersey City's boss Robert "Little Bob" Davis, Hauge elected Street and Water Commissioner. In 1913 Hauge was elected to the five-person city commission. Ironically, Hague and his political friends ran in 1913 on a platform to reform Jersey City government. Hague was elected commissioner of public safety in 1916, a position that gave him control over the police and fire departments. From this position Hague was able to make appointments to two vital city departments and build a patronage system that supported his political career. In the election of 1917 political allies of Hague were elected to the city commission. Following the 1917 election, the city commission unanimously selected Hague as mayor. Once in office, he immediately began to pad payrolls, help elect men loyal to him, pack the state courts, and appoint his followers to state boards.

Hague served as mayor of Jersey City from May 15, 1917, until his retirement on June 17, 1947. During these years he made political friends and enemies at the national level. He unsuccessfully supported a fellow Irish Catholic, Al Smith, for the Democratic presidential nomination in 1924. At the 1932 Democratic National Convention he tried to gather votes for Smith but eventually was forced into backing the party's nominee, Franklin D. Roosevelt. In 1948 he angered Harry Truman with his advocacy of General Dwight D. Eisenhower as the Democratic nominee. Hague decided not to run for mayor in 1947, but made sure that his nephew, Frank Hague Eggers succeeded him. After a heated election, Eggers was defeated two

years later by John Kenny. With his nephew's loss in the 1949 electoral race, Hague lost much of his political power. In 1952 the state Democratic organization ousted him from his post as national committeeman.

Hague's career earned him a well-earned reputation for corruption. His methods for retaining power included controlling newspapers, intimidating opponents, and making false arrests. He followed the practice perfected by Tweed, and allowed the city to buy goods and services at high prices, pocketing cash from suppliers. In addition, Hague's associates purchased land that was later condemned and bought by the city at exorbitant prices. Hague's electoral fraud was legendary. In the 1925 New Jersey governor's race, people voted with addresses that turned out to be vacant lots, the Republican candidate failed to receive a single vote in some wards although some voters claimed they had voted for the candidate, and in one district there were more votes tallied than registered voters (Cook 1973, 116). During the 1930s Hague acquired a personal fortune that ran into the millions of dollars, even though he never earned more than $8,000 a year legitimately as the mayor of Jersey City. At the time of his death on January 1, 1956, his wealth was estimated at over $10 million. Hague enjoyed palatial homes and a private suite at the Waldorf-Astoria, an exclusive New York City hotel.

The New Jersey political machine had great longevity, yet suffered a serious blow when Richard Nixon was elected in 1968. Nixon sent federal prosecutors to New Jersey, and after a months-long investigation a federal grand jury issued indictments to Hague's successors. In contrast to earlier convictions, which involved only minor penalties because of the Jersey politicians' "distinguished" careers, punishments for the politicians now were relatively harsh and included prison sentences. The judge presiding at one of the trials stated:

It is impossible to estimate the impact—and the cost—of these criminal acts to the decent citizens of Newark, and indeed, to the citizens of the State of New Jersey, in terms of their frustration, despair and disillusionment. . . . Their [the accused politicians'] crimes, in the judgment of the Court, tear at the very heart of our civilized form of government and of our society. The people will not tolerate such conduct at any level of government, and those who use their public office to betray the public trust in this manner can expect from the courts only the gravest consequences. (Cook 1973, 133)

Chicago and the Daley Machine

Richard J. Daley (1902–1976), the longtime Democratic mayor of Chicago, carried out many of the practices that were perfected by earlier bosses. Daley firmly believed in the Tammany Hall tradition of ministering to the personal needs of constituents as a roadmap to success; the great social and emotional issues of the times were secondary to the day-to-day concerns of individual voters. Like other bosses, he had little use for altruistic philosophies or ideology. Great causes were for liberals and intellectuals—impractical amateurs—to discuss. These views are similar to those held by William Tweed and New York's Tammany Hall. Tammany politicians regarded reformers as "morning glories" that looked lovely in the morning but withered in a short time. In contrast, regular machines and regular machine politicians went on flourishing forever, like fine old oaks. In retrospect, Daley's machine proved this statement to be true, standing like a fine oak while other politicians faded away.

The grandson of Irish immigrants, Richard Daley was born in 1902 to a working-class family (his father was a sheet metal worker). He was active in sports, participated in social activities, and rose to leadership of a neighborhood social organization. The Hamburg Social and Athletic Club was part sports club, part gang, and part a process of acculturation into the adult community. Like Tweed with his fire company, Daley used his membership in the neighborhood organization to launch his political career.

Upon graduation from high school in 1919, Daley began to work in the Chicago stockyards and was also selected to become a precinct captain for Chicago alderman Joseph ("Big Joe") McDonough. Daley also began to work in McDonough's city council office as a secretary. In this capacity, Daley was described as one of a corps of glorified gofers. In 1923, Daley began taking pre-law and law school classes four nights a week at DePaul University. He became president of the Hamburg Club in 1924, a position he held for fifteen years. After eleven years Daley received his law degree.

Daley's rise in both appointed and elected offices was steady after he became secretary for the county treasurer (his old patron "Big Joe" McDonough) in 1931. Assuming most of the responsibilities of the county treasurer, Daley learned a great deal about government, taxes, and the inner workings of the political system while McDonough was frequenting racetracks and speakeasies. Daley's work for McDonough fit a pattern he followed throughout his career: apprentice to powerful men and make yourself indispensable by taking on dull but necessary jobs. Daley held onto the office of secretary McDonough until McDonough died unexpectedly in 1934 (Cohen and Taylor 2000, 61). In 1935 Daley was elected to the lower house of the state legislature. He moved to the state senate in 1938, served loyally for eight years, and at the request of party leaders ran unsuccessfully for Cook County sheriff in 1946.

After his only electoral defeat in 1946, the following year Daley fought a successful battle to become a member of the Central Committee of the Cook County Democratic Party. With this electoral victory he became a powerful figure in

Chicago's Democratic politics. As the leader of one of the city's most reliable wards, he enjoyed high status among the Catholic Irish and made many allies. He was appointed state revenue director in 1949, but his main interests were with the city of Chicago. Like Tweed, Daley preferred to seek power at the city level rather than at a higher level of government. In 1950, Daley quit his state position to run in a special election for Cook County clerk. His success in the election rewarded him for his long years of service. Daley's rise to power was far from meteoric, yet he remained faithful to his party and took his responsibilities seriously.

As one of more than 3,000 precinct captains spread across Chicago's fifty city wards, Daley was faithful to the moral code of Chicago's Democratic machine. Among the tenets of this creed were the following: (1) Be faithful to those above you in the hierarchy, and repay those who are faithful to you; (2) Back the whole machine slate, not individual candidates or programs; (3) Be respectful of elected officials and party leaders; (4) Never be ashamed of the party, and defend it proudly; (5) Don't ask questions; (6) Stay on your own turf and keep out of conflicts that do not concern you; (7) Never be first, since innovation brings with it risk; and (8) Don't get caught (Cohen and Taylor 2000).

Daley, the prototype of the loyal machine soldier, became chair of the Cook County Democratic Central Committee in 1953 and two years later, at the age of fifty-two, he became mayor of Chicago. Reelected five times, he served for more than twenty years, becoming a figure of national importance to Democratic presidents and would-be presidents. When he died in 1976, his political machine was well entrenched. Daley was widely heralded as the "last boss" because in an age when the old political machine seemed to be disappearing (for example, in New York, Boston,

and elsewhere), it flourished in Chicago (Allswang 1977, 118).

Daley became known as a presidential kingmaker when John F. Kennedy was elected in 1960. Kennedy acknowledged his debt to Daley by inviting him and his family to the White House on Kennedy's first day in office (Rakove 1975, 71). The alleged "vote stealing" in Illinois during the 1960 campaign is attributed to Daley's loyalty to Kennedy, a fellow Irish Catholic, and Daley's desire to defeat state Republican opponents. His ability to shrug off allegations leveled against him attests to the power of his organization and his support from all kinds and classes of voters. Chicago citizens from the South Side ghetto to the wealthy North Shore suburbs defended their mayor and were unconcerned with the allegation of vote fraud (Allswang 1977, 129).

As the prototypical "machine man," Daley viewed politics as a full-time profession. The Chicago machine and its boss subscribed to the infamous views of "Tammany philosopher" and turn-of-the-century New York ward boss George Washington Plunkitt, who claimed that the reason reformers do not last in politics is that they are not trained in the business of politics. Plunkitt equated politics to a grocery store or drugstore. He claimed that he survived in the business of politics because of his experience, which began with his work at political polling stations when he was twelve years old. Experience in the political game was a main reason why the career politician "answers to the gong" every time while the reformer "goes down and out in the first or second round" (Riordon 1948, 26).

Daley was widely recognized as a man of the people. Even after he gained enormous power, he refused to move away from his modest neighborhood house. Daley instilled in all his children fundamental values that he learned from his devout Irish Catholic parents. He sent his children to church two blocks away from that house, to local Catholic parochial schools instead of expensive boarding schools, and to "subway" Catholic universities such as Loyola and DePaul. Unlike Tweed, Daley did not furnish his children with lavish weddings or engage in conspicuous consumption. He was a man of simple tastes who preferred White Sox games, fishing, and parades to literature, music, and French cooking. He raised his oldest son, Richard M. Daley, for a career in politics, law, and public service. Richard M. Daley was elected mayor of Chicago in 1989 and was reelected in 1991, 1995, 1999, 2003, and 2007. His 2007 reelection set him to become the longest-running mayor in Chicago history should he remain in office past 2010.

Richard J. Daley became synonymous with Chicago, the city he exemplified. By the late 1960s, however, many critics felt that his time had passed. One such critic claimed that Chicago under Daley was government for and by a few thousand elite who used Daley to manipulate the poor masses. According to this perspective, Daley's purpose was to preserve the social status quo, to stimulate business (particularly in the central business district), and to build housing for the upper and middle classes. Only minimal benefits were seen as going to the common folks. Critics claimed that social problems, including racial conflict, were sublimated; improvements were marginal; and benefits went disproportionately to the powerful. Critics of Daley's management style contended that Daley presented a handsome image for Chicago but glossed over the desperate social and economic problems of the poor (Rakove 1975, 79).

Supporters of Daley point to his ability to protect private property from crime, foster an environment conducive to economic growth, and please contractors, banks, and downtown interests both economically and in terms of civic pride. For Daley's admirers, he made Chicago a city that "worked"; it

was clean, its books were balanced, its credit rating was good, and its mayor was even applauded by the city's four Republican newspapers (Allswang 1977, 146).

Application of Case No. 1 to Ethics and Responsible Governance

Breaches of Responsibility: The Public Interest

Machines had characteristics that both attacked and enhanced the public interest. According to Banfield and Wilson (1967, 40, 46), two conflicting perceptions of the public interest existed in urban areas: (1) a view derived from the immigrant ethos that focused on providing material benefits, and (2) a view derived from the middle-class ethos that favored efficiency, impartiality, honesty, planning, strong executives, and virtue. Richard Hofstadter (1955, 9) noted such differences in his discussion of the clash between the needs of immigrants and the sentiments of Americans derived from early English settlers. In this clash of the two groups, alternative political values vied for dominance. One set of values, founded upon Yankee Protestant political traditions, demanded disinterested activity of the citizen in public affairs and argued that political life ought to be run in accordance with general principles apart from personal need. The other set of values, founded upon the backgrounds of non-English immigrants, focused upon their lack of familiarity with independent political action, acceptance of systems of tight hierarchy, and the high value placed on family needs. The non-English perspective accepted political relations chiefly in terms of personal obligations and placed strong personal loyalties above allegiance to principles or moral codes.

From the Yankee Protestant middle-class perspective, the public interest was damaged by political machines since machines pursued private rather than public values. From the perspective of immigrants, however, political machines were beneficial and served their needs. Describing the immigrant perspective, sociologist Robert Merton ([1957] 1976, 25–30) argued that political machines served three important functions. First, political machines humanized and personalized assistance to the needy. This was accomplished through the precinct captain's provision of food baskets, jobs, legal advice, college scholarships, and basic friendship to those in need. The manner in which assistance was given was also important. In contrast to the impersonal bureaucracies found in welfare agencies, legal aid clinics, free hospitals, and relief departments, machine precinct captains did not ask questions or demand compliance with rules of eligibility.

For many constituents, the loss of respect that came with dealing with the formal organizations was too high a price to pay for assistance. For example, many settlement house workers were educated, upper-class women who belonged to a different ethnic group from those seeking aid. Poor immigrants saw these workers as condescending, impersonal, and uppity. In contrast, the precinct captain was likely to come from the same ethnic neighborhood as their constituents and was better suited to serve their needs. Members of the urban machine provided needed help to the "deprived classes" without any questions, formal rules, regulations, or rigid adherence to the law. Serving the poor enhanced the legitimacy of government officials (among the poor), increased the stability of the state, and reduced class tensions. The machine therefore can be viewed as not only serving the public, but also as helping to preserve the political system.

A second useful function played by the political machine related to its interactions with business. According to Merton, large businesses, such as public utilities, railroads, electric light companies, and communications companies, wanted a strong government so that they could operate without too much disruption. Machine bosses tightened the linkage between business and government. In a 1908 article, "An Apology to Graft," muckraker journalist Lincoln Steffens argued that the machine boss should not be blamed for corruption. Rather, the economic system that enriched men who corruptly bought timber, mines, oil fields, and franchises was to blame. He noted that business and machine politicians had mutual interests, recognizing that little would get done without business becoming an integral part of machine corruption: "You cannot build or operate a railroad, or a street railway, gas, water, or power company, develop and operate a mine, or get forests and cut timber on a large scale, or run any privileged business, without the corruption of the government" (quoted in Merton [1957] 1976, 27). The machine therefore served the public interest through its role as an intermediary between business and the public.

The third set of functions provided channels of social mobility for those excluded from typical avenues of advancement. Merton claimed that American society as a whole placed tremendous importance on both money and power as a definition of success. In certain subpopulations of American society, the desire for money and power was inculcated into the values of the people. However, many individuals had little access to conventional and legitimate means of attaining the desired money or power. The political machine allowed these individuals to move up in American society both socially and economically.

Merton observed that immigrants had great difficulty finding places for themselves in American society. He contended that politics and criminal rackets became an important means of social mobility for those individuals who were blocked from advancement in more "respectable" channels. The political machine was able to help whole groups of people, such as the Irish, who were previously excluded from the "American dream." Merton stated, "It is in the machine itself that these individuals and subgroups find their culturally induced needs more or less satisfied. . . . Seen in the wider social context we have set forth, it [the machine] no longer appears merely as a means of self-aggrandizement for profit-hungry and powerful *individuals*, but as an organized provision for *subgroups* otherwise excluded from or handicapped in the race for getting ahead" ([1957] 1976, 29).

From the perspective of the public interest, it therefore appears that political machines can be interpreted from alternative outlooks. From the perspective of the Protestant Yankees, machines acted counter to the interests of "good" citizens since they squandered the public treasury, enriched themselves individually, set poor examples for others to emulate, assisted criminal enterprises, and attacked cherished American values such as honest and fair elections. On the other hand, Merton as well as others argued that machines served the important functions of legitimizing the political system and helping poor immigrants.

Breaches of Responsibility: Natural Law

As discussed in Chapter 2 natural law is identified as unchanging, inscribed in the consciences of human beings, superior to man-made law, discovered through reason, and found in laws made by humans. Natural law can be observed in some of the behavior of political machines. For example, political machine behavior helped supply their constituents with basic needs such as food, clothing, shelter, and jobs. While machine politicians did not always follow the letter of the law,

the machine organizations provided the means of survival for those without visible means of support. Intuitively, it could be argued that machine actions were in accord with the higher natural law of assisting the destitute and helping them to survive in what for some was a harsh, foreign, and hostile new environment.

In contrast to this justification, it can also be argued that the greed of certain machine leaders violated basic principles of economic justice. Some machine leaders lived like kings, plundering public treasuries and skimming off tax money whenever possible. While turn of the twentieth century bosses became wealthy, large proportions of their constituents were living in severe poverty. William Marcy Tweed and his associates represent stark examples of the insatiable appetite of corrupt politicians. Tweed's lifestyle and fall from grace are well documented (Lynch 1927; Mandelbaum 1965; Callow 1966).

Tweed became the symbol of political corruption, thievery, and greed in the mid-nineteenth century. He actions became legendary. For example, in 1870 at a meeting of the New York City Board of Audit, which was composed of Tweed and two others, payment of more than $6 million for the construction of a new county courthouse was authorized. It later turned out that more than $5.5 million of the money allocated was fraudulent and divided among members of the Tweed Ring. The total price paid by taxpayers for the courthouse, furnishings, and equipment was more than $12 million. Some critics estimated that $3 million would have been a high price for the building and its contents.

New York reformer Samuel J. Tilden contended that the amount of fraudulent billing in 1873 alone by Tweed and his associates approximated $28 million. This represented a sharp increase from the 1871 estimates of fraudulent billing of almost $3.5 million. Tweed's method of plundering the government treasury was relatively straightfor-ward. Tweed established that all money paid to contractors and merchants who worked for, or sold supplies to, New York City must be, at a minimum, evenly divided between creditors and the Tweed Ring. The share for Tweed and his associates was to be as large as circumstances permitted (Lynch 1927, 338–339).

The magnitude of machine corruption under Tweed eventually drew the attention of New York's economic elite, who noted that Tweed, who was penniless in 1861, was a multimillionaire in 1870. As Tweed's extravagance became better known, people began to ask how a public servant on a salary of $7,500 a year could afford such a lavish lifestyle. He was the third-largest landowner in the city, occupied one of the finest mansions on Fifth Avenue, owned another expensive home in Greenwich, Connecticut, and possessed a steam yacht equipped with Oriental rugs, a library, monogrammed linens, sterling silver, a crew of twelve, and an orchestra for large parties (Callow 1966, 249; Hershkowitz 1977, 158). The event that, according to some New York City reporters, marked the beginning of the end for Tweed was the marriage of his twenty-one-year-old daughter Mary in 1871. The New York press covered the wedding extensively, observing that the Tweed family was a "Christmas tree" of diamonds. Boss Tweed wore his "familiar planet-diamond" on his shirtfront and Miss Mary Tweed sparkled with diamonds on her ears, arms, bosom, neck, and satin shoes. Influential politicians, judges, congressmen, and the superintendent of police attended the wed-ding. Tweed's associates gave the bride and groom gifts estimated to be worth $700,000 (Callow 1966, 250–251).

The wedding extravaganza and other purchases were out of proportion to the status of the Tweed family. Average taxpayers as well as social elites began to resent being taxed to enrich a relatively small group of corrupt politicians. Citizens who promoted "good government" felt that the nobility and ideals of the American government had been stained by the excesses of Tweed. The wealthy elite felt infringed upon by grasping individuals of lower social status who dominated the political machines of the time.

One could surmise that the conspicuous con-sumption of machine politicians crossed some boundaries of propriety. On the other hand, urban machines helped the survival of various destitute individuals who were newcomers to America. The legacy of political machines remains mixed. They represent both an affront to America's civic culture and an example of how democracy can work to mitigate the problems associated with abject poverty.

Breaches of Responsibility: The Rule of Law

The sanctity of the law is a fundamental pillar of free societies. Machine politics, however, bred disregard and even disdain for the universality of the legal system. Machine leaders such as New Jersey boss Frank Hague even went so far as to replicate the famous utterance of France's King Louis XIV that "I am the law" (Cook 1973, 127). To the extent that bosses controlled the political process they could disregard the law; however, even Boss Tweed learned that there were limits to this practice. Many machine politicians eventually found themselves behind bars, imprisoned by a system they had wantonly abused. The periodic triumph of good-government reformers over ma-chine politicians marked a victory of the rule of law and the forces that supported the law.

The fall from power of Boss Tweed is a highly instructive illustration of the power of the rule of law in America. Tweed's arrogance and extravagant behavior mobilized good-government forces eager to bring him down. These civic activists perceived machines as representing lower-class, "non-Yankee" immigrants who did not adopt the principles of American Protestants. Immigrants fit Richard Hofstadter's characterization of the non-Yankee ethos. According to Hofstadter immigrants were unfamiliar with independent political action, family oriented and likely to prioritize individual needs over general principles. American Protestants generally believed that non-Protestant immigrants were more willing to sell their votes for material rewards than to vote their principles.

An account of Tweed's fall demonstrates that the ethos of the rule of law persisted even in a machine stronghold such as nineteenth-century New York City. The Tweed Ring's stranglehold on power was relatively short-lived. Having raided the public treasury from 1866 to 1871, the Tweed Ring reached its high point in July 1871, when the *New York Times* began carefully documenting the abuses of Tweed's machine. Five months later the ring was virtually destroyed by a combination of newspapermen, ambitious anti-Tweed politicians, resentful machine insiders, good-government reformers, bankers, and moralists (Callow 1966, 253). Tweed's excesses activated the middle as well as upper classes to oppose him. In overstepping the existing borders of corruption and in living an opulent lifestyle Tweed's support among poor immigrants eroded (Allswang 1977, 55).

There is probably no one reason that can be cited for Tweed's downfall. Contributing to his demise was a combination of factors such as greed, ostentatious displays of wealth, and the appointment to office of individuals who were disloyal to the machine organization. Disloyal and unhappy with the size of their payoffs, members of the machine turned on their leaders and passed damaging information to the media. This information empowered both the *New York Times* and the magazine *Harper's Weekly* to attack Tweed with added credibility.

The two media companies then led highly visible crusades against the Tweed Ring.

Thomas Nast's political cartoons in *Harper's* were particularly troublesome for Tweed. Tweed insisted that he did not care about news articles since his constituents did not know how to read, but they could not help seeing pictures. Members of the Tweed Ring offered Nast $500,000 in gold if he would leave the country and stop drawing cartoons of "the boss." Nast replied that he made up his mind long ago to put some of the ring's fellows behind bars (Lynch 1927, 364). The publisher of the *New York Times*, George Jones, was also offered a bribe of $500,000 to clamp down on the newspaper's stories. Jones declined the bribe, saying that he "didn't think the devil would ever bid higher than that" (Callow 1966, 268).

The confrontation with Tweed and his associates exposed significant class differences within the city. Advocates of clean government represented, for the most part, middle- and upper-class interests such as bankers, merchants, journalists, and less corrupt politicians. These interests felt they previously held the power, but that they were now in the process of being replaced by immigrants and other poor as well as lower-middle-class citizens. The media stoked fear that new immigrants were a threat to the American system of governance and did not have the same political principles as American Protestants. Reformers declared that the country was safe only in the rightful hands of the educated, wealthy, and virtuous, who would uphold the rule of law and protect the rights of hardworking Americans.

Individuals on the lower rungs of society were associated with decaying morals, the Roman Catholic religion, and a fondness for the corner saloon. For New York City reformers of 1871, machines were not Robin Hoods to the needy (taking from the rich and giving to the poor) but rather Robin Hoods to the degenerate. Machines were characterized as wasting taxpayers' money by giving jobs to immigrants, bailing out drunks from jail, and corrupting the unemployed with food. Reformers considered machines as parasites since they took money from the productive in society and gave it to themselves with a bit going to the unproductive. Reformers believed that such parasitic behavior would undermine the Protestant ethic of civic responsibility, setting the nation on a downward course (Callow 1966, 264).

The reformers, newspapers, and "responsible" citizens eventually were able to triumph over Tweed. Motivated by the media, New York elites called for a public meeting. The public meeting was well attended and held in Cooper Union on September 4, 1871. The banker James Brown called the meeting to order and nominated former mayor William F. Havemeyer to preside. Havemeyer made an opening speech that was highly critical of the gross corruption of the Tweed administration. At the conclusion of the meeting the names of seventy gentlemen who agreed to serve on a nonpartisan "Committee of Seventy" was announced. Havemeyer, became vice-president and later president of this committee. The explicit goal of the committee (heavily represented by business interests) was to bring down Tweed and his associates.

Acting in accordance with advice from the Democrat Samuel J. Tilden, a member of the Committee of Seventy filed a taxpayer's suit against the city, forbidding the mayor from raising any money by taxation and from making any further payments from city funds. Panic ensued and a special state attorney general was named to bring suit against Tweed and others to recover money that had been stolen (Lynch 1927, 381).

The election of 1871 was disastrous for the Tweed Ring. There was an unusually large turnout, and many who had previously been apathetic registered their indignation at the ballot box. Reform candidates captured numerous offices as aldermen,

assistant aldermen, and state senators. Tweed retained his seat in the state senate, but his essential lieutenants were swept from power. The *New York Times* contended that the election was won by the strong vote of the "neutral population, who seldom voted—the gentlemen and quiet citizens." For the *Times*, the 1871 election represented a moral struggle in which good triumphed over evil. The victory was trumpeted by the *Times* as a sign that "immortal principles on which this Government is founded, although they may be momentarily stifled by dishonest factions, will constantly rise triumphant, while the men who assailed them will pass away to everlasting infamy" (Callow 1966, 278).

The 1871 election was a victory for the rule of law over a cabal who overplayed its hand. One of New York's leading citizens stated during the height of the controversy:

> I am still a believer in the irresistible force inherent in our legal and political system. Whatever way, under God, we may be rescued, it must be by the law, or we will only add to our disgrace . . . At all events, let us first have recourse to the law, before even a whisper is heard that men of thought and education and high standing in the community have lost faith in the efficacy of our institutions. (Lynch 1927, 373)

Questions for Student Group Discussions

1. Did the negative deeds of political machines outweigh their positive deeds?
2. What are the ethical lessons of machine politics?
3. Was the rise of political machines inevitable in rapidly growing democracies?
4. Why did the reformers triumph over the Tweed machine?
5. How are machine principles antithetical to ideals of responsible governance?
6. How did the Daley machine differ from the Tweed machine?

7. What recommendations can you offer to reduce machine influences on government?

8. Are some forms of political corruption inevitable? What can be tolerated and what cannot be tolerated?

9. Did machines violate or represent principles of democracy?

10. Are there machines in American politics today? Where are they most likely to be found?

Case No. 2: Tom DeLay, Money Laundering, and Influence Peddling

DeLay's Political Rise

The background of Tom DeLay is somewhat similar to that of old-time machine bosses. DeLay was born in Laredo, Texas, in 1947 into a family dominated by a father who was described as big, tough, gregarious, and alcoholic. According to DeLay and his siblings, their father, Charlie, would routinely drink a fifth of scotch whiskey in a night. When Tom was nine, his father moved the family to Venezuela, where he landed a job in the oil fields. Five years later, the family moved back to Texas. Eventually Tom's father succeeded in the oil-drilling business, building a multimillion-dollar company called Storm Drilling.

Tom attended high school in Corpus Christi, where he met his future wife, Christine Furrh. She came from a hardscrabble south Texas background and later taught high school. She never enjoyed living in Washington and after her husband was elected to Congress she preferred to live full-time in the Houston area. Tom played football in high school; despite weighing only 140 pounds, he could knock down bigger boys. He spent two years as a pre-med student at Baylor University before being expelled for drinking

and vandalism. The vandalism charge stemmed from his painting rival Texas A&M University's buildings with the Baylor colors of green and gold. Tom and Christine married in 1967 and had a daughter in 1972.

In 1970, DeLay received a Bachelor of Science degree with a major in biology from the University of Houston. After three years of working for a chemical company, he founded Albo Pest Control, a company that was known as a struggling operation. DeLay faced tax liens by the Internal Revenue Service for not paying payroll and income taxes, and he paid out settlements to associates who claimed they were cheated. His work in pest control was the origin of one of his nicknames, "the Exterminator." The Environmental Protection Agency's ban on pesticides was an early source of DeLay's continuous opposition to government regulation.

In 1978 DeLay was elected to the Texas House of Representatives, where he gained a reputation as a playboy known as Hot Tub Tom. He roomed with other male legislators in a condo that was called Macho Manor. By his own admission he was drinking eight to twelve martinis a night at receptions and fund-raisers. He also admitted that later, when he was first elected to the U.S. Congress, he would stay out drinking until the bars closed and then get up sober and go to work. Both of DeLay's brothers had problems with alcoholism. His older brother Ray served two years in a South Dakota penitentiary for grand theft. His younger brother Randy gave up drinking and became a lawyer and lobbyist. After the death of his father in 1988, Tom cut off contact with his three siblings and stopped attending family gatherings. He does not openly discuss this estrangement (Perl 2001).

In 1985, DeLay became a born-again Christian, gave up drinking hard liquor, and became involved with helping troubled youth (Wikipedia 2007d). He traced his religious conversion to his freshman year in Congress, when a Republican colleague, Frank Wolf of Virginia, urged him to watch a religious video about Christian fatherhood. In the video, child psychologist and Christian family spokesperson James Dobson discussed the damage done by fathers who were too busy to love their children. After watching the video, DeLay admitted that he was "totally self-centered" with "golf or my business or politics" always coming first in his life (Perl 2001).

As a practicing Christian, DeLay attended church in a suburb of Houston, participated in Bible study class, and taught a weekly adult class based on the writings of Watergate figure Charles Colson. Colson's writings contend that only Christianity can truly reform America's government and culture. DeLay's personal religious convictions easily carried over to the political realm. In 1999, DeLay asserted that virtually all man-made government programs, philosophies and "-isms" favored by Democrats and liberals were doomed utopian dreams because they are not inspired by God. He asked the following question in a 1999 election speech made to the Christian Coalition, "Will this country accept the worldviews of humanism, materialism, sexism, naturalism, postmodernism or any of the other -isms? Or will we march forward with a biblical worldview, a worldview that says God is our creator, that man is a sinner, and that we will save this country by changing the hearts and minds of Americans?" (Perl 2001). DeLay viewed the 2000 presidential election as a battle for souls in a struggle between good and evil.

Tom DeLay was elected to the U.S. House of Representatives in 1984 from the Texas 22nd Congressional District. He quickly made a name for himself through criticism of both the National Endowment for the Arts and the Environmental Protection Agency. In 1988, DeLay was appointed deputy whip of the House of Representatives. When the Republican Party gained a majority of

the House in 1995, DeLay was elected majority whip, winning out over a candidate backed by Speaker of the House Newt Gingrich. DeLay nevertheless faithfully supported Gingrich's agenda and survived the turmoil of Gingrich's resignation in 1998. When Representative Dick Armey left the position of majority leader in 2003, DeLay assumed the role of majority leader without much opposition.

DeLay became known as a cultural warrior in the House, consistently favoring conservative policy positions. He opposed abortion, supported teaching creationism in public schools, supported an anti–flag-burning amendment to the Constitution, supported President Ronald Reagan's Strategic Defense Initiative (nicknamed "Star Wars"), opposed campaign finance reform, opposed Bill Clinton, and most strongly opposed environmental legislation. DeLay's opposition to the Environmental Protection Agency (EPA) led him to characterize the EPA as "the Gestapo of government." DeLay consistently championed business rights and fought to hold down minimum wages, eliminate occupational health measures, and protect corporations from consumer lawsuits. He opposed bills that sought to phase out the use of chlorofluorocarbons (CFCs) and supported efforts to repeal parts of the Clear Air Act.

Perhaps the biggest factor in the rise of Tom DeLay was his ability to raise money and use the money to get what he wanted. DeLay provided a great deal of support—both money and consulting expertise—for Republican candidates running in the 1994 midterm elections. He carefully picked races in which he thought he would get the most return for the amount of money he contributed. In order to help candidates, DeLay set up a candidate's school that provided candidates with tapes, talking points, and a video. He traveled extensively in the campaign. When one of the eighty candidates DeLay supported would call for help, DeLay's allies contacted friendly lobbyists who would contribute money. DeLay admitted after the election that he lost count of how much money he had raised after it surpassed $2 million (Dubose and Reid 2006, 87).

DeLay influence grew substantially after the 1994 election when the Republican Party took control of both the U.S. House of Representatives and the U.S. Senate for the first time since 1953. DeLay was considered to be the leader of the Republican House freshmen. These freshmen Republicans were overwhelmingly conservative (Dubose and Reid 2006, 88). DeLay furthered his stature as a fiscal conservative who was deeply committed to tax cuts when he criticized President George H.W. Bush for reneging on his "watch my lips—no new taxes" pledge. He also gained credibility with conservatives for supporting Newt Gingrich's blueprint for future success; the ten-point Contract with America. DeLay welcomed the growing numbers of oil and gas, timber, pharmaceutical, and insurance company lobbyists who embraced the Republican Party that now controlled Congress. Lobbyists from these groups replaced the influence formerly held by Democratic lobbyists who represented the construction industry, the entertainment industry, and trial lawyers. DeLay observed that it was understandable that lobbyists would write legislation because they had the expertise. This became an accepted mantra as lobbying interests gained immense power.

DeLay's power was linked to his ability to raise money from lobbyists who were seeking something or trying to avoid something. Campaign finance reformer Fred Wertheimer notes that all politicians raise money, but for DeLay raising political money was what he was about "as if political money is in his DNA" (Dubose and Reid 2006, 125). From the start, DeLay recognized that to increase his influence he would have to increase the amount of his contributions to other Republican candidates. After attaining his position as majority whip in

January 1995, he hired a professional fund-raiser for his political action committee, Americans for a Republican Majority (ARMPAC). Before long, DeLay was cultivating a relationship with Enron Corporation CEO Kenneth Lay, who generously contributed to ARMPAC. This allowed DeLay to compete financially with Newt Gingrich's political action committee. Before the collapse of Enron, the energy corporation had contributed about half a million dollars to ARMPAC.

By 2004, DeLay's fund-raising machine was capable of extracting large amounts of money from business and delivering benefits to clients. DeLay was able to set himself apart from other money raisers. He did not host "the huge cattle calls" where a donor was only expected to drop off a $1,000 check before moving to the next event. Instead, DeLay's specialty was "small gatherings in exclusive restaurants, where donors got 'face time' as they very publicly handed $20,000 checks to fundraising operatives" (Dubose and Reid 2006, 134).

DeLay's Political Fall

DeLay's fall was relatively swift, with a variety of questionable actions precipitating the descent. DeLay's questionable behavior included his insistence that lobbyists hire Republicans if they wanted to deal with him (K-Street Project), his association with convicted felon Jack Abramoff, his expensive trips paid for by corporations and lobbyists, his decision to pay large amounts of money to his wife and daughter for assistance in elections, and finally his tampering with the electoral process. The K-Street Project was a project of the Republican Party to pressure Washington lobbying firms to hire Republicans in top positions, and to reward Republican lobbyist with access to influential leaders. The project was launched in 1995 by DeLay and Republican strategist Grover Norquist. Congressional scholar

Norman Ornstein notes that the act of placing Delay's staffers with lobbyists represented "Tammany Hall all over again" (Dubose and Reid 2006, 258). It was reported that DeLay's daughter and wife were paid $500,000 over four years by political organizations controlled by Tom DeLay (N. Thompson 2005). In 2004, Texas prosecutor (District Attorney for Travis County) Ronnie Earle subpoenaed DeLay's daughter, Danielle Ferro, to explain what she had done for the DeLay-controlled Texans for a Republican Majority Political Action Committee (TRMPAC) as a $27,600 consultant. A DeLay spokesperson claimed that all she did was buy some flowers (Dubose and Reid 2006, 265).

In 2004, DeLay was admonished by the House Ethics Committee a total of three times. DeLay was rebuked by the ethics committee on October 6, 2004, for soliciting contributions from corporations in exchange for action benefiting the corporations. Specifically, the ethics committee admonished DeLay for his dealings with top officers of the Kansas City, Kansas-based energy company, Westar Energy Inc. Some of the officers of Westar wrote memos in 2002 citing their belief that the $56,000 in campaign contributions to political committees linked to DeLay would get them "a seat at the table" where key legislation was being drafted (Babington 2004). The ethics committee cited DeLay's participation in Westar's golf fund-raiser on June 2–3, 2002, as objectionable in that it created an improper appearance.

This golf tournament raised money for the DeLay-controlled political action committees, ARMPAC and TRMPAC. A House Ethics Committee report noted that the golf tournament "took place just as the House-Senate conference on major energy legislation ... was about to get underway." The legislation was of critical importance to the attendees. The ethics committee's report said that DeLay was "in a position to significantly influence the conference."

The bipartisan Ethics Committee concluded that DeLay's participation in the golf fund-raiser was objectionable because "at a minimum, his (DeLay's) conduct created at least the appearance that donors were being provided with special access to Representative DeLay regarding the then-pending energy legislation" (Babington 2004).

A second objection cited by the House Ethics Committee related to DeLay's improper use of federal resources in a Texas redistricting controversy in 2003. During this ultimately successful attempt at redistricting favorable to Republicans, DeLay used federal assets—the Federal Aviation Administration (FAA)—to search for Democratic state legislators who were attempting to boycott a redistricting vote. The Ethics Committee specifically faulted DeLay for asking the FAA to locate a private plane that Republicans believed was carrying Texas Democratic legislators. Democratic lawmakers were leaving the state to prevent a quorum that Republicans needed to pass the Texas redistricting plan. The Ethics Committee stated that using federal executive branch resources to resolve state issues raised serious concerns about federalism and the separation of powers. The Ethics Committee further contended that matters of the Texas House of Representatives were the responsibility of the legislators, officers, and employees of the state of Texas, not the federal government. Finally, a third ethics violation related to a job endorsement in return for a vote on the Medicare prescription drug bill (Babington 2004).

DeLay's biggest problem, however, concerned the money-laundering charge brought against him by Ronnie Earle, the district attorney of Travis County, Texas. In what Earle described as an attempt to "steal an election," DeLay was indicted in September 2005. The indictment directly led to his resignation as majority leader, since under Republican rules members of the House of Representatives must give up leadership posts if indicted. In January 2006, DeLay announced that he would not try to reclaim his leadership post. In April, he announced that he would not run for reelection despite polls indicating that he could beat his Democratic opponent. DeLay remained defiant to the end. In his farewell address to Congress on June 8, he stated that he "scraped and clawed for every vote, every amendment and for every word of every bill that I believed in my heart would protect human freedom and defend human dignity. I have done so at all times honorably and honestly . . . as God is my witness and history is my judge" (CQ Transcripts Wire 2006).

In his 2007 book *No Retreat, No Surrender,* DeLay attempts to refute all the charges leveled against him. Consistent with his conservative roots, he notes that his entire political life has been devoted to "forcing government back into its constitutional cage so that the American people may achieve their intended magnificence." His dream was to move government off center stage "in order to free the God-given greatness of a people" and to "assure the glory of America for generations yet to come." He states that he remained "unyielding about my fight in Congress, my fights in the courts, and my fight for the hearts and minds of the American people" (DeLay and Mansfield 2007, 174, 178–179).

Application of Case No. 2 to Ethics and Responsible Governance

Breaches of Responsibility: The Public Interest

The actions of Tom DeLay suggest that he may have represented the conservative views of his Houston congressional district well but that he overreached in representing the public as a whole. DeLay's plan was to tap into corporate wealth in order to gain power for Republican candidates. This plan not only violated Texas law but violated the public interest due to its potential to corrupt the electoral process and to allow money to unfairly distort the electoral playing field.

Expanding the influence of money further damages the concept of open, free, and fair elections. Since money is the mother's milk of elections, absence of money is a clear disqualifier that reduces the pool of potential leaders. Money facilitates the rule of the wealthy few to the detriment of the many. Money in elections shifts advantages to those who already are advantaged and shifts opportunity away from others. It is disingenuous to believe that corporations and others who contribute large sums of money do not expect something in return. What they get is access, special consideration, and at times votes to pass or kill specific pieces of legislation. These practices harm the public interest in that government spends more attention in benefiting those already privileged and less attention in extending aid to the less privileged.

When Republicans took control of Congress in 1994, DeLay earned a reputation as the person who brazenly strong-armed corporate lobbyists for funding. Along with Republican strategist Grover Norquist, DeLay created a plan that pressured Washington lobbying firms to hire Republicans in top positions and then rewarded Republican lobbyists with access to influential government officials. To the detriment of the large disinterested public, DeLay facilitated a return to the classic form of machine politics. Reporters for the *Washington Post* described his lasting contribution as empowering party discipline, empowering lobbyists, and returning politics to attitudes prevalent in the machine era:

> His take-no-prisoners style of fundraising—in which the classic unstated bargain of access for contributions is made explicit and without apology—has been adopted by both parties in Congress, according to lawmakers, lobbyists and congressional scholars.

Democrats, likewise, increasingly are trying to emulate DeLay-perfected methods for enforcing caucus discipline—rewarding lawmakers who follow the dictums of party leaders and seeking retribution against those who do not. Most of all, DeLay stood for a blurring of the line between lawmakers and lobbyists so that lobbyists are now considered partners of politicians and not mere pleaders. (Birnbaum and VandeHei 2005)

Breaches of Responsibility: Natural Law

Tom DeLay's acceptance of God's laws in 1985 marked a significant turning point in his life. He began to view politics in apocalyptic terms as a struggle between good and evil, with himself championing the causes of good and fighting fiercely against the forces of evil. This was evident in the impeachment of President Bill Clinton, which occurred in the U.S. House of Representatives while DeLay served as majority whip. DeLay attacked Clinton relentlessly on talk radio, on television, in position papers, and in Congress, calling Clinton a lying, cheating, sexually immoral disgrace to the office. DeLay stated that he viewed the impeachment as an unavoidable personal responsibility. He prayed for strength prior to the vote (Perl 2001).

DeLay's acceptance of God's laws, as he interpreted them, solidified his political base with the Christian Coalition. He embraced socially conservative positions such as ending abortions, limiting the rights of homosexuals, curbing contraception, ending constitutional separations of church and state, and adopting the Ten Commandments as a principle for public schools. These public policy positions resonated with religious fundamentalists who viewed such behavior as consistent with God's will on earth or consistent with natural law.

DeLay became a faithful ally of religious fundamentalists, castigating "fashionable elites" in the media and entertainment world. From De-Lay's view of the world, the "fashionable elites" had staged a "cultural coup d'etat" to eliminate religious and moral values from American life. Salvation for the country would be possible only with a return to the moral values that underpinned the country. For DeLay, President George W. Bush did not promote the conservative social agenda aggressively enough. DeLay encouraged Bush to build a more God-centered nation whose government would promote prayer, worship, and the teaching of values (Perl 2001).

DeLay's behavior, however, seems to highlight limitations of natural law as a guide to societal action. DeLay seems to have felt sincerely that he was fighting for good to triumph over evil. However, his zealous pursuit of the good (as he saw it) led to his violations of election law and caused the American public to question whether his interpretation of God's will was accurate or even applicable to a nation based on secular as well as religious beliefs.

DeLay caused many Americans to remember the aphorism to "be wary of those who seem too good as well as those who seem too bad." DeLay and his fellow travelers seemed to have derived their behavior from the concept that the end justifies the means. For some, DeLay's behavior was a consequence of dogmatic pursuit of idealized goals, reflecting a lack of flexibility required of pluralistic societies, and an inquisition-like distrust of nonbelievers.

DeLay's case highlights the fact that natural law theory empowers and motivates those who personally identify God's will and then strive to impose their interpretation of that will on others who are not as enlightened. Such a worldview, however, subsumes other guides to public sector behavior, such as the public interest and the rule of law, and dredges up vexing questions such as whether natural law exists, who interprets it if it does exist, whether collective societies can coexist with individualistic interpretations of unwritten laws, and whether gut-level interpretations of God's will are an effective guide to action. While DeLay was the avowed political champion of Christian conservatives, his passion to defeat political opponents led to behavior that crossed certain boundaries of legality.

Breaches of Responsibility: The Rule of Law

On September 28, 2005, Delay was indicted by a Travis County, Texas, grand jury for conspiring to violate state election law. DeLay indignantly denied any wrongdoing; however, the Travis County District Attorney claimed that the facts clearly showed otherwise. The indictment charged DeLay with money laundering and conspiracy—specifically, that his statewide political action committee, TRMPAC, accepted corporate contributions and laundered the money by making contributions to the Republican National Committee, which in turn gave the money to Republican candidates for statewide races. Texas law specifically forbids corporate contributions for state legislative races.

The broad issue underlying the indictments was whether DeLay's political money unfairly altered the playing field in a manner that ultimately led to Republican control of the U.S. House of Representatives. The narrower issue in the indictment of DeLay stemmed from his conspiring to violate Texas state election law that makes it a felony to spend corporate money on election campaigns. The 100-year-old law was enacted in order to protect average voters from the influence of robber barons (Dubose and Reid 2006, 262).

In addition to the criminal charges leveled against DeLay, he was also implicated in a civil case brought against the treasurer of TRMPAC by five Democratic candidates for the Texas state legislative who were defeated in 2002 by Republican candidates who had accepted money from TRMPAC. DeLay was involved through his service on the board of TRMPAC, writing a cover letter for its fund-raising brochure, calling or meeting with donors, and attending TRMPAC fund-raising events. At these events DeLay sometimes solicited donors' views on upcoming federal legislation. It was revealed at the civil trial that TRMPAC took corporate money in 2002 from companies with business before the Texas legislature or the U.S. Congress and used the money for illegal campaign activities such as phone banks and polling. Spending corporate or union money on candidates has been illegal in the state of Texas since 1905.

TRMPAC was a great success in that all seventeen of the state legislative candidates that it backed in 2002 were elected, including five new Republican state legislators. The election of the five Republicans helped secure the first Republican majority in the Texas House of Representatives in 130 years. As a result, the Texas legislature was called into session in 2003 to redraw the state's congressional districts. As a result of the redistricting, more Republicans were elected to the U.S. House of Representatives in 2004, ultimately giving the national Republican Party control of the U.S. Congress.

Specifically, the indictment brought against Tom DeLay by the Travis County district attorney charged that TRMPAC collected money from several corporations, then sent a check for $190,000 to the Republican National Committee, made payable to the Republican National State Elections Committee, along with a list of candidates who should receive the money. All the individuals on the list were state-level Republicans. Figure 3.1 describes the questionable transfers of money by TRMPAC as well as the apparent consequences of the transfers.

85

Figure 3.1   **Money Laundering Scheme**

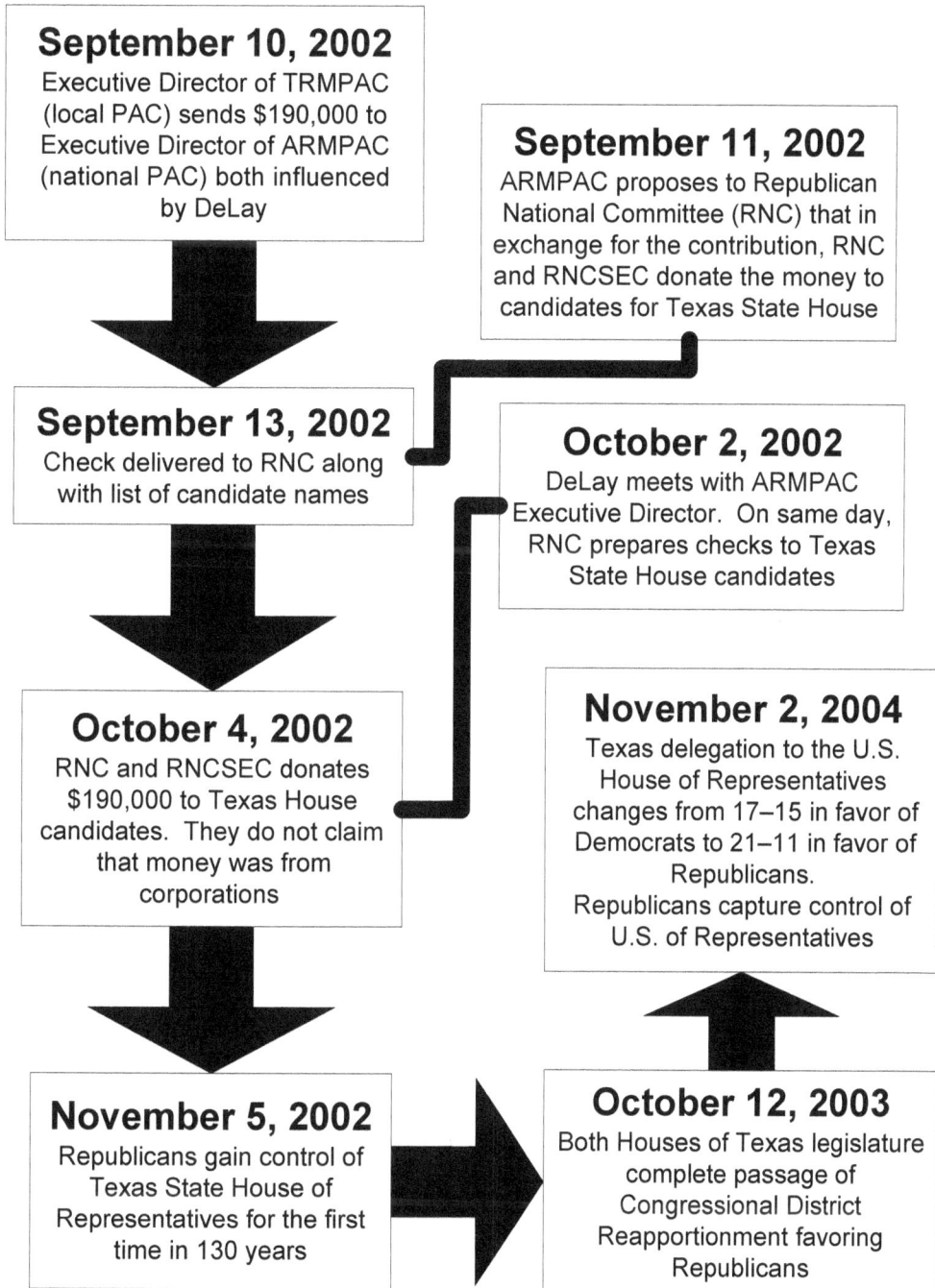

September 10, 2002
Executive Director of TRMPAC (local PAC) sends $190,000 to Executive Director of ARMPAC (national PAC) both influenced by DeLay

September 11, 2002
ARMPAC proposes to Republican National Committee (RNC) that in exchange for the contribution, RNC and RNCSEC donate the money to candidates for Texas State House

September 13, 2002
Check delivered to RNC along with list of candidate names

October 2, 2002
DeLay meets with ARMPAC Executive Director. On same day, RNC prepares checks to Texas State House candidates

October 4, 2002
RNC and RNCSEC donates $190,000 to Texas House candidates. They do not claim that money was from corporations

November 2, 2004
Texas delegation to the U.S. House of Representatives changes from 17–15 in favor of Democrats to 21–11 in favor of Republicans.
Republicans capture control of U.S. of Representatives

November 5, 2002
Republicans gain control of Texas State House of Representatives for the first time in 130 years

October 12, 2003
Both Houses of Texas legislature complete passage of Congressional District Reapportionment favoring Republicans

As indicated by Figure 3.1 the money-laundering scheme to avoid the Texas ban on corporate contributions had wide-ranging implications both for the country as a whole and for Tom DeLay personally. On October 19, 2005, a Texas court issued a warrant for Tom DeLay's arrest. On December 5, a charge of conspiracy to violate election law was thrown out of court, but two charges against DeLay, of money laundering and conspiracy to commit money laundering, remained (Bernstein 2005; Moreno and Smith 2005). The conspiracy to commit money-laundering charge was dropped in 2006 upon appeal. At the end of 2007, a trial date for the remaining money-laundering charge had not yet been set. DeLay found that even though he once occupied a position of great power, his breaches of the rule of law were too egregious for the system to tolerate.

Questions for Student Group Discussions

1. What ethical lessons can you derive from the DeLay case?
2. Was DeLay justified in his money-raising activity because he believed in his cause?
3. What do you think was the most serious of DeLay's offenses? Why?
4. How do you think DeLay affected Republican candidates in the 2006 election?
5. Did DeLay's actions run counter to his Christian beliefs?
6. How can DeLay's behavior be interpreted from the perspective of natural law?
7. Did DeLay's actions advance or damage the public interest?
8. How does the DeLay case relate to the concept of responsible governance?
9. Was DeLay a victim or a villain?
10. How was DeLay similar to and at the same time different from Boss Tweed?

Chapter 4

Images of Responsibility

Honesty and Patronage in Government

This chapter focuses on the concepts of misrepresentation (lying) and incompetence as irresponsible actions. The chapter asserts that both these forms of behavior are linked to negative perceptions of government leaders and low approval ratings. At the national level, the low approval levels experienced by a variety of presidents provide some evidence of the difficulties of leadership in the United States. Past presidents have been burdened by unpopular wars, sex scandals, and general perceptions of incompetence. They have also been linked to faulty assumptions and/or statements. The credibility gap of Lyndon Johnson's administration, the Watergate break-in of the Nixon administration, the poor economy and hostage crisis of the Carter administration, the faulty statements about sex of the Clinton administration, and the unfound weapons of mass destruction of the Bush administration are just a few examples of misrepresentation or incompetence associated with American chief executives.

Public opinion data reveals wide variance in public perceptions of U.S. presidents. Invariably public perceptions of chief executives are more negative toward the end of their administrations than in the earlier period. For example, toward the ends of their administration, Presidents Johnson (August–December 1968, Gallup Poll), Nixon (January–July 1974, Gallup Poll), Carter (June–July 1979, Gallup Poll), George H.W. Bush (July–August 1992, Gallup Poll), and George W. Bush (June 2007, Newsweek Poll) all suffered from approval levels that ranged between 20 and 29 percent. With the exception of a 22 percent approval rating for Harry Truman in 1952, Richard Nixon's 23 percent approval rating represented the lowest approval rating since Gallup began polling in 1935. Public opinion for Johnson, Ford, Reagan, and Clinton sank to between 35 percent and 37 percent approval at various points in their administrations.

Three presidents registered approval levels of 80 percent or above early in their administrations—92 percent for George W. Bush (October 2001, ABC Poll), 89 percent for George H.W. Bush (February–March 1991, Gallup Poll), and 80 percent for Lyndon Johnson (February–March 1964, Gallup Poll). Three presidents enjoyed job approval levels in the seventies—73 percent for Clinton (January 1998, CBS Poll and December 1998, USA Poll), 74 percent for Ford (August 1974, Gallup Poll), and 75 percent for Carter (March 1977, Gallup Poll). At the peak of his popularity, 68 percent approved of Reagan's job performance. At the high point of the Nixon administration, Nixon received a 67 percent rating (2007, Roper Center). Clearly these leaders enjoyed the confidence of the American people at some point, yet their popularity waned.

All these presidents suffered through one or more public relations disasters that eroded their popularity and the trust with which the American people regarded them.

This chapter investigates the role of public opinion in democracies, the value of trust, breaches of trust (Vietnam and Watergate), and the ethos of merit in public service. Two case studies illustrate how the concepts of honesty and merit in public service were violated during the Clinton and Bush administrations. The construct of honesty is described through the lens of the Monica Lewinsky/ Clinton impeachment episode. The public sector response to Hurricane Katrina highlights issues of merit, patronage, and incompetence. Both dishonesty and incompetence illustrate a lack of responsibility in governance. Responsible governance, in contrast, reduces dishonesty and fosters competence as a norm of acceptable conduct.

The Role of Public Opinion in Democracies

In theory, democracy refers to government of the many, not the few. Responsible governance, acting under the mandate of democracy, therefore must be responsive to the sentiments of the majority. It also has an obligation to educate citizens without confusing or obfuscating issues so that voters can make informed decisions. While some democratic theorists are quite optimistic about the ability of citizens to clearly identify their interests, others are much less sanguine about the capacities of citizens to make prudent, wise, and balanced decisions (see Chapter 2).

With the advent of television and mass marketing, election campaigns more and more resemble private sector approaches to manipulating images in order to sell products. Voters are seen as consumers to be won over by clever advertising campaigns, well-placed messages, and skillful discrediting of opponents. Candidates with well-financed campaigns have a decided advantage over others. Money not only buys time over the airwaves, but also buys the pollsters, campaign workers, and public relations people that have become so essential for success.

Today, clever politicians use the mass media in order to create certain images for their candidate and other images for opponents. From the perspective of responsible governance, such electoral manipulation is highly dysfunctional since it can misinform voters and lead them to vote in a manner that is detrimental to their interests. The aim of responsible governance is to increase the levels of transparency and honesty in government, allowing voters to fulfill the mandate of democracy by clearly identifying their interests. This obviously is a formidable task. Recent history indicates that more and more money is being spent on elections. Whether or not this spending has produced a better-informed voter, however, is open to question.

Trust is an essential feature of democracies. People trust their leaders to do the right thing, to foster the interests of society collectively rather than to advance their own personal interests. Elections in the United States indicate shifts in political power between alleged reformers and those the reformers wish to purge. Urban history is marked by conflict between corrupt machine politicians and good-government reformers. At times, corrupt machine politicians have characterized themselves as reformers in order to displace other machine politicians. At other times, candidates more representative of an ethos of honest public service have succeeded. History indicates that American politics has often been a dirty business. However, history also indicates the capacity for self-reflection, self-correction, and reform. For example, reformers in the past have placed greedy government officials (such as Boss Tweed) in prison and warned other politicians that there were boundaries of legality that could be crossed only at their own peril.

The ultimate check on political dishonesty and irresponsible governance is the ballot box. Political realignments in American history indicate that wholesale change is possible at periods of widespread disenchantment with current leaders. Change has occurred as a result of voters' perceptions of dishonesty or incompetence in government. For example, the perceived inability of the Hoover administration to deal with the Great Depression led to the 1932 electoral landslide of Franklin D. Roosevelt. Watergate led to the election of a large number of Democrats in 1974. The perceived incompetence of the Carter administration (saddled with the Iran hostage crisis and botched rescue mission) helped Ronald Reagan achieve a mandate in 1980.

President George W. Bush's precipitous fall in popularity coincided with public perceptions of his incompetence in foreign policy (an inconclusive war in Iraq) and his dishonesty concerning the reasons for going to war. Confusion over the presence of weapons of mass destruction in Iraq as well as uncertainty about the legality of the treatment of detainees cast a cloud over the honesty of members of the administration. The administration's poor response to the disaster of Hurricane Katrina contributed to a sense of incompetence. Revelations about the conduct of high-level Federal Emergency Management Administration (FEMA) leaders further undermined perceptions of competence.

The competence of the director of FEMA, Bush appointee Michael Brown, specifically came into question after the hurricane. Brown's performance and Bush's initial support for him, exemplified in the president's statement, "Brownie, you're doing a heck of a job," cast further doubt on the president's ability to meet the demands of his office. Furthermore, the perceived inadequacies of Brown brought

attention to the entire issue of political appointees.

The question of political versus merit appointments has been debated in the public administration literature. The mandate of executive leadership justifies widespread use of political appointments. These appointments permit executives to exert influence on government agencies and adjust priorities according to the views of the elected leader. The mandate of neutral competence, on the other hand, stresses the ethos of merit and the ability to perform specific jobs. With the growth of antigovernment sentiment after Katrina, the bureaucracy came under attack.

The concept of merit appears to have made a comeback after the Hurricane Katrina public relations debacle. For example, few Americans were relieved that the conservative political views of the director of FEMA were in line with those of President Bush. Many more citizens were concerned that the government did not seem to have a decisive plan to help Americans who were in danger. The government seemed ineffective, inefficient, confused, and impotent. While the themes of cutting taxes, reducing government size, and reducing waste were effective campaign slogans for a number of presidents, the reality of Katrina forced these messages to temporarily recede from public discourse. The American public demanded a competent, effective response from their government to address the plight of homeless victims of the hurricane.

Paradoxically, despite low opinions about many public sector leaders, people's expectations of the government are still relatively high. In general, the public demands safe streets, good schools, sound money, protection from enemies, affordable health care, safe air travel, honest elections, honest facts, low unemployment, affordable housing, safe food, safe pharmaceutical drugs, relatively honest stock markets, rescue from natural disasters, and a host of other "deliverables." The public puts its trust in the government to supply these "products"; if they are not provided or are provided in a shoddy manner, trust erodes. This erosion of trust can have very negative consequences. Responsible governance must therefore strive to increase the levels of trust in government. This is a tricky proposition and by no means a simple task.

Trust in Government

General Perceptions of Trust

Trust is a very fuzzy concept. We cannot touch or physically feel it, yet we can sense it and attempt to measure the extent to which it is present. Trust has been linked to economic development (Fukuyama 1995) as well as good governance (Carnevale1995; Braithwaite and Levi 1998). Trust is usually based on knowledge of the behavior of others. In regard to the relationship of trust to governance, John Locke observed that society turns over power to leaders with an explicit or implicit trust that they will act for the public good. The core of the relationship between citizens and their governors is trust (Harding 1998, 9).

Trust is relational. Citizens maintain trust in their government as long as there is some semblance of a quid pro quo or understanding that for certain types of behavior they can expect something of comparable value in return. Citizens understand that they have obligations to the state. These obligations may take the form of paying taxes, serving in the armed forces, serving on jury duty, driving within acceptable speed limits, and abiding by the zoning restrictions of a jurisdiction. In return for fulfilling these obligations, American citizens expect certain freedoms and rights, such as freedom of speech, freedom of religion, the right of due process, and the right to bear arms. These rights are identified in the U.S. Constitution.

It is recognized that trust is not given in perpetuity and can be removed over time. For example, according to the American National Election Studies, (ANES) trust in the federal government declined significantly between 1958 and 2004. The American National Election Studies is the leading academically run nation survey of American voters. It was formally established by a National Science Foundation grant in 1977 and continues studies going back to 1948. It has been based at the University of Michigan since its origin; since 2005 it has been run in partnership with Stanford University.

In 1958, in response to the question "How much of the time do you think you can trust the government in Washington to do what is right—just about always, most of the time or only some of the time?" 16 percent of those surveyed responded that they could trust the government just about always. In contrast to this figure, only 4 percent of those surveyed in 2004 believed they could trust the government just about always. A decline in trust was also discovered in the "most of the time category." In 1958, 57 percent of respondents claimed they trusted the government "most of the time." This belief in government declined to 43 percent by 2004. Trust in government reached a low point in 1994, with only 2 percent of respondents claiming to have trust in the federal government "just about always" and 19 percent claiming that they had faith in the federal government "most of the time" (American National Election Studies 2007).

Political science professor, Francis Fukuyama (1995, 9–10) contends that the absence of trust or "social capital" (the ability of people to work together for common purposes in groups and organizations) leads to poor economic performance. Declines in social capital and trust are also associated with negative political implications. Fukuyama relates declines of trust to social changes in American society, including the rise of violent crime, the rise of civil litigation, the breakdown of family structure, and declines in neighborhoods, churches, unions, clubs, and charities. In addition, Fukuyama says that there is a general sense among American people of a lack of shared values.

The decline in shared values and trust noted by Fukuyama can be observed in specific indicators such as the large U.S. prison population and the large number of American lawyers. Both prisons and litigation represent costs that can be linked to social factors such as the breakdown of trust in American society. The United States, according to Fukuyama, is in a deficit situation in the sense that it has been depleting its previously established fund of social capital. According to Fukuyama, social capital has been eroding in concert with an erosion of the American savings rates. Savings are necessary to replace physical plants and infrastructure. Social capital is necessary to hold societies together.

Fukuyama defines trust as the expectation that arises within a community of regular, honest, and cooperative behavior, based on commonly shared norms. These norms can relate to large value questions, such as the meaning of justice, or to more narrowly defined standards of behavior, such as those defined in codes of professional conduct.

Governments have the capacity to enact policies that either deplete or enhance social capital and trust. The primary task of responsible administrators is to work toward enhancing trust. Enhancing trust will rebuild the reservoir that must be called upon in times of crisis. Trust, once lost, is difficult to restore. A necessary prerequisite for building social capital, a popular concept today, is the establishment of trust in society (Fukuyama 1995, 26).

Perceptions of Trust: Margaret Levi and David Carnevale

Trust is the glue that holds relationships together at both the individual and societal levels. Margaret Levi (1998, 85) notes that trust does not arise in a vacuum; an array of factors, such government's protecting citizens from violent crimes, oversight of honest elections, and truthful reporting of events can influence trust in a positive direction. Governments influence trust by enforcing laws, applying reasonable sanctions against lawbreakers, and providing specific guarantees to citizens. If citizens doubt the government's commitment to enforcing laws and if guarantees are not credible, capacity to generate trust diminishes. Politicians can attempt to regain trust through ethical and effective behavior. They can exhibit this positive behavior through their commitments and actions within organizations. Competent and honest organizations in turn can reduce corruption, reduce inefficiency, and increase the probability of cooperation within the organization.

The state's overall capacity to govern has been linked to its capacity to generate trust and cooperation. Levi states that trust

> affects both the level of citizens' tolerance of the regime and their degree of compliance with government demands and regulations. Destruction of trust may lead to widespread antagonisms to government policy and even active resistance, and it may be one source of increased social distrust. Legitimate (and "virtuous") government may depend on leaders' keeping faith with the citizens who have given them authority to act on the public's behalf. Failures of government representatives to uphold compacts, to achieve stated ends, or to treat potential trustworthy citizens as trustworthy can have disastrous effects on the extent to which citizens trust in government and trust each other. (1988)

Actions that produce cynicism toward government include breaking promises, incompetence, and antagonistic behavior of government officials toward their clients. Citizens are likely to trust government if they believe that it acts in their interest, it is fair, and their trust is reciprocated. Citizens can make an assessment of costs and benefits before they decide to comply or not to comply with government directives. At times, citizens may comply with government requests even when the individual costs exceed benefits. This is more likely to occur when citizens believe that their government is trustworthy and fair. Compliance also increases when it is believed that others are doing their part (Levi 1998, 88).

Levi states that individuals need to have evidence that governments are fair in order to give their trust. For example, young men who volunteer to go to war or are drafted generally trust the government's claim that the war is justified, that their service is necessary, and that the military organization is relatively efficient. Citizens who pay their taxes assume that the government is doing the right thing with their money. According to Levi, fairness comprises the following four components:

1. Coercion—Citizens are likely to trust a government that ensures that others do their part. For example, the willingness of a person to make sacrifices in the name of the general good often rests on the state's capacity and readiness to secure the compliance of others.
2. Universalism—Another indicator of fairness is government reliance on universal (affecting or including all) criteria in recruitment and promotion of workers. The concept of inclusion is also applied to the regulation of institutions. Regulation should not be selective but applied to all institutions evenhandedly.
3. Impartial institutions—Those who believe the process is fair are likely to accept the occasional unfavorable outcome. For example, citizens who believe in the impartiality of institutions are inclined to support electoral outcomes. If trust is high, citizens who are unhappy with the

current outcomes believe that they will be able to revisit issues later. Abortion, immigration, and affirmative action are examples of policy issues that continue to be considered and reconsidered by American institutions.
4. Participation—Government can enhance its reputation for fairness by involving citizens in the process of making policy. It is possible, however, that once citizens become more involve they might come to distrust the government. (1998, 90–92)

David Carnevale (1995, 3–5) places a lack of trust at the heart of the approval, credibility, and legitimacy problem facing the United States. He therefore views reconstructing faith in the government as a major task for the nation's leaders. Carnevale summarizes the importance of trust as threefold. First, trust is essential since it is what holds the social fabric of organizations together. Second, trust is truth since trust enables employees and managers to directly confront reality. Third, trust is survival because facing up to the truth reduces defensive behavior and facilitates learning.

Carnevale's analysis focuses on individual organizations; however, it can easily be applied to entire societies. Trust is viewed as essential for restoring the confidence of the American people in their institutions and leaders. Truth is necessary for restoring trust. Truth, however, is often in short supply. Recent American history indicates relatively high levels of distortion, misinformation, or obfuscation. Examples abound. President Lyndon Johnson was criticized for the lack of credibility in his statements about progress in Vietnam ("light at the end of the tunnel"). President Richard Nixon was dishonored by the illegal Watergate break-in and effort to cover it up. President Bill Clinton's sex scandal and vigorous denial of "having sexual relations with that woman" scarred his presidency.

The trustworthiness of President George W. Bush was damaged by a lack of clarity about the reasons for going to war in Iraq (missing weapons of mass destruction) and the treatment of prisoners there. These actions and others committed by a string of presidents have eroded the approval, credibility, and legitimacy of American leaders. Further details of events that contributed to this erosion of trust are described below.

Causes for Mistrust

Vietnam

The negative effects of the war in Vietnam have been amply documented. It cannot be ignored as a period in American history that not only deeply divided a generation, but also greatly increased the levels of distrust in government. In retrospect, a wide number of incidents surrounding the war in Vietnam could be chosen to convey misrepresentations and misappropriations of trust. "Backdoor escalation" and the absence of a clear call for war from Congress are among the numerous factors that led to Lyndon Johnson's downfall. From a troop level of 16,000 at the time of the Kennedy assassination in 1963, the numbers of American soldiers in Vietnam grew to 184,000 at the end of 1965 and reached a peak of 537,000 in 1968, the last year of the Johnson administration.

Over time, Johnson lost the support of the American people through his statements and actions. He often announced troop increases with little or no sense of urgency. The true costs of the war were hidden from full view as Johnson promised both a war on poverty and communism. Spending expanded greatly without comparable increases in taxes. In his 1966 State of the Union address, he argued that the nation could have both "guns and butter" (Lyndon Baines Johnson Library and Museum 1966). Great confusion surrounded the justification for escalating the war in Vietnam. Critics contend that Johnson, in fact, made up the incident that legitimated the large increase in the numbers of American troops.

The Facts of the Gulf of Tonkin Incident

The Gulf of Tonkin incident has been written about in great detail and it still remains a subject of controversy (Goulden 1969; Galloway 1970; Windchy 1971; McNamara 1995). Basic information relating to the incident reveals that on the afternoon of July 30, 1964, four South Vietnamese patrol boats with crews trained by the United States left their base in Da Nang, South Vietnam, on a mission to attack two islands off the coast of North Vietnam. The attacks were part of a U.S. program of covert operations against North Vietnam known as Operations Plan 34A. Operations Plan 34A was approved by the Joint Chiefs of Staff on August 14, 1963. Operating under this authority, attacks by the South Vietnamese patrol boats commenced on July 31, 1964. According to Secretary of Defense Robert McNamara (1995, 129), events in the Tonkin Gulf involved two separate operations: Plan 34A activities and what were known as DESOTO patrols. Plan 34A involved CIA support for two types of operations: (1) placing South Vietnamese agents into North Vietnam to conduct sabotage and gather information, and (2) hit-and-run attacks against North Vietnamese shore and island installations.

DESOTO patrols differed from these Plan 34A operations in that the DESOTO mission was aimed at electronic reconnaissance carried out by specially equipped U.S. naval vessels. These vessels operated in international waters and were responsible for collecting radio and radar signals that emanated from shore-based stations around Russia, China, and North Vietnam.

The attack that occurred on the two North Vietnamese islands in July 1964 was part of Plan 34A operations. Unrelated to the Plan 34A attack, the vessel USS *Maddox* was engaged in intelligence-gathering DESOTO operations. Based on speeches of Senator Wayne Morse, a Senate Foreign Relations Committee report, a dispatch of interviews of officers and men, and testimony before the Senate Foreign Relations Committee, analysts concluded that at the time of the attacks on the North Vietnamese islands, the *Maddox* was approximately 110 miles from the islands (Galloway 1970, 48–66). On August 1, 1964, about forty-four hours after the raid on the two islands, the *Maddox* came within four miles of one of the islands before altering its direction. The next day, August 2, the *Maddox* intercepted a message indicating possible hostile action by the North Vietnamese. The captain of the vessel, John J. Herrick, cabled his superior that, given the intercepted information, continuance of the patrol presented an unacceptable risk. The Seventh Fleet commander, Vice Admiral Roy Johnson, ordered Herrick to resume his itinerary "when considered prudent" (McLaughlin 2004).

Heading back to the vicinity of the North Vietnamese islands, Herrick detected North Vietnamese patrol boats and cabled the nearby aircraft carrier *Ticonderoga* that his ship was being approached by high-speed craft that apparently intended to conduct a torpedo attack. Herrick said that he intended to open fire in self-defense if necessary. The log of the *Maddox* indicates that it fired six salvos at the approaching North Vietnamese vessels before fire was returned from a distance of less than three miles. At this distance, two enemy craft fired one torpedo each at the *Maddox*. Both missed by 100 to 200 yards. According to a statement by McNamara, machine-gun fire was also directed at the *Maddox*; however, there was no injury to U.S. personnel and no damage. Four fighter jets from the *Ticonderoga* joined the attack. Two of the North Vietnamese vessels were damaged and a third was sighted "dead

in the water" after a direct hit. The evidence for this "first" incident is fairly clear. Evidence for a "second" incident, however, is not.

On August 3, President Lyndon Johnson ordered the destroyer *C. Turner Joy* to join the *Maddox* and both ships were ordered to respond to any future attacks with the objective of not only driving off the North Vietnamese force but to "destroy it." Coincidentally, on the night of August 3–4, four South Vietnamese patrol boats attacked a radar installation on the North Vietnamese mainland. About the same time as this attack, Captain Herrick informed his superiors that he had learned that North Vietnam would consider his DESOTO mission as directly involved in the 34A operations. Herrick requested more air support from the aircraft carrier *Ticonderoga*. Herrick also suggested to his superiors that his patrol should be terminated but was quickly informed that his patrol should continue in order to demonstrate U.S. resolve in international waters.

On the night of August 4, the *Maddox* identified at least five torpedo boats thirty-six miles away to the northeast, although radar normally reaches only twenty to twenty-five miles. Later the *Maddox* reported new radar contact with two surface vessels and three unidentified aircraft. Additional unidentified vessels were also reported and their intentions were perceived as "hostile." At a distance of 6,000 yards, the vessel *C. Turner Joy* opened fire. According to a statement by Secretary McNamara, the U.S. ships reported that they avoided many torpedoes and that they sank two of the attacking vessels. Various discrepancies between these reports and what actually happened, however, were evident.

North Vietnam denied that the August 4 incident ever occurred, claiming that it was a fabrication created by the United States to justify its escalation of the war. While the *C. Turner Joy* located enemy vessels on its radar, the *Maddox* could not identify any vessels. The *Maddox* reported twenty-two enemy torpedoes; however, the *C. Turner Joy* failed to detect one. It was subsequently reported that six hours before the alleged attack, the *Maddox* reported a "material deficiency" in its sonar. Furthermore, North Vietnamese vessels of the type reported by the *C. Turner Joy* only carried two torpedoes each and there was no suggestion that as many as eleven vessels were involved.

Three hours after U.S. firing ceased, Captain Herrick cabled his superiors that the "review of actions makes many recorded contacts and torpedoes fired appear doubtful. Freak weather effects and overeager sonarmen may have accounted for many reports. No actual visual sightings by Maddox. Suggest complete evaluation before further action" (Goulden 1969, 152).

The reaction to the incident raised a different question. Even if enemy vessels were sighted and the enemy vessels launched their torpedoes, historians questioned American accounts of the incident that led to passage of the Gulf of Tonkin resolution. Author John Galloway concludes that the crucial point of the Gulf of Tonkin incident was not whether torpedoes were fired, but "whether the incident warranted the retaliatory bombing of North Viet Nam and passage of a 'functional equivalent of a declaration of war.' At issue also is the role of the Johnson Administration and the military in precipitating the crisis, their evaluation of the incident, and of course, the candor of the Administration in reporting the affair to Congress and the American people" (1970, 65–70). These are serious questions that perhaps have become even more relevant in light of the Bush administration's questionable justification for the war in Iraq. Allegations that the government manufactured evidence to justify serious military action do not instill trust or confidence in governance.

Critical questions surrounding the Gulf of Tonkin incident include (1) whether the second

incident actually happened, (2) whether the incident was provoked, and (3) whether the incident was blown out of proportion in order to justify an escalation. The attack by the U.S.-allied South Vietnamese vessels on the North Vietnamese radar installations in August 1964 appears to have heightened tensions. News of this attack nevertheless did not reach Washington until after key decisions were made by the White House, the Pentagon, and the State Department (Goulden 1969, 139).

On December 1, 2005, the largest U.S. intelligence agency, the National Security Agency (NSA), declassified more than 140 formerly top-secret documents on the Gulf of Tonkin incident. These documents included oral history interviews, reports, articles, chronologies, and information gathered by interception of signals. The document release confirmed what historians have long contended: that there was no second attack by the North Vietnamese on August 4, 1964. Classified signal intercepts used by U.S. officials actually were referring to the first Gulf of Tonkin engagement on August 2 (National Security Archives 2004, 2005).

There is some indication that President Johnson was more than a bit skeptical about what actually happened in the Gulf of Tonkin on August 4, the alleged "second" engagement. Reporter Joseph Goulden stated that during a lengthy monologue on the military handling of the Vietnam War, Johnson brought up the August 4 incident as an example of what he had to put up with at the Pentagon. Johnson noted that for all he knew the navy was "shooting at whales out there" (1969, 160).

The Political Implications of the Gulf of Tonkin Incident

President Johnson's reaction to the August 4 incident was swift. Having been informed of "a second deliberate attack" by "an undetermined number of North Vietnamese patrol boats" in international waters, he called a meeting of the National Security Council, which selected North Vietnamese targets to bomb. Key congressional leaders were then gathered for a ninety-minute briefing, where they all supported the resolution proposed by the president.

On the evening of August 4, 1964, President Johnson addressed the nation on both radio and television. He somberly announced that "aggression by terror against the peaceful villagers of South Vietnam has now been joined by open aggression on the high seas against the United States of America." Johnson then told the audience that retaliatory bombings were "now in execution" (Galloway 1970, 69). The Pentagon later released details of air strikes at four North Vietnamese patrol boat bases and at an oil storage depot that was linked to the torpedo boat base.

During the national address, the president noted that he had informed congressional leaders that he would request Congress to pass a resolution making it clear that the government was united in its determination to take necessary measures in support of peace and freedom in Southeast Asia. On August 5, Johnson sent a message to Congress officially requesting passage of a congressional resolution expressing support for all necessary action to protect American armed forces and to assist nations covered by treaty.

On August 6, the Tonkin Resolution, having passed the appropriate committees, was debated on the Senate Floor. The *New York Times* reported that there was no atmosphere of impending crisis and that the chamber was not even one-third full most of the time. On August 7, the Senate passed the resolution with a vote of 88–2; it was later approved in the House of Representatives by a vote of 416–0. Here is the full text of the resolution:

> SEC. 1. Whereas naval units of the Communist regime in Vietnam, in violation of the principles of the Charter of the United Nations and of international law, have deliberately and repeatedly attacked the United States naval vessels lawfully present in international waters, and have thereby created a serious threat to international peace; and whereas these attacks are part of a deliberate and systematic campaign of aggression that the Communist regime in North Vietnam has been waging against its neighbors and the nations joined with them in collective defense of their freedoms; and whereas the United States is assisting the peoples of southeast Asia to protect their freedom and has no territorial, military, or political ambitions in that area, but desires only that these peoples should be left in peace to work out their own destinies in their own way: Now, therefore, be it *Resolved by the Senate and House of Representatives of the United States of America in Congress assembled,* That the Congress approves and supports the determination of the President, as Commander in Chief, to take all necessary measures to repel any armed attack against the forces of the United States and to prevent further aggression.
>
> SEC. 2. The United States regards as vital to its national interest and to world peace the maintenance of international peace and security in Southeast Asia. Consonant with the Constitution of the United States and the Charter of the United Nations and in accordance with its obligations under the Southeast Asia Collective Defense Treaty, the United States is, therefore, prepared, as the president determines, to take all necessary steps, including the use of armed force, to assist any member or protocol state of the Southeast Asia Collective Defense Treaty requesting assistance in defense of its freedom.
>
> SEC. 3. This resolution shall expire when the President shall determine that the peace and security of the area is reasonably assured by international conditions created by action of the United Nations or otherwise, except that it may be terminated earlier by concurrent resolution of the Congress. (Galloway 1970, 181–182)

The political ramifications of the Gulf of Tonkin incident were mostly positive for the president in the short run. Immediate criticism was minimal. One dissenter, Senator Ernest Gruening of Alaska, denounced the war as an inevitable consequence of U.S. "unilateral military aggressive policy." The other dissenting senator, Wayne Morse of Oregon, proclaimed that the resolution was a "predated declaration of war" and was therefore unconstitutional. Senator Morse stated that "history will record that we have made a great mistake in subverting and circumventing the Constitution of the United States." He claimed that Congress had just given the president war-making powers in the absence of a declaration of war (Goulden 1969, 75).

On August 5, Johnson followed up his radio and television speech with a triumphal trip to Syracuse University, where he spoke in front of a huge banner that proclaimed in foot-high letters: SYRACUSE LOVES LBJ. He was frequently interrupted by applause as he declared that "aggression unchallenged is aggression unleashed."

Johnson received immediate support as a consequence of the "rally around the flag" phenomenon—rallying around the leader in a crisis. In July 1964, before the Gulf of Tonkin incident, a Harris poll had reported 58 percent of Americans critical of the president's handling of Vietnam. After the American air raids of August 5, 72 percent of those surveyed approved of Johnson's handling of Vietnam. Before the raids, 59 percent of Americans thought Johnson could handle Vietnam better than his presidential opponent Barry Goldwater. After the American raids, the proportion of Americans who believed Johnson could better handle Vietnam soared to 71 percent (Galloway 1970, 25).

According to Goulden, the Gulf of Tonkin incident was useful to Johnson for the following reasons: (1) it gave the United States a pretext to draw blood from North Vietnam and demonstrate U.S. resolve, (2) it boosted the morale of the South Vietnamese, who had complained that North Vietnam was immune from the devastation of the war, and (3) it temporarily united Congress and the American people behind the president (1969, 20). Goulden notes, however, that Johnson's short-term gain was offset by his long-term loss of the confidence of the American people and Congress: Johnson was "the overall loser at Tonkin; consid-ered more broadly, we all are the losers, for Tonkin came to be a synonym for national disunity and distrust" (1969, 19).

The highly respected "Senator Sam," Sam Ervin of North Carolina, summed up the attitude of many in the Senate. He observed that in all generations, some presidents have sent American troops abroad, usually on a small scale, without authorization of Congress, an act that has been used to justify the theory that the president has that power. Ervin's reply was that unauthorized use of troops was like murder and larceny, since "people have been committing murder and larceny in all generations, but that has never made murder meritorious or larceny legal" (Goulden 1969, 20). In retrospect, the Gulf of Tonkin resolution did not inspire confidence nor was it an exemplar of responsible governance. The rationale for President Johnson's speech to the nation was later shown to be false. Even if the rationale was true, many questioned its proportionality or the fact that a relatively small naval engagement became the constitutional justification for a declaration of war. What the resolution lacked in constitutionality, it made up in its ability to bypass thorough debate.

Watergate

The Facts of Watergate

Watergate, coming quickly on the heels of Vietnam, further eroded public confidence in the institutions of government. Like the war in Vietnam, it has been voluminously discussed and written about, and it remains a significant event in terms of ethics and responsibility of government officials. Some have called it the biggest scandal in U.S. history, with all the elements from "small scale dirty tricks" to "corruption at the highest levels of government" and "a president committing impeachable crimes" (Rosenthal 1997).

The origins of the Watergate scandal can be traced to the night of June 17, 1972, when five burglars were arrested in the offices of the Democratic National Committee located in the Watergate apartments and office complex in Washington, DC—hence the name Watergate. Four of the Watergate burglars were part of Miami's Cuban exile community and veterans of the Bay of Pigs invasion of Cuba in 1961. The fifth burglar, James McCord, had worked for the CIA as a technician for twenty years; he was also a colonel in the Air Force Reserve and a security director for President Richard Nixon's Committee for the Re-election of the President (often abbreviated as CRP or CREEP). The men were found with what police classified as burglary kits as well as two sophisticated devices capable of picking up transmissions. One of the devices was described as about the size of a silver dollar and capable of being hidden underneath a telephone or desk. Two ceiling panels near the office of Larry O'Brien, the Democratic Party chair, had been removed in such as way as to make it possible to slip in a bugging device. All five men were charged with felonious burglary and possession of implements of crime.

When they were caught, the five "burglars" were in possession of almost $2,300 in cash, mostly hundred-dollar bills. These bills, unfortunately for President Nixon, were traced to money collected by his reelection committee. Following the arrest, O'Brien contacted Attorney General Richard Kleindienst and demanded that the entire matter should be turned over to the FBI (Woodward and Bernstein 1972a).

In October 1972 the FBI found that the Watergate break-in stemmed from a campaign of political spying and sabotage conducted on behalf of Richard Nixon's reelection campaign. The FBI further declared that the operation was directed by officials of the White House and members of CRP. Information from both the FBI and the Department of Justice revealed that specific activities were aimed at all the major Democratic presidential contenders and represented a basic strategy for Nixon's reelection. Federal agents noted that hundreds of thousands of dollars of Nixon's campaign contributions were set aside for an extensive undercover campaign to discredit Democratic presidential candidates and disrupt their campaigns.

According to Federal investigators, undercover work against opponents is normal during election campaigns, but the work carried out by Nixon's supporters was unprecedented in scope and intensity. Undercover activities included assembling dossiers on Democratic candidates and their families, forging letters and distributing them under the candidates' letterheads, leaking false information to the press, disrupting campaign schedules, and seizing confidential campaign files. Probably the best example of campaign sabotage on the part of Nixon's forces was the fabrication by a White House aide of a letter to the editor of the *Manchester Union Leader*. This allegedly fabricated letter was published February 24, 1972, just two weeks before the New Hampshire primary. The letter alleged that a member of Muskie's staff had had slurred Americans descended from French-Canadians. Its effect was devastating on the leading Democratic candidate, Senator Edmund Muskie of Maine (Woodward and Bernstein 1972b).

Nixon's fortunes began to fall after the FBI linked him to the Watergate break-in. Significant events in Nixon's descent included the establishment of a Senate Committee to investigate the Watergate break-in, the cooperation of White House counsel John Dean in the investigation, the discovery of tape-recordings of conversations in the White House, Nixon's unwillingness to turn over the tapes to the Watergate Committee, and his belligerent attitude toward the investigation. Perhaps the most memorable statement of the entire Watergate saga occurred in November 1973

Table 4.1

Chronology of Watergate Events

June 17, 1972: Five men are arrested at the Watergate office building on charges of breaking into the Democratic National Committee headquarters.

October 9, 1972: FBI agents link Watergate burglary and bugging to a Nixon campaign of spying and sabotage.

January 8, 1973: The five "burglars" plead guilty to all charges.

February 7, 1973: A U.S. Senate Committee, headed by Senator Sam Ervin Jr., is formed to investigate matters related to the Watergate break-in.

June 25, 1973: In testimony before the Senate Watergate Committee White House counsel, John Dean describes a program to cover up the Watergate break-in. Dean alleges Nixon participated in the cover-up.

July 16, 1973: A tape recording system in the White House is revealed by a former White House aide.

July 26, 1973: Following Nixon's refusal to turn over White House tapes, the Senate Watergate Committee subpoenas several of them.

November 17, 1973: In a televised session with Associated Press managing editors Nixon announces, "I'm not a crook."

March 1, 1974: An indictment is returned against seven former presidential aides. Nixon is named as co-conspirator, but is not indicted.

May 9, 1974: Impeachment hearings begun by House Judiciary Committee.

July 24, 1974: In a unanimous ruling the Supreme Court orders Nixon to hand over the tapes.

July 27, 1974: The House Judiciary Committee votes 27–11 to approve an article of impeachment that charges Nixon with obstruction of justice.

August 5, 1974: Nixon releases three tapes including one that indicates he ordered a cover-up as early as June 23, 1972, and lied to the public about it.

August 9, 1974: Nixon resigns; Gerald Ford takes oath of office.

September 8, 1974: Ford pardons Nixon for all offenses he committed or may have committed.

Sources: Various newspaper accounts.

in Orlando, Florida, when Nixon spoke before 400 Associated Press managing editors. In a question and answer session, Nixon declared, "People have got to know whether or not their President is a crook. Well, I'm not a crook. I've earned everything I've got." Nixon added that he had never profited from his public service and defended his record in the Watergate case (Kilpatrick 1973). A rough chronology of significant events of what we know as Watergate is found in Table 4.1.

The Political Implications of Watergate

Watergate had a clear impact on American politics. Nixon's dirty tricks campaign had an immediate impact on Senator Muskie, the Democratic front-runner early in 1972, and led to the nomination of George McGovern, whom some considered to be a much weaker threat to Nixon. A letter to the editor of the *Manchester Union Leader* implied that Muskie was prejudiced. In childish writing with poor spelling, the author of the allegedly forged letter claimed to have met Muskie in Florida and asked him how he could understand the problems of African-Americans, given Maine's small black population. According to the letter, a member of the Muskie staff responded while in Florida that they had the minority group "Cannocks" [*sic*] in Maine. The authenticity of the letter sent to the *Manchester Union Leader* was later questioned. A *Washington Post* writer claimed that a White House communications official told her that he wrote the "Canuck letter" himself. However, the White House official later denied that he wrote the letter. William Loeb, the publisher of the Manchester paper, unsuccessfully attempted to find the author of the letter.

On the Saturday before the March 7 New Hampshire primary, Senator Muskie delivered his "crying speech" in which he lambasted the publisher of the *Manchester Union Leader* for impugning the character of Muskie's wife. An editorial in the newspaper alleged that Jane Muskie enjoyed excessive drinking and telling dirty jokes. Reporters from the *Washington Post* and *Boston Globe* described Muskie breaking down "three times in as many minutes" and "weeping silently" during the speech. Muskie later claimed that the tears were snow melting on his face. The so-called crying speech of Muskie damaged his image of stability and strength.

The *Washington Post* also reported that the Canuck letter might have been written by Ken Clawson, deputy director of White House communications. Muskie charged that his presidential effort was plagued by a systematic campaign of sabotage. *Time* magazine reported in 1972 that information in the Justice Department's files establishes a direct link between the Nixon White House and a Los Angeles attorney named Donald H. Segretti. Segretti was paid more than $35,000 from the CRP funds to subvert and disrupt Democratic

candidates' campaigns. Segretti admitted to Justice Department officials that that he was hired, among other things, to disrupt the primary campaigns of Democratic candidates (Time 1972).

Muskie won the New Hampshire primary but finished with only 48 percent of the Democratic primary vote, a margin much smaller than predicted. His standing began to slip immediately. The second-place showing of George McGovern energized his campaign and by March 1972 Muskie's candidacy was essentially finished (Woodward and Bernstein 1972b; Wikipedia 2007e).

Aside from derailing Edmund Muskie's political ambitions, the political fallout from Watergate was devastating. Watergate led to the resignation of a president and his disbarment from the legal profession. It also led to the resignation and disbarment of a vice president (Spiro Agnew), an attorney general who went to jail (John Mitchell), a former secretary of commerce who went to jail (Maurice Stans), a former chief of staff who went to jail (H.R. Haldeman), a president's counsel (John Dean) who went to jail, and a special counsel to the White House (Charles Colson) who went to jail. In all, over two dozen administration figures were imprisoned because of Watergate (Genovese 1999, 125).

The electoral consequences were also highly negative for the Republican Party. In the 1974 election, just three months after the Nixon resignation, Democrats gained five seats in the U.S. Senate and forty-nine seats in the U.S. House of Representatives. Watergate led to a renewed awareness of the danger of unchecked executive power. As a consequence of this concern, laws were passed limiting the powers of the chief executive. These laws shifted the balance of power between Congress and the president in the direction of Congress. Legislation motivated by the abuses of Watergate included the War Powers Act (1973), the Budget Control and Impoundment Act (1974), the Federal Election

Campaign Act (1974), the Freedom of Information Act (1974), the Ethics in Government Act (1976), and the Government in Sunshine Act.

The Watergate scandal also ushered in a period when reporters and the press became more involved in uncovering scandal. For example, the 1974 drunken driving accident of Congressman Wilbur Mills was reported and he was forced to resign from his position as the chair of the U.S. House Committee on Ways and Means. During the 1988 presidential campaign, newspapers circulated a picture of Democratic candidate Gary Hart with Donna Rice, a model, sitting on his lap aboard a yacht named *Monkey Business.* It was reported that Hart had spent a night on the yacht with Rice. Soon after the story broke, Hart dropped out of the race for the presidency. The sexual scandals involving President Bill Clinton were major news; in contrast, President John Kennedy's extramarital affairs were not widely reported. It appears that Watergate at least contributed to a new attitude on the part of the press that is less reverent, less forgiving, and more inclined to the "gotcha" politics that characterize the American political landscape today.

A clear legacy of Watergate is its impact on trust in government. Presidential scholar, Michael Genovese states that after Watergate the "delicate bonds of trust" necessary for a properly functioning democracy "degenerated into a slash-and-burn type of politics in which a 'take no prisoners' attitude dominates." He concludes that Watergate went beyond presidential corruptions of the past that mostly involved isolated crimes or greed for money. He sees Watergate as representing a systematic and comprehensive attempt to degrade the rights of citizens and the democratic electoral process (1999, 113, 125).

A special report by a panel of the National Academy of Public Administration (NAPA) also addresses the Watergate scandal. The report claims that practitioners as well as scholars in the field of public administration have an interest in the quality of governmental institutions, because all citizens share a concern about government competence and dependability. In order to secure this competence and dependability, integrity of leaders in every branch of government is necessary. The report proclaims, "without such integrity, government cannot gain and retain the confidence of the people it serves" (Mosher 1974, 3). According to the NAPA panel, the governmental climate of 1973 constituted a critical threat to many of the values and protections Americans associate with a democratic system of government. These protections include the following:

1. The right to participate or be represented in decisions affecting citizens.
2. The right to equal treatment.
3. The right to know.
4. Free and honest elections.
5. Assurance of constitutional protections such as those in the First and Fourth Amendment.
6. A balance of countervailing powers to prevent usurpation by any single power—as among the branches of government, political parties or sectors of parties, interest groups, and geographic sections.
7. Ethical conduct of public officials in pursuit of the public interest. (Mosher 1974, 11)

The NAPA report observes that Watergate represented a cause for both concern and hope. Watergate led to "growing disillusionment, cynicism, and even contempt for government" among the citizenry. At the same time, Watergate provided "an opportunity for reexamination and reform, not of the electoral process alone, but also of other related practices and institutions." Watergate could thus represent not merely an extension of long-term negative trends in politics but a "watershed" and a point from which improvements could be made (Mosher 1974, 7).

Competence in Government

Disregard for merit represents a serious threat to responsible governance. Perceptions of incompetence not only reduce trust in government but also decrease legitimacy and stability. It is well known that bureaucracy and the public sector in general have been under attack for some time. Politicians from George Wallace to Ronald Reagan to George W. Bush have benefited from attacking "incompetence" in government. "Outsider" state governors have often fared better in national elections than "insider" Washington politicians tainted by their association with the national government. For example, California governor Ronald Reagan, Arkansas governor Bill Clinton, and Texas governor George W. Bush all were successful in their presidential election campaigns against insider Washington opponents.

Often, as outsiders were elected to run the national bureaucracy, their popularity faded. Though Reagan is remembered for his genial personality, he suffered from charges that he was unaware and removed from details during his administration, allowing subordinates to do too much without consultation with the president. His image initially suffered from the Iran-Contra scandal, the secret arrangement to provide funds to the Nicaraguan contra rebels from profits gained by selling arms to Iran. In an investigation by the Reagan-appointed Tower Commission, it was determined that, as president, Reagan's disengagement from the management of his White House had created conditions which made possible the diversion of funds to the Nicaraguan contras. The Commission found no evidence linking Reagan to the diversion. Consistent with his image as the "Teflon" president, few if any of the negative revelations

from the Iran-Contra affair "stuck" to him and in 1989 he left office with the highest approval rating of any president since Franklin D. Roosevelt (Wolf 2007).

Clinton was linked to the Monica Lewinsky sex scandal. His statement before the American public that he did not have sexual relations with "that woman" was harmful to the image of the president as a truth teller. Impeached by the House of Representatives, he avoided conviction in the Senate. His ability to stay in office until the last hour of the last day attests to his well-regarded political skills (see Case No. 3). George W. Bush's popularity declined as he became associated with a failed war in Iraq, an inadequate response to Hurricane Katrina (see Case No. 4), and abusive treatment of prisoners in Iraq (see Case No. 6). Although he was reelected in 2004, by 2007 public perceptions of his performance were highly negative.

Such high-profile political "failures" exacerbate an underlying perception among the people that government officials are venal, corrupted, or just not too bright. Such cases also lead to a general perception that we the people should not expect too much from our government leaders. Incompetence in performance therefore should not come as a surprise.

Incompetence in government can arise from a variety of factors, including burnout in career bureaucrats who have tired of their jobs or ignorance in political appointees who enjoy the status of their position but possess very little knowledge about the operation they supervise. Patronage—the appointment to office of relatives or political friends—has a long tradition in the United States. It has some benefit in enabling chief executives to implement policy. It also is somewhat responsive to citizens' desires in that the leaders elected by the people can influence unelected career civil servants. Patronage, however, often leads to inadequate delivery of goods and services and frequent misuse of government revenue. The ethos of good-government movements, merit hiring, and civil service arose to counter the abuses of patronage that prevailed in the nineteenth century. Pioneers in the ideal of competence in the public sector include Woodrow Wilson, Max Weber, and Frederick W. Taylor. These authors fostered the view that government can be run like a business in terms of efficiency and effectiveness.

Pioneers of the Ideal of Government Competence

Woodrow Wilson

Woodrow Wilson is best known as the president of the United States during World War I. Before his election, however, he was president of Princeton University and a leading intellectual of the Progressive movement. Consistent with the thinking of reformers of his day, Wilson advocated abolishing the spoils system and instituting a merit system. The two main themes of his article "The Study of Administration" are that (1) public administration (the running of a government) should be premised on a science of management, and (2) public administration should be separate from traditional politics (Wilson [1887] 1991). His academic arguments fitted well with the writings of the father of scientific management, Frederick Winslow Taylor.

The separation between politics and administration was a common theme of reformers of Wilson's day, who argued that political appointments should be based on fitness and merit rather than partisanship. In the dichotomy between politics and administration, politics set the tasks for administrators and the administrators used their professional expertise to carry out the tasks. Politics do not interfere with the day-to-day operation of administration and administrators do not engage in partisan politics. Political hacks are not given jobs based on their loyalty to the party. Merit hires

are expected to know something about effectively delivering services or running organizations.

In his classic article, Wilson strongly urges government administrators to perform their tasks with the "utmost possible efficacy" and at the least possible cost. He contends that the country needs to know more about administration in both the public and private arena. He asserts that the business of government could be made "less unbusinesslike, to strengthen and purify its organization, and to crown its dutifulness" ([1887] 1991, 13).

Wilson notes that Americans and the British are less versed in the science of administration than the French and Germans. The British and Americans were thought to be better versed in the art of curbing executive power (checks and balances) than in the art of perfecting executive methods. Great Britain and the United States were thought to be more concerned with making government just and moderate than in making it well ordered and effective. As a consequence of this orientation, America was viewed as behind many monarchies in administrative organization and administrative skills.

Wilson sees civil service reform as a necessary first step toward fuller administrative reform. Civil service reform could improve the moral atmosphere of official life and help establish public office as a public trust. By eliminating partisanship from public sector employment and by "sweetening its motives," reforms could "improve its methods of work." Wilson concludes that a technically schooled civil service was indispensable and that American administrators could learn about efficiency from the French and Germans without catching their "disease" of autocracy. The future president states, "if I see a monarchist dyed in the wool managing a public bureau well, I can learn his business methods without changing one of my republican spots. He may serve his king; I will continue to serve the people; but I should like to serve my sovereign as well as he serves his" ([1887] 1991, 23).

Max Weber

Sociologist Max Weber was the first person to articulate the concept of bureaucracy. According to Weber, bureaucracy was the mirror opposite of today's stereotype: bureaucracies were thought to be efficient and the most rational method known to administer modern societies. Weber identifies the following features of what he calls the "ideal type" of bureaucracy:

1. Administration is carried out on a continuous basis, not simply at the pleasure of the leader.
2. Tasks in the bureaucratic organization are divided into functionally distinct areas.
3. Offices are arranged in the form of a hierarchy.
4. The resources of the organization are distinct from those of the individual members of the organization. Official activities are distinct from the sphere of private life.
5. The officeholder cannot sell the position or pass it on by heredity.
6. Administration is based on written documents.
7. Control in the organization is based on impersonally applied rational rules.

In addition to these characteristics, Weber also outlines the following terms of employment for modern bureaucratic organizations:

1. Officials are personally free and are appointed on the basis of a contract.
2. Officials are appointed, not elected. An official elected by the governed is not a purely bureaucratic figure.
3. Officials are appointed on the basis of professional qualifications.
4. Officials have a fixed money salary and pension rights.

5. The official's post is his sole or major occupation.
6. A career structure exists with promotion based on merit.
7. The official is subject to a unified control and disciplinary system.
8. The methods of compelling workers to behave properly are clearly defined. (Fry 1989, 31)

Weber views bureaucracy as the ultimate in rationality, efficiency, and impartiality. Bureaucracy is rational in that it involves control based on knowledge, has clearly defined spheres of competence, and operates according to rules. It is efficient because of its precision, speed, consistency, availability of records, and minimization of interpersonal friction. Bureaucracy is impartial in that it attempts to exclude irrational feelings and sentiments in favor of the detachment of the professional expert. Weber contends that by eliminating incalculable emotional elements, bureaucracy suits the attitudes demanded by modern culture. The demands for legal equality and guarantees against arbitrariness require the type of rational objectivity found in bureaucracies (Fry 1989, 33).

Frederick W. Taylor

Frederick Winslow Taylor (1856–1915) was an American mechanical engineer who sought to improve industrial efficiency. Sometimes called "the father of scientific management," he was one of the intellectual leaders of the efficiency movement and his ideas were highly influential in the Progressive era. Taylor's ideas attracted the support of people in government as well as the private sector. Dwight Waldo notes that scientific management and the study of public administration arose concurrently and developed similar doctrines. They both sought to extend the spirit of science to an ever-widening range of concerns. At least two major figures in public administration, Frederick Cleveland and W.E. Mosher, were ardent advocates of extending scientific management to administration in the public sector (Waldo 1984, 54).

Taylor wanted management to become a science that would promote the desired conditions of coordination, harmony, efficiency, and economy. These conditions, Taylor believed, could be achieved by those trained in the scientific method of gathering relevant facts. Taylor contended that not only was there "one best way" to accomplish tasks, but there was also "one best man" to achieve efficiency. Different tasks required different qualities and different types of training. The task of the human relations official was to find the proper person for a specific job and, if the person's abilities were potential rather than immediate, to provide the proper training. Scientific management therefore entailed the use of science for both selection and training (Waldo 1984, 58).

Taylor claimed that scientific management was not an efficiency device, a group of efficiency devices, a scheme for paying workers, a bonus system, or a piecework system. Scientific management represented a whole new way to look at work and to manage workers. In his words, "Scientific management does not exist and cannot exist until there has been a complete mental revolution on the part of the workmen working under it, as to their duties toward themselves and toward their employers, and a complete mental revolution in the outlook for the employers toward themselves and toward their workmen." This new mental revolution will allow workers and managers to stop fighting since, under its efficiencies, each side would have more than ever before (Taylor [1916] 1996, 70).

The new style of management would be far superior to its predecessor because scientific management evokes the workers' initiative, hard work, goodwill, and best efforts. The greatest gain,

however, derives from the duties that are voluntarily assumed by management. The new duties of management, divided into four groups, have been called the principles of scientific management.

The first principle of scientific management is gathering the knowledge that, in the past, has been in the heads of workers, recording it, tabulating it, reducing it to rules, and finally applying the rules to the workplace. The gathering of the mass of knowledge is done by conducting time and motion studies.

The second principle of scientific management is the scientific selection of workers and their progressive development. Managers should take great care in the selection of workers. It becomes the duty of managers to study the workers under them and to train employees to be able to do better and still better work than before. Workers could then receive higher pay.

Taylor's third principle is enhancing cooperation between managers and workers. The clearest way to enhance cooperation, according to Taylor, is to do something nice for workers—for example, providing better treatment, more kindly treatment, more consideration for workers' wishes, and an opportunity for workers to express their wants freely. An equally important part of this equation is to make workers do what they should. If they do not do what they should, they should leave the company.

The fourth principle of scientific management involves a sharing of work between management and labor. This sharing, according to Taylor, would eliminate strikes that previously existed. Taylor states that workers' complaints have to be heeded, just as much as managers' complaints that the workers do not do their share. Scientific management therefore is thought to represent cooperation as well as a genuine sharing of work that never existed before (Taylor [1916] 1996, 74).

Taylor's theory of scientific management is important to the concept of responsible governance for a variety of reasons. It focuses on selecting the best individual for the job. Its emphasis on efficiency supports the notion that responsible government provides goods and services at reasonable cost. Its reference to science implies that rationality can create effective public sector organizations. Taylor's theory exemplifies the ideal of rewards for ability that characterizes the ethos of merit.

The Ideal of Merit

Few would argue that a good recipe for organizational prosperity is to discourage high performance based on merit and to promote incompetence. Nevertheless, a good deal of friction has developed between those who support public sector appointments based purely on professional qualifications and others who embrace patronage.

The ethos of merit or neutral competence has not always been dominant. Herbert Kaufman (1956, 1057) contends that administrative institutions in the United States have been organized and operated in pursuit of three differing values: (1) the value of representativeness, (2) the value of neutral competence, and (3) the value of executive leadership. Each of these was dominant at different periods of American history. The value of neutral competence fell from favor, according to Kaufman, because it encouraged self-directing groups acting without much oversight within the bureaucracy. This produced fragmentation in government: the formation of independent islands of decision making, agencies pursuing contradictory policies, and the creation of specialists who resented efforts by laymen to intervene. In reaction to these problems, students of government began to advance the idea that chief executives had to be empowered to take charge of the machinery of government.

Recently, criticism of neutral competence and bureaucracy in general has grown more intense.

Perceived problems of the federal bureaucracy include a lack of productivity and accountability. Public sector workers are thought to be difficult to motivate since salaries are limited and it is difficult to remove employees who do not perform adequately. Under the civil service system, pay and promotion are based on time on the job rather than productivity. Salary adjustments usually involve across-the-board pay increases, and job tenure guarantees are granted to virtually all career civil service employees. This system makes it difficult for supervisors to generously reward or severely punish their subordinates on the basis of their job performance (Johnson and Libecap 1994, 154).

Public choice writers view the bureaucracy as both opportunistic in pursuit of its self-interest and influential in shaping policy away from the desires of elected officials. Johnson and Libecap assert that because monitoring is costly, senior bureaucratic officials are assumed to be able to alter policy to fit their preferences. These authors advocate reform of the bureaucracy but view true reform as difficult to attain. Constraints on reform include the power of public sector unions to block change and the widely held belief that changes in the present civil service system would allow the "evils" of patronage to reappear (1994, 157).

Conclusions

Many people see irresponsible governance as the norm. Our popular culture commonly feeds off the misbehavior of the rich or powerful. High-profile politicians do not escape this scrutiny. Sex, lying, and abuse of power are commonly associated with political scandal. Vietnam and Watergate illustrate that there is ample reason to distrust leaders. Prior irresponsibility, however, does not negate the possibility of improvement and future responsibility. Exposure of abuse is the best antidote to more permanent abuse.

The following two case studies provide examples of dishonesty and incompetence. Clinton's lies to the American people and the Bush administration's managerial ineptitude in response to Hurricane Katrina obviously did nothing to enhance the trust of constituents. Responsible governance, in contrast, acts to restore rather than deplete the reservoir of trust that exists between the people and their representatives. This bond of trust, however, is tenuous and can be broken at any time.

CASE NO. 3: The Clinton Impeachment

The impeachment of William Jefferson Clinton marked the first time that an elected president was impeached in the history of the United States. It was the first time since 1868 that the U.S. Senate considered removal of a president. The impeached Andrew Johnson (who was not elected but succeeded to the presidency after Abraham Lincoln was assassinated in 1865) avoided conviction by the narrowest of margins when the Senate ballot failed to reach the required two-thirds majority by the margin of one vote. The vote in the Senate to remove President Clinton was not as close; one of the articles of impeachment failed to gain a majority of votes and the other split the Senate by a vote of 50–50. Nevertheless, events leading up to the impeachment captivated the nation's attention and dominated the news. The scandal included all the ingredients of a sensational story: sex between a powerful man and a much younger woman, the president caught in a lie under oath, a constitutional struggle between branches of government, and emotional appeals to "justice" as well as the "rule of law" from parties involved in the controversy.

The Lewinsky Affair

The facts of the Lewinsky affair are relatively well known by now. In 1995, Monica Lewinsky, graduated from a private liberal arts college located in Portland, Oregon (Lewis and Clark College) and in June of 1995 was hired to work as an intern at the White House. In November of 1995, according to audiotapes secretly recorded by her friend Linda Tripp, Lewinsky and President Clinton began a sexual relationship. Her relationship with the president was brought to light through a sexual harassment lawsuit brought by Paula Jones.

On May 6, 1994 (two days before the deadline of the three-year statute of limitations), Jones filed a civil suit against Clinton in Arkansas seeking damages for willful, outrageous and malicious conduct at the Excelsior Hotel in Little Rock on May 8, 1991. Her court papers accuse Clinton of sexually harassing and assaulting her, then defaming her with denials. At the time Clinton was governor of the state and Jones was a rank and file employee of the Arkansas Industrial Development Commission, an agency within the executive branch of the state of Arkansas. After the suit was filed, Clinton's lawyers argued for delay, ideally until he left office; however, the Supreme Court unanimously ruled in *Jones v. Clinton* that the case could continue while the president was still in office. In the aftermath of the 9–0 Supreme Court decision, the president and his advisers downplayed the ruling, stressing the need to focus upon the public agenda and legislation for the country. They decided, nevertheless, to contest the Jones lawsuit and in January 1998 Clinton delivered a pretrial deposition.

The president was aware that Jones's lawyers intended to ask about his relationships with other women in order to establish a pattern of continuous behavior. His decision to contest the Jones lawsuit was consistent with previous damage limitation strategies of appearing honest, forthright, and the victim of circumstance, as opposed to being the perpetrator of any wrongdoing. Clinton's supporters sought to discredit Jones, his lawyer, Robert Bennett, describing her as "tabloid trash" (Busby

2001, 49). In 1998, Clinton agreed to pay Jones $850,000 to drop the case and effectively end the sexual harassment lawsuit. Prior to the settlement, Clinton was questioned by Jones's attorneys who were trying to show a pattern of behavior by Clinton of sexual involvement with state or government employees. In his deposition for the Jones lawsuit, Clinton denied having "sexual relations" with Monica Lewinsky.

Monica Lewinsky was one of a number of women who were included on a list of potential witnesses prepared by Paula Jones's attorneys. Her name, along with the others, was submitted to the president's legal team. Clinton suspected that the source of Lewinsky's name was either the Secret Service agents who guarded him or Linda Tripp, a former White House employee who had become a confidante of Lewinsky.

On January 12, 1998, Tripp approached the Office of the Independent Counsel (OIC), headed by Kenneth Starr, and claimed that she possessed tapes detailing an intimate relationship between the president and Monica Lewinsky. She informed the OIC of her concerns about being prosecuted for perjury and obstruction of justice. After Lewinsky had submitted an affidavit in the Paula Jones case denying any physical relationship with Clinton, she attempted to persuade Tripp to lie under oath in the Jones case. Lewinsky's affidavit (provided to avoid direct testimony in the Jones case) stated that Lewinsky never had a sexual relationship with the president, that he did not propose sexual relations, and that he did not offer her a job or other benefits in exchange for a sexual relationship. Tripp however did not follow Lewinsky's advice and notified FBI agents that Lewinsky had an affair with the president and that a dress with the irrefutable proof of semen stains was still in Lewinsky's possession. Tripp gave attorneys for Starr's office more than a dozen tape recordings of phone conversations she had with Lewinsky.

Tripp was required to submit an affidavit concerning any knowledge of a sexual encounter between the president and a former White House aide, Kathleen Willey. On January 21, 1998, Tripp submitted an affidavit to Jones's lawyers claiming that there had been a sexual encounter between Clinton and Willey in late 1993 and that Monica Lewinsky also had a relationship with the president. Tripp claimed that Lewinsky recorded conversations between Lewinsky and Clinton, and in the affidavit asserted that Lewinsky played at least three tapes containing the president's voice. Tripp also noted that Lewinsky had shown her gifts that were exchanged between the president and Lewinsky. Tripp maintained that Lewinsky told her she was going to deny everything, and that the president would deny everything. Lewinsky urged Tripp to deny that she had told her anything about a relationship with the president (Busby 2001, 61).

Prior to Linda Tripp's submission of her affidavit to Jones's attorneys, she received a three-page document from Lewinsky, commonly referred to as the "talking points" memo. Many of the points in the memo were not true and Tripp chose a different path to follow in her damaging affidavit (Busby 2001, 61).

On January 17, 1998, President Clinton was questioned in a deposition about sexual relations he may have had with government employees. Contents of the deposition were not to be made public; within a matter of days, however, leaks about his alleged relationship with Lewinsky began to circulate in Washington. Clinton denied ever having had a "sexual affair" or "sexual relations" with Lewinsky. This statement was consistent with Lewinsky's affidavit but was not helpful to Jones's lawyers, who were trying to establish that Clinton was a habitual womanizer and had made unwanted advances to their client (Busby 2001, 64).

In advance of Clinton's January 17 deposition, the Office of Independent Counsel already had information from Tripp suggesting that Clinton had engaged in a private relationship with Lewinsky and that Lewinsky intended to lie about it. It then appeared to Starr that he had grounds to extend his initial mandate (which involved investigation of real estate dealings in Arkansas) to cover the Monica Lewinsky matter. His request to expand his mandate was granted by Attorney General Janet Reno on January 16, 1998. This expansion of authority allowed Starr to investigate allegations of the president's perjury, obstruction of justice, and other matters. Before long, Starr would submit a document, the Starr Report, to the House of Representatives recommending impeachment of the president (Busby 2001, 63).

The Starr Report

The investigation that was conducted by the independent counsel, Kenneth Starr, generated a great deal of controversy. For example, Harvard law professor Alan Dershowitz denounced the Starr Report as posing a far greater danger to the American system of governance than anything charged against President Clinton. According to Dershowitz, Starr went too far in his investigation of the president's behavior. Dershowitz concluded that Starr exhibited a partisan determination to force the president out of office and that one unelected prosecutor should not be empowered to bring down a president on the basis of un–cross-examined, one-sided accounts of sexual misbehavior and alleged efforts to cover it up. Dershowtz stated:

> Prior to this report, no self-respecting prosecutor would include such material in an indictment or present it at a trial. If he tried, the judge would strike it as gratuitous, prejudicial and irrelevant. But Kenneth Starr did not submit his report to any judge. He alone made the decision what to publish, and his decision evidences a partisan determination to embarrass the President out of office. Starr's tactic seems to be to render the President incapable of governing by exposing his sex life to public ridicule." (1988, 221)

Despite Dershowitz's views, members of the U.S. House of Representatives held the Starr Report in sufficient esteem to conduct an impeachment inquiry.

The Starr Report was submitted to the House of Representatives on September 9, 1998. The report included eleven grounds for the impeachment of President Clinton, which are listed in Table 4.2.

The president's legal team issued an initial response to the charges even before seeing them. When the Starr Report was made available, the president's legal team issued a more detailed response. The Preliminary Memorandum Concerning Referral of Office of Independent Counsel identified the president's confession of wrongdoing, but argued that his actions did not warrant impeachment because they could not be equated with the "high crimes and misdemeanors" specified in the Constitution (Busby 2001, 130). The memorandum stressed the high level of criminality and wrongdoing required for impeachment and contended that the president had done little more than act in an inappropriate manner, in a private capacity (Busby 2001, 131). The core of Clinton's defense was condensed into four simple points:

1. The president did not commit perjury.
2. The president did not obstruct justice.
3. The president did not tamper with witnesses.
4. The president did not abuse the power of his office.

The Preliminary Memorandum was made public on the same day that the Starr Report was publicly released by the House of Representatives, September 11, 1998. A second document in defense of the president, Initial Response to Referral of Office of Independent Counsel, was released the next day. It directly addressed the eleven charges advanced by Starr. Both of Clinton's responses to the Starr Report

Table 4.2

Grounds for Impeachment Cited in Starr Report

1. President Clinton lied under oath in the Jones deposition of January 1998 by denying a sexual affair, a sexual relationship, or sexual relations with Monica Lewinsky.

2. President Clinton lied under oath about his sexual relationship with Monica Lewinsky during his grand jury testimony in August 1998.

3. President Clinton lied during the Jones deposition about being alone with Lewinsky and about the exchange of gifts.

4. President Clinton lied in the Jones deposition about his discussion with Lewinsky regarding the Jones case.

5. President Clinton conspired with Lewinsky to conceal the truth about their relationship and conceal subpoenaed gifts.

6. President Clinton obstructed justice by lying under oath and encouraging Lewinsky to lie and file an affidavit to prevent her testifying.

7. President Clinton attempted to obstruct justice by aiding in a job search for Lewinsky, which encouraged her to continue to withhold information about the relationship.

8. President Clinton lied under oath in the Jones deposition about his discussion with Vernon Jordan.

9. President Clinton tampered with a witness by attempting to influence the testimony of his secretary Betty Currie.

10. President Clinton tried to obstruct justice by misinforming his aides and refusing to testify for seven months—and did thereby deceive, obstruct, and impede the grand jury.

11. President Clinton abused his constitutional authority.

Source: Busby 2001.

alleged that the independent counsel was politically biased and overly preoccupied with sexual issues. Clinton's lawyers also argued that the OIC report was presented as fact without giving Clinton's lawyers any opportunity to cross-examine any witnesses and that it failed to substantiate the legal charges raised (Busby 2001, 132). Through these two responses, the White House hoped to avert the onset of impeachment proceedings in the House of Representatives. These efforts, however, failed to avert a majority vote in the House of Representatives to let the matter move to the trial phase in the Senate.

Impeachment, Trial, and Aftermath

On September 11, 1998, two days after receiving the Starr Report, the House of Representatives ap-

proved House Resolution 525, authorizing a review of the Starr Report by the House Judiciary Committee. The committee was charged with determining whether sufficient grounds existed to recommend to the full House of Representatives that an impeachment inquiry should be commenced.

Impeachment is a fairly complicated, multistep process. The term "impeachment" refers to only half the process of removing a president from office. Under the terms of the U.S. Constitution, the House of Representatives has the responsibility of impeaching or bringing charges of wrongdoing against the president. These charges are contained in articles of impeachment that explain the nature of the perceived transgressions. If the articles of impeachment are agreed to by a majority of the House of Representatives, the Senate then undertakes a trial phase. The Senate examines the charges brought forward by the House and determines whether the charges are in keeping with the Senate's understanding of the nature of impeachment as outlined in the Constitution. House managers instruct the Senate; the chief justice of the Supreme Court presides over the trial in the Senate. The senators vote on the charges and must approve them by a two-thirds majority in order to remove the president from office. The Senate must vote on each article of impeachment separately and if any single article is approved, then the president is required to leave office (Busby 2001, 139).

On October 8, 1998, the full House of Representatives voted to commence impeachment procedures. Clinton reacted to this vote by repeatedly referring to the American people and the policies that affected their daily lives. He claimed that he trusted the American people and that he would do his job for the people. His comments were in line with public opinion polls that indicated a reluctance to see the president impeached. In contrast, Henry Hyde, chair of the House Judiciary Committee, contended that, despite public opinion and the November 1998 election that favored Democrats, his duty to the Constitution had not changed and that he must proceed with the impeachment.

Relations between the members of the House Judiciary Committee and the president became strained. On November 5, the committee presented the president with eighty-one written questions about the Lewinsky scandal. The tone of the questions was terse, with all eighty-one inquiries beginning with the phrase "Do you admit or deny. . ." Clinton's response was delivered to the Judiciary Committee before the end of November, but his answers were viewed as unsatisfactory. Many of the responses simply repeated information previously submitted to Kenneth Starr.

On November 19, Starr testified before the House Judiciary Committee. He claimed that the evidence spoke for itself and that, if examined in an apolitical manner, it would clearly indicate that the president had abused the power of his office. On December 11, Clinton publicly apologized for his behavior and argued that a vote to censure him would be appropriate. He stated that he was "profoundly sorry" for all that he did in words and deeds. He admitted that he never should have misled the country, Congress, his friends, or his family. From December 10–12, the articles of impeachment were debated in the House Judiciary Committee. All four of the articles passed in the vote of the Judiciary Committee.

Two broad themes emerged from the debate in the judiciary committee. Republicans stressed the rule of law, Clinton's apparent reluctance to cooperate, and the weak message that any verdict, other than impeachment, might send to future presidents. Democrats, on the other hand, contended that impeachment was not warranted by Clinton's actions, would harm the American system of government, and would increase partisan rancor. A final argument advanced by Democrats was that censure was a viable alternative. On December 19, 1998, the House voted on the four articles that were approved by the Judiciary Committee. Table 4.3 summarizes the articles and votes in the full House.

Articles II and IV were defeated, but Articles I and III were approved by a majority vote and sent on to the Senate for a possible conviction and removal of the president. On January 7, 1999, the trial began in the U.S. Senate. After Representative Hyde read the two articles of impeachment that had been approved by the House of Representatives, all 100 senators were sworn in as jurors by Chief Justice William Rehnquist. Arguments on the floor of the Senate resembled those made previously in the House of Representatives. An attempt to have Monica Lewinsky appear to give evidence directly failed by a vote of 70–30 (Busby 2001, 165). Three individuals—Monica Lewinsky, Clinton's friend

Table 4.3

Impeachment Votes in House of Representatives

Article I: The president provided perjurious, false, and misleading testimony to the grand jury regarding the Paula Jones case and his relationship with Monica Lewinsky.
Yea 228; Nay 206

Article II: The president provided perjurious, false, and misleading testimony in the Jones case in his answers to the written questions and in his deposition.
Yea 205; Nay 229

Article III: The president obstructed justice in an effort to delay, impede, cover up and conceal the existence of evidence related to the Jones case.
Yea 221; Nay 212

Article IV: The president misused and abused his office by making perjurious, false, and misleading statements to Congress.
Yea 148; Nay 285

Source: Busby 2001.

Vernon Jordan, and White House aide Sidney Blumenthal—gave written depositions.

On February 12, the Senate voted on both articles of impeachment. Article I: charging that the president provided perjurious, false, and misleading testimony to a grand jury, received 45 guilty and 55 not guilty votes. Article II: charging that the president tried to obstruct justice in an effort to delay, impede, cover up, and conceal evidence, received 50 guilty and 50 not guilty votes. The necessary two-thirds vote was not attained and Clinton therefore was not removed from office.

Clinton responded to his acquittal with a brief statement to reporters. The president wanted to put the scandal behind him and was ready to dismiss it as a footnote to his administration. Although he apologized for the great burden that his words and actions had imposed on Congress and the American people, he asked all Americans to rededicate

themselves to the work of serving the nation and building a future together. His statement lasted barely a minute. Bitterness and acrimony, however, remained among those who sought to convict the president. For example, David Schipper, the investigative counsel for the House Judiciary Committee, condemned the Senate for its failure to convict the president.

At the end of March Clinton discussed the scandal in an interview with Dan Rather of CBS News. The president raised four issues: (1) every person must bear the consequences of his or her conduct, and when you make a mistake you pay for it, no matter who you are; (2) the Constitution works, the requirement of a two-thirds majority in the Senate preventing partisanship from playing a decisive role in the removal of a president; (3) the American people almost always get it right if you give them enough time to think through things; and (4) it is important that elected officials follow the guidance and will of the people, not losing sight of the function of a representative democracy. These four lessons reflect various aspects of the scandal: morality, partisanship, public opinion, and representative democracy (Busby 2001, 216).

Clinton did not escape being damaged by the scandal. On January 19, 2001, the day before his departure from the presidency, he issued a statement to the effect that he "tried to walk a fine line between acting lawfully and testifying falsely" but failed to "fully accomplish this goal"; that he "knowingly violated" directives in the Paula Jones deposition; and that "certain of my responses to questions about Ms. Lewinsky were false." In addition to the statement, as part of an agreement, between Clinton and Robert Ray (who succeeded Kenneth Starr as the new Independent Council) Clinton agreed to pay a $25,000 fine to the Arkansas Bar Association, agreed to a five-year suspension of his license to practice law, and promised not to seek reimbursement for legal fees. The independent council agreed to end previous inquiries into Arkansas real estate dealings and end investigations into other matters. This agreement between Ray and Clinton effectively prevented charges from being placed against Clinton after he left the office of the presidency (Busby 2001, 218; Koven 2003, 200).

In retrospect, the jury still seems to be out in regard to the implications of the Clinton impeachment. Responsibility in the context of the impeachment can be viewed as defending a duly elected official from partisan attacks, on the one hand, and, on the other hand, as fulfilling the constitutional directive to protect the people from officials engaged in high crimes. It could be argued that both Clinton's defenders and his attackers acted in a manner that was consistent with their perceptions of correct behavior and that supported the public interest as well as the rule of law.

Application of Case No. 3 to Ethics and Responsible Governance

Breaches of Responsibility: The Public Interest

The public is served when its leaders represent its interests. The president, as a symbol of respect, has a responsibility to act in a manner that will bring dignity and honor to the citizenry of the nation. The public interest can therefore be served by effective policy and by leaders that citizens respect. One can argue that these do not necessarily have to coexist, yet the public interest is best served when both appear simultaneously.

In one sense discrediting public leaders suggests the strength of democracy. It demonstrates the power of the people to humble the arrogant, safeguard liberty, and protect themselves against tyranny. The constitutional system of checks and balances provides a framework whereby Congress

can investigate wrongdoing and if necessary remove the wrongdoers. In the Clinton example, Congress impeached the president (similar to an indictment) but refused to remove him. The other constitutional check on the executive branch of government, the courts, became involved in the scandal when Paula Jones filed a sexual harassment lawsuit in 1994. As was the case with Richard Nixon, the Supreme Court eventually became involved, ruling in 1997 that a sitting president of the United States has no immunity from civil law litigation for facts unrelated to his office.

The Clinton impeachment can be viewed as a proper exercise of the constitutional checks and balances. It can also be viewed as an attempt to invalidate an election and therefore a threat to democracy. The Clinton scandal did more than expose sex in the White House. If nothing else, the Clinton scandal raised public awareness about how the government works. Like Watergate, it raised constitutional questions about checks and balances. It raised questions about the rights of the chief executive and the obligations of Congress. It generated debate about the value of truthfulness and how lying and cover-ups can be counterproductive. After Clinton, political figures may be more careful about their public statements and more discreet about their behavior. The result may be more transparency, candor, and honesty in American politics.

The Clinton scandal, however, was damaging to the public interest on a variety of fronts. It wounded the image of the nation's leader and thereby increased distrust for all politicians. As distrust increases, the social bond that holds Americans together weakens. As noted in Chapter 2, representatives of the government have an ethical obligation to citizens—to encourage civic virtues and maintain concern for the common good, the broad, shared interests of society. To a certain extent, the Clinton scandal reflected the protection of private interests rather than the promotion of the common good.

Clearly, ridicule and derision of public leaders erode support for institutions while respect for officeholders enhances the legitimacy of a regime. Exposure of the Clinton-Lewinsky affair bolstered the public interest by identifying wrongdoing and leading to corrective action (impeachment). For some people, this process restored faith in the system. On the other hand, awareness of abuse can erode faith and trust in government (Koven 2003, 210).

Breaches of Responsibility: Natural Law

Natural law refers to rational or intuitive interpretations of right and wrong. Natural law also relates to one's understanding of God's precepts. A number of authors have discussed the Clinton scandal in terms of its relationship to religious and moral principles. One spin on the scandal, presented by Clinton in his speech at a religious leaders' prayer breakfast, was that he had sinned but that he was genuinely sorry and determined to change. Clinton consistently portrayed the scandal as an example of moral transgression as opposed to legal wrongdoing. A core of Clinton's assertions was that he was involved in a sex scandal and nothing more, that the scandal did not constitute a serious violation of law (Busby 2001, 216).

Clinton's claims of moral transgression were on full display at the prayer breakfast on September 11, 1998. He noted that he was up late the previous night thinking and praying about what he should say, that he had been on "quite a journey" to get to the "rock bottom truth" and that he agreed with others who contended that he "was not contrite enough" in his nationally televised speech to the nation. There was no "fancy way" to say that he had sinned and that his sorrow was genuine. He claimed that two things were necessary to be for-

given: genuine repentance and an understanding that he must have God's help to be the person he wanted to be. He announced that he would "continue on the path of repentance seeking pastoral support" and that he was grateful for those who stood by him by arguing that the "bounds of privacy had been excessively and unwisely invaded" by his political opponents. This invasion, however, could "be a blessing" because if his repentance was genuine then "good can come of this for our country, as well as for me and my family" (Fackre 1999, 186).

Not everyone was as willing to accept the "good" for the country emanating from the Lewinsky-Clinton scandal. For example, Yale University law professor Stephen Carter stated that Clinton as an evangelical Christian needed to understand that the premise of forgiveness is true repentance. According to Carter, more than apology and accepting responsibility were required; true repentance necessitated a "determination to turn and walk the path for good." Walking this path would require Clinton to abandon his habit of resorting to legalism and obfuscation; apologize to his family, to the surrogates he sent to defend him, to Lewinsky, and to the American people; and stop lashing out as though others were to blame for his humiliation (Carter 1999, 170).

Carter felt that the president must exercise genuine moral leadership and that his televised speech to the nation on August 17, 1998, lacked contrition. In the speech Clinton had admitted to "a relationship with Miss Lewinsky that was not appropriate" yet asserted that "at no time did I ask anyone to lie, to hide or destroy evidence, or to take any other unlawful action." According to the president, his silence about the matter was motivated by his desire to protect himself and his family from embarrassment, his opposition to a "politically inspired lawsuit," and his concerns about the legitimacy of an independent counsel investigation.

He proclaimed that Starr's investigation had gone on too long, cost too much, and hurt too many innocent people. Clinton concluded, "This matter is between me, the two people I love most—my wife and our daughter—and our God. I must put it right, and I am prepared to do whatever it takes to do so. . . . It's nobody's business but our own. Even presidents have private lives. It is time to stop the pursuit of personal destruction and the prying into private lives and get on with our national life" (Fackre 1999, 184).

Commentators such as Carter, however, did not condemn the investigation of Clinton and public pronouncement of his indiscretions. Instead, Carter viewed the revelation of the Lewinsky affair as potentially "a godsend." He stated that sometimes getting caught is the only way to learn a lesson and the president "will never have a better opportunity to seek spiritual solace." Carter concluded that the Clinton scandal "may also be heaven-sent for the rest of us because sometimes it takes a rude shock to wake the nation's conscience. . . . That conscience needs awakening because our sense of right and wrong is ultimately what makes America a special place. This depressing scandal might represent our best chance at reinvigorating our shared belief in an American moral code" (Carter 1999, 171).

The connection between Clinton's behavior and American morality was also identified by others. Religious leaders such as Pat Robertson and Jerry Falwell as well as political leaders such as Senator Joseph Lieberman, the Democratic vice presidential candidate in 2000, openly condemned the president's behavior. Former Secretary of Education William Bennett claimed that the ideals of American citizenship were under assault by a corrupting president. After the Senate failed to oust Clinton, conservative activist Paul Weyrich predicted a cultural collapse in America (Koven 2003, 206).

Breaches of Responsibility: The Rule of Law

Kenneth Starr sought to frame the Clinton scandal within the context of the rule of law and perjury rather than sex and immorality. Ultimately, the most serious challenge to Clinton's presidency was legal, stemming from the Paula Jones lawsuit, statements he made in the lawsuit, later testimony before a federal grand jury, and claims of executive privilege. Jean Bethke Elshtain, Laura Spelman Rockefeller Professor of Social and Political Ethics at the University of Chicago, notes that legal questions remained at the heart of Clinton's problems. She stresses the need to distinguish between "contrition chic" and serious acts of public and political forgiveness and to examine the relationship between contrition and the rule of law. Forgiveness does not invalidate legal questions relating to the performance of the duties of office. According to Elshtain, the law embodies what is best about Americans. Abandoning standards of law-abiding behavior therefore is destructive to democracy:

> [I]f we believe a President has behaved dishonorably and may even have broken the law (but that's okay because the subject is one "everybody" lies about), and we also claim that he is an effective leader nonetheless, then we have moved into a zone of amoral Machiavellianism that ill befits us as a people and that undermines a political system in which law has always been construed as more than a prohibitive or penal exercise. Rather, the law, ideally, embodies what is best, most capacious, and most hopeful about us as a people. . . . Few of us would want our lives examined with a fine-toothed comb and the results of that examination made public. At the same time, it is deadly to a decent democratic process to abandon altogether standards of minimally decent, honorable, and law-abiding behavior in our public figures. . . . Those who undertake public office have special responsibilities. They are neither below nor above the law. But we rightly care, or at least we used to, more about what they do *under cover of their office* than what the clerk in the department

store does, or the traffic cop or the farmers. Why? Because they have accepted and are charged with particular, clear responsibilities not incumbent upon the rest of us. We all have a duty to follow the law, unless it is blatantly unjust. But not all of us have a duty to uphold it. (Elshtain 1999, 14–17)

The matter of the rule of law came up repeatedly during the impeachment in the U.S. House of Representatives. In his opening statement, Representative Henry J. Hyde of Illinois, the seventy-four-year-old chair of the House Judiciary Committee, declared that "no man or woman, no matter how highly placed, no matter how effective a communicator, no matter how gifted a manipulator of opinion or winner of votes, can be above the law in a democracy." On December 18, 1998, Hyde asserted that the issue at hand was not a question of sex or a question of lying about sex, but a question of lying under oath—a public act, not a private act. Arguing that the focus of attention should be on the "willful, premeditated, deliberate corruption of the nation's system of justice," Hyde asserted that the compact between the president and the American people had been broken; that the nation's chief executive had corrupted the rule of law by his perjury and obstruction of justice.

In his closing argument, Hyde reminded his colleagues that a bedrock principle of democracy is that no one is above the law. To erode this principle evokes the arbitrary behavior of absolute rulers under the "divine right of kings" theory of governance. Under this conception of governance, those who governed were absolved from adhering to the basic moral standards to which the governed were held.

According to Hyde, to tolerate one law for the ruler and another for the ruled would break faith with Americans' ancestors "from Bunker Hill, Lexington and Concord to Flanders Field, Normandy, Iwo Jima, Panmunjon, Saigon and Desert Storm." The rule of law is one of the great achievements in our civilization because the alternative to the rule of law is the rule of raw power. Hyde pronounced

that Americans are heirs to the Ten Commandments and Mosaic law, a moral code for a free people; to Roman law, the first legal system that united people of different cultures and religions in a political community; to the Magna Carta, by which freemen of England began to break the unchecked power of royalty; to parliamentary development, in which the rule of law gradually replaced royal prerogative as a means for governing; to 1776, when America's founders pledged to defend the rule of law; to a civil war that vindicated the rule of law over the appetite of some people for owning others; and finally to the twentieth century's great struggles against totalitarianism.

Hyde affirmed that the rule of law protects citizens from the arbitrary exercise of power by the state, safeguarding liberty and allowing citizens to honor the freedom of others while strengthening the common good. Hyde denied that he and his fellow members of the House of Representatives were "Clinton haters," "frivolous," or "mean-spirited." Instead, they believed "in conscience that the President willfully obstructed justice, and thereby threatened the legal system he swore a solemn oath to protect and defend." These were not trivial or partisan matters but "matters of justice." In contrast to the image of "Clinton haters," Hyde portrayed House members as lovers of the rule of law, equal justice before the law, and honor in public life.

In his closing thoughts, Hyde stressed that political prisoners, the families of executed dissidents, and those yearning for freedom knew that the impeachment was about the rule of law. He felt that the members of the House of Representatives had a responsibility to those across the river in Arlington Cemetery who died defending the rule of law. He instructed members of the House to go to the Vietnam Memorial and press their hands "against some of the 58,000 names carved in the wall—and ask yourself how we can redeem the debt we owe all those who purchased our freedom with their lives."

His answer was to "work to make this country the kind of America they were willing to die for. That's an America where the idea of sacred honor still has the power to stir men's souls" (Hyde 1999).

Questions for Student Group Discussion

1. Do you think Clinton should have been impeached? Why or why not?
2. Was Clinton's behavior purely a private matter?
3. How much privacy should be granted to presidents? When do private matters become public?
4. What type of personal character do you expect from America's elected leaders? How do you define character?
5. Do you think Clinton was a victim of overzealous enemies? Why or why not?
6. Do you think Clinton got what he deserved or should have gotten worse? Why or why not?
7. Are the public's expectations for America's leaders too high?
8. What specific actions do you think merit impeachment of a president?
9. Why did Clinton retain fairly solid support among average citizens, but less support among members of the House of Representatives?
10. What do you think are the lessons of the Clinton impeachment?

CASE NO. 4: FEMA's Response to Hurricane Katrina

An Overview

Hurricane Katrina was a crucial event in stemming the political call for reduced government. American

citizens watched in amazement the televised images of victims of the flood waiting on their roofs for food, water, or rescue. Who would help them? There was little question that the public viewed the government as a necessity in times of emergency. The question before the American people was not whether assistance should be private, nonprofit, or governmental or why people had not picked themselves up by their bootstraps. The question was why needed assistance appeared to be so little, so late, and so poorly delivered.

The inadequacy of the response to the storm raised other troubling questions as well. Who was to blame? Were important government positions filled by folks with good political connections but little knowledge about their jobs? Was a system in place that allowed federal, state, and local leaders to work together? What should have been done differently? Will Americans be protected from future disasters? The basic facts of the case do not inspire confidence in the competency and capability of the public sector. Katrina was one of the largest natural disasters in the nation's history. It is also synonymous with one of the nation's largest screwups. The appearance, if not the reality, of incompetence, confusion, and indecisiveness surround the very words "Hurricane Katrina." Whether these statements are exaggerations or reality is to some extent explained below through a detailed account of the storm, the damage, and the response. This review of the facts of the case sheds light on the larger issues of competence and government responsibility.

The Facts of the Case

The Storm

On August 23, 2005, the National Hurricane Center (NHC) noted that a tropical depression had formed over the Bahamas. On August 24, the tropical depression, now a tropical storm, was given the name Katrina. Tropical storms are classified as such by winds between 39 and 73 miles per hour. On August 25, Katrina was upgraded to a Category 1 hurricane and forecast to make landfall in Florida. "Category 1" refers to the Saffir-Simpson scale, which categorizes hurricanes based upon their intensity, from "Cat 1" storms with winds between 74 and 95 miles an hour to the highest "Cat 5" hurricane with winds greater than 155 miles an hour.

On August 25, as predicted, Hurricane Katrina made landfall near the Miami-Dade and Broward County line with sustained winds up to 80 miles an hour, more than a dozen deaths, power outages affecting over 1.4 million people, and areas of severe flooding. On August 26, Katrina weakened to a tropical storm as it passed over Florida, but intensified into a Category 2 hurricane soon after entering the warm waters of the Gulf of Mexico. The NHC projected that the storm would continue to intensify, that the eye of the storm would pass just east of New Orleans, and that Katrina's storm surge would produce tides fifteen to twenty feet above normal at the point where the eye of the storm made landfall. Aware of the impending danger, Louisiana governor Kathleen Blanco and Mississippi governor Haley Barbour quickly declared a state of emergency for their respective states. Governor Barbour issued an executive order to prepare to use the Mississippi National Guard for disaster relief operations (Townsend 2006, 24).

On August 27, Katrina strengthened to a Category 3 hurricane and nearly doubled in size. The NHC warned that the storm was still expected to intensify with powerful storm surges. As the storm strengthened in the Gulf of Mexico, Governors Blanco and Barbour implemented their "contraflow" traffic plans. Under these plans, major roadways and interstate highways would close their inbound lanes and expand the number of lanes that took traffic away from the imperiled areas. Local governments across the northern Gulf Coast issued evacuation orders. The mayor of New Orleans, Ray Nagin, called for a voluntary evacuation of the city and declared a state of emergency. Shelters began to open throughout the region, including the New Orleans Superdome, which was opened to people with "special needs" (Townsend 2006, 26).

On August 28, Katrina was upgraded to a Category 5 hurricane. The National Weather Service in Slidell, Louisiana, issued an urgent warning about the impending devastation. President George W. Bush called Governor Blanco to urge mandatory evacuation for New Orleans. The Superdome was designated as a shelter of last resort for the general population. By midnight, estimates placed 10,000 to 12,000 people at the Superdome. As the storm approached landfall, about 80 percent of New Orleans's 484,000 residents fled. Many of the old, sick, black, poor, and those without their own vehicles remained in the city awaiting the storm. In addition, thousands of other citizens made a personal decision to stay because they did not want to fight the traffic, they believed that hurricanes were in the Lord's hands, they wanted to look after their neighborhood, they wanted to finish chores, or they sought the thrill of riding out the storm (Brinkley 2006, 62).

On August 29, the hurricane made landfall in three places as it veered eastward along the Gulf Coast. The first area to feel the full fury of the storm was Buras, Louisiana, a hamlet near the mouth of the Mississippi River about sixty-three miles southeast of New Orleans. All the inhabitants had been evacuated and virtually all of the 1,146 houses were flattened. As the hurricane swept along, it dropped about an inch of rain an hour (Brinkley 2006, 133).

Storm surges smashed the entire Mississippi Gulf Coast, including the Mississippi towns of Gulfport and Biloxi. Damage was attributed to a variety of factors, including Katrina's Category 5 strength at sea, the height of its storm surge and its size. When it hit land, Katrina was only a Category 3 storm, but its storm surge was great enough to flood the area (Brennan and Koven 2007). At one time, winds around the eye of Katrina were clocked at 200 miles an hour. Katrina lost its hurricane strength more than 150 miles inland near Meridian, Mississippi. It was downgraded to a tropical depression near Clarksville, Tennessee, but its remnants were still distinguishable in the eastern Great Lakes region on August 31. It moved rapidly to the northeast and affected both Ontario and Quebec.

Since hurricane records were first kept in 1851, only three Category 5 storms are known to have hit the United States—the Labor Day hurricane of 1935 in the Florida Keys, the 1969 Hurricane Camille in Mississippi, and the 1992 Hurricane Andrew in Dade County, Florida. The Category 4 Galveston hurricane of September 8–9, 1900, was the deadliest in U.S. history. Between 8,000 and 12,000 people died in the Great Galveston Hurricane, which motivated Texans to move to higher land in Houston (Brinkley 2006, 74).

The Damage

An official government report concluded that Hurricane Katrina caused 1,326 deaths, displaced more than 700,000 people, and destroyed or damaged an estimated 300,000 homes. Disaster declarations covered over 90,000 square miles (Department of Homeland Security 2006, 4–5). Katrina was the most expensive natural disaster in the history of the United States. Costs included those associated with the forced evacuation of more than 75 percent of the Gulf's manned oil platforms. The storm cost $96 billion in property damage: $67 billion from housing damage, $7 billion from damage to consumer durable goods, $20 billion from damage to business

property, and $3 billion from damage to government property.

When damage to housing was defined as ranging from total destruction to destruction of parts of roofs and floors, it was estimated that nearly three-fourths of the housing in New Orleans was damaged. An exact count does not exist for types of housing damaged, yet it is believed that most of the damaged units were occupied by the poor, minorities, and renters (Gilderbloom 2008).

Most of the damage was caused after a number of the levees in New Orleans were breached. The deputy director of the Louisiana State University Hurricane Center reported that 87 percent of all the water that flooded the greater New Orleans metro area was caused by levee failure rather than rainfall. Water poured out of the breached levees for more than sixty hours until approximately 80 percent of New Orleans was flooded and the city's water level equaled the water level in the adjoining Lake Pontchartrain (van Heerden and Bryan 2006, 95).

When one of the levees abruptly collapsed, a "wall of water" exploded into part of the city. A variety of reasons was given for the collapse of the levees. Although Katrina was only a Category 3 storm when it hit land, high waves and storm surge had been produced when it was out at sea as a Category 4 and Category 5 storm. Another factor that contributed to the collapse of the levees was the erosion of wetlands in the path of the storm (van Heerden and Bryan 2006, 85). Some critics blamed the oil companies that constructed oil pipelines and shipping channels through coastal Louisiana, making the area more subject to erosion and providing less protection to the city (Brinkley 2006, 15). Other critics blamed the quality of the levees and wondered why New Orleans's flood protection system differed so much from the first-rate dike system in the Netherlands (Brinkley 2006, 115).

Spending priorities also played a role in the disaster. Officials from Louisiana State University's Coastal Studies Institute had been warning people all over the world that New Orleans was a nightmare waiting to happen. One institute official claimed that New Orleans faced so many problems, such as inadequately funded schools, political corruption, and collapsing infrastructure, that it could not address the issues of wetlands. Brinkley (2006, 16) observed that it was difficult to save wetlands when you were not safe on your block.

The displacement of people caused by the hurricane was the largest since the dust bowl migration from the southern Great Plains in the 1930s (Fox Facts 2006). The toll of suffering fell disproportionately on the elderly, the poor, and minorities. In Louisiana, about 71 percent of those who died in the storm were older than sixty and 47 percent were older than seventy-five. Some were found in nursing homes allegedly abandoned by their caretakers (Department of Homeland Security 2006, 8).

The Government Response to Hurricane Katrina

The response to Hurricane Katrina has been categorized as a disaster within a disaster. The size and scope of the devastation in the aftermath of Katrina required good coordination between the various levels of government, decisive leadership, caring administrators, and practical knowledge of disaster plans, to name just a few of the factors that could have improved the response.

In September 2005, the House of Representatives created a bipartisan committee to investigate the preparation for and response to Hurricane Katrina. The committee's report, titled *A Failure of Initiative*, concluded that all three levels of government failed to meet their obligations to the public and that the response to Katrina constituted

"a litany of mistakes, misjudgments, lapses, and absurdities all cascading together, blinding us to what was coming and hobbling any collective effort to respond" (Ink 2006, 800).

According to the report, the inadequate response of the government was primarily the result of a failure of policy implementation, not a failure of public policy. The report was critical of the slowness to act on the part of the Department of Homeland Security (DHS) and concluded that proactive steps should have been taken earlier. Other problems with the response to the hurricane were: (1) information moving poorly across departments or between jurisdictions; (2) poor coordination between the Defense Department, DHS, and the state of Louisiana; (3) a lack of joint training with other groups; (4) government red tape that delayed needed medical help; and (5) a failure of initiative (Ink 2006, 801–802).

In retrospect, many things could have been done differently. The mayor of New Orleans waited until Katrina escalated to a Category 5 storm before ordering a mandatory evacuation. Michael Brown, the director of the Federal Emergency Management Administration, waited until five hours after Katrina hit to request the federal government to send 1,000 Homeland Security employees to the Gulf Coast. Brown directed fire and emergency service personnel not to respond unless they were requested and lawfully dispatched by state and local authorities. The military did not set up a task force to respond to the hurricane until two days after the storm made landfall. President Bush was slow to respond to Governor Blanco's request for aid. Almost 700 municipal and school buses in operation prior to the hurricane could have been used in evacuating the remaining New Orleans residents. After the hurricane hit, however, the buses were flooded and out of commission. New Mexico's governor, Bill Richardson, offered Governor Blanco the assistance of his state's National

Guard, yet the paperwork needed to implement the plan was delayed for four days in Washington. Two days after the storm hit, President Bush, cutting short his vacation, surveyed damage through the window of Air Force One but did not land (Brinkley 2006; Dyson 2006).

The head of the American Bus Association tried unsuccessfully to reach FEMA two days after the storm hit land, wanting to know how many buses would be needed for evacuation. FEMA, however, had outsourced the job and buses were not ordered until eighteen hours after the hurricane made landfall. An 844-foot ship, the USS *Bataan*, was in the Gulf of Mexico before the storm with helicopters, marines, physicians, 600 hospital beds, food, and the ability to make 100,000 gallons of drinkable water a day. The *Bataan*'s helicopters were used to rescue stranded citizens, but its other assets were not used (Dyson 2006, 120).

Nearly 500 airboat pilots who volunteered to go to New Orleans to rescue storm victims and transport supplies were prevented by FEMA from entering the city. The Red Cross was also denied entry because FEMA claimed the city was unsafe. FEMA rejected an offer of assistance from Chicago that included 36 members of the firefighters' technical rescue teams, eight emergency medical technicians, more than 100 police officers, 29 clinical health workers, 117 non-clinical health workers, a mobile clinic, and 140 Streets and Sanitation workers. FEMA blocked a 500-boat citizen flotilla that tried to deliver aid, kept the Coast Guard from delivering diesel fuel, turned back a German plane transporting rations, failed to properly use hundreds of volunteer firefighters, and used about 1,000 firefighters from other communities merely to distribute flyers.

FEMA's performance did not go unnoticed. On September 4, 2005, in an appearance on the television news show *Meet the Press*, the president of Jefferson Parish in Louisiana stated:

The aftermath of Hurricane Katrina will go down as one of the worst abandonment of Americans on American soil ever in U.S. history. . . . Bureaucracy has committed murder here in the greater New Orleans area, and bureaucracy has to stand trial before Congress now. . . . FEMA needs to be empowered to do the things it was created to do. It needs to come somewhere, like New Orleans, with all of its force immediately, without red tape, without bureaucracy, act immediately with common sense and leadership, and save lives. (Dyson 2006, 126)

The Political Implications of Hurricane Katrina

The image of President Bush flying over New Orleans without stopping to offer a kind word or the immediate promise of assistance plagued his presidency. Bush's behavior came to symbolize an uncaring, disengaged leader. Tulane University historian Douglas Brinkley asserts that Bush's failure to put his heels down in Louisiana and Mississippi in the days following Katrina was one of the low marks of his presidency. No one expected the president to "pick up a bucket, and start bailing water," but when he finally appeared he had to recover from his "high-altitude disconnect." According to Brinkley, Bush should have "smelled the death," "touched the floodwater," and "showed he cared a bit more" (2006, 408).

Republican strategists privately called the image of Bush (the "tourist") peering down on the flood's destruction one of the most damaging images of his presidency. A *Newsweek* poll conducted soon after the hurricane found for the first time less than half (49 percent) of respondents stating that Bush had strong leadership qualities. This number was down from 63 percent in the previous year. His job approval rating was 38 percent, the lowest of his presidency up to that time. About two-thirds of the respondents (66 percent) also stated they were dissatisfied with where the country was heading (Fineman 2005).

Application of Case No. 4 to Ethics and Responsible Governance

Breaches of Responsibility: The Public Interest

The government has a responsibility to protect the general public and to provide assistance to those harmed by major natural disasters. In order to accomplish these tasks, a minimal level of competency is required. The Katrina case revealed that experience and competence are not always in good supply and are sometimes disregarded when filling high-level government positions. Arguably, excessive cronyism and the hiring of incompetents can waste government resources (in the case of "do nothing" appointments), seriously damage the reputation of public sector organizations (by the inappropriate behavior of appointees), and, worse, deprive the public of desperately needed goods and services. The head of FEMA, Michael D. Brown, was not the sole cause of what many perceived as an inadequate response to the disaster. Nevertheless, his behavior encouraged the media to look behind the curtain at hiring practices in the federal government as well as at the questionable qualifications of Brown.

The use of political patronage by the Bush White House in hiring Michael Brown as head of FEMA should not be seen as an anomaly. For example, the Bush administration also nominated the president's personal attorney, Harriet Miers, for a position on the Supreme Court and appointed Julie Myers (the niece of the former chair of the Joint Chiefs of Staff, General Richard Myers) to head the Immigration and Customs Enforcement division of the DHS (Koven 2007, 295). Bush's loyalty to longtime associates such as U.S. Attorney General Alberto Gonzales and adviser Karl Rove is well known. Consistent with the ethos of the urban machine, George Bush rewarded friends with cushy jobs and expected loyalty in return.

A review of Brown's behavior and background is instructive in exploring how well the public is served by government hiring practices. Brown's apparent lack of qualifications, misrepresented résumé, jocular manner, and concern for personal appearance tarred both him and the administration that appointed him. Appointed to the FEMA post in 2003, Brown quickly became synonymous with incompetence and strange behavior. A variety of factors cast serious doubt on his character and judgment. For example, controversy arose over the truthfulness of his résumé. Michael Brown's biography (posted on the FEMA Web site) states that he served as an assistant city manager in the city of Edmond, a small town in Oklahoma, and had oversight responsibilities over emergency services. A public relations representative from Edmond, however, denied that Brown had authority over other employees. The representative characterized him as an intern who worked for the town while he was a student at Central State University (later renamed University of Central Oklahoma). In early September 2005, an article in *Time* magazine questioned Brown's credentials. The *Time* article observed that Brown listed himself under the "honors and awards" section of his profile at FindLaw.com (which is information on the legal Web site provided by lawyers or their offices) as "Outstanding Political Science Professor, Central State University." However, Brown was only a student at Central State. Under the heading of "Professional Associations and Memberships" on FindLaw, Brown states that he has been director of the Oklahoma Christian Home, a nursing home in Edmond. An administrator with the Christian, however, informed a reporter for *Time* magazine that Brown is "not a person that anyone here is familiar with." His padded resume apparently went undetected when he was appointed head of FEMA in 2003. Brown claimed that the *Time* article distorted his record, but did not provide proof to refute the story or file a libel suit (Fonda and Healy 2005; Brinkley 2006, 246).

Brown's prior work was uneven at best. In the 1980s he practiced law in Oklahoma, working for an attorney who later described him as "not serious and somewhat shallow." Brown was one of the two attorneys (out of thirty-seven) who were let go when the firm split up. Brown ran for Congress in 1988 against a Democratic incumbent and lost by a wide margin. Immediately before joining FEMA (from 1999 to 2001), Brown was the Judges and Stewards Commissioner for the International Arabian Horse Association (IAHA). Some members of the IAHA nicknamed him "The Czar" for his imperious attitude. After numerous lawsuits were filed against the organization, by members of the IAHA who were disciplined by Brown, he resigned (Brennan and Koven 2007).

It is useful to know a bit of the history of FEMA to gain insight into how someone such as Brown could be appointed as its director. The organization was created in 1979 by President Jimmy Carter, but was held in low regard by the incoming Reagan administration. Tulane's Douglas Brinkley notes that by 1981 the agency already smacked of patronage. Appointing a person as director of FEMA therefore was "akin to giving a donor or friend the ambassadorship to Luxembourg—a cushy, largely honorary position." FEMA was perceived by some as a bureaucratic joke. When Hurricane Hugo hit the Carolinas in 1989, South Carolina senator Fritz Hollings called FEMA employees "the sorriest bunch of jackasses I've ever known" (Brinkley 2006, 247).

Brown's appointment was directly related to the fact that he was an old college friend of Joseph Allbaugh. Allbaugh, a fellow Oklahoman, was Bush's chief of staff when Bush was governor of Texas. Allbaugh also served as Bush's campaign manager during the 2000 presidential election.

After Bush was elected, Allbaugh was appointed head of FEMA. While he excelled at raising money and troubleshooting, he knew almost nothing about disaster relief. Allbaugh retired from the post in 2002 after FEMA was absorbed into the new Department of Homeland Security. His former job was given to his old friend, Michael Brown.

From a public relations perspective, Brown's performance in the disaster relief spotlight was far from reassuring. A few gaffes stand out as emblematic of his overall character and questionable performance. For example, there was only one FEMA employee in New Orleans when the hurricane struck on August 29. On August 31, this employee e-mailed Brown: "Sir, I know that you know the situation is past critical. Here are some things you might not know. Hotels are kicking people out, thousands gathering in the streets with no food or water. Hundreds still being rescued from homes. . . . We are out of food and running out of water at the dome [New Orleans Superdome], plans in works to address the critical need." In a response that probably would not encourage Woodrow Wilson's vision of scientific and efficient management, Brown e-mailed back, "Thanks for the update. Anything specific I need to do or tweak?"

On September 1, 2005, Brown told Paula Zahn of CNN that he was unaware that New Orleans officials had housed thousands of evacuees in the convention center. Major news outlets had been reporting this fact for at least a day. An e-mail from Representative Charlie Melancon, (whose district was devastated by the hurricane), relating to critical medical equipment went unanswered for four days (Brennan and Koven 2007). Brown was also criticized for flippant remarks. On the morning of the hurricane he asked the deputy director of FEMA, "Can I quit now?" A few days later he asked an acquaintance to "please rescue me." In the midst of the damage he wrote about his "problems finding a dog-sitter." In an e-mail to his deputy public affairs director Brown joked that he was "a fashion god" and that his attire was from Nordstrom (CNN 2005).

On September 9, 2005, Michael Brown was relieved of his responsibilities for overseeing storm relief efforts. His relief duties were handed to a Coast Guard official, Thad Allen. Some people saw Brown as the scapegoat for the Bush administration since he became the public face of FEMA. Despite the controversy that surrounded him, Brown seemed unrepentant. After the storm, in testimony before a House investigative panel, Brown blamed the Louisiana governor, the mayor of New Orleans, "dysfunctional" state officials, the military, and DHS for the problems of Katrina. He admitted to making only two mistakes: not holding regular media briefings and not being able to persuade Governor Blanco and Mayor Nagin to "get over their differences." He concluded that he was happy to be a scapegoat if it meant the FEMA he knew could be "reborn" and "get back to where it was" (Hsu 2005).

Breaches of Responsibility: Natural Law

As previously noted, natural law refers to laws that are not manmade. These laws can be identified through either rationality or intuition. Its application, however, is subject to enormous variation in interpretation. From one perspective, Katrina demonstrated that the government failed to live up to basic precepts of loving thy neighbor, taking care of the needy, and doing unto others as you would like them to do to you. From this perspective, it is simply inconceivable that such a wealthy, predominantly Christian nation would be so unresponsive to citizens in desperate need.

There has been speculation that race and class played some role in the quality of the government's response to the hurricane. If this was indeed the case, then the public sector's reaction violated not only manmade, U.S. laws of impartial justice but also the natural laws of caring for the needy. Dyson suggests that race played a role in the failure of the federal government to respond in a timely manner. He claimed that the poor blacks of the Mississippi Delta lacked social standing and racial status. These factors made it unlikely that they would evoke much empathy from President Bush or FEMA director Brown: "the black poor simply didn't register as large, or count as much, as they might have had they been white. If they had been white, a history of identification—supported by structures of care, sentiments of empathy, and an elevated racial standing—would have immediately kicked in" (2006, 24–25).

Class or income level may have also played a role in the government's response. For example, the *Atlanta-Constitution*'s editorial page editor, Cynthia Tucker, expresses the view that Americans have turned their backs on the impoverished. She notes that the hurricane "exploded the conventional wisdom about a shared American prosperity, exposing a group of people so poor they didn't have $50 for a bus ticket out of town. If we want to learn something from the disaster, the lesson ought to be: America's poor deserve better than this" (Dyson 2006, 147).

An alternative tack on natural law was taken by others who chose to link the hurricane to God's will. An Israeli rabbi stated (some say jokingly) that Katrina was God's punishment for Bush's support for withdrawing Jewish settlers from the Gaza Strip. Minister Louis Farrakhan argued that Hurricane Katrina represented God's way of punishing America for its warmongering and racism. A black Baptist pastor suggested that New Orleans faced divine retribution because of its voodoo and devil worship. The executive director of the Christian group Restore America characterized New Orleans as a place where immorality is flaunted.

Other conservative Christian ministers claimed that God punished New Orleans because of its abortion clinics, annual gay pride parade, and dependence on welfare (Dyson 2006, 181).

Breaches of Responsibility: The Rule of Law

Images of anarchy, lawlessness, and total confusion are associated with the hurricane. FEMA was responsible by law to rescue those in need. Under the Stafford Act of 1974 and the National Response Plan, FEMA was directed to provide disaster assistance for individuals and communities and to coordinate emergency support functions, including the care of people, housing, the delivery of services, urban rescue, and long-term recovery. The National Response Plan was formulated in December 2004 by the Department of Homeland Security in order to create a unified approach to domestic incidents. The intent of the plan was to prevent, prepare for, respond to, and recover from terrorism, natural disasters, and other major emergencies.

The critical issue in terms of the rule of law was not whether laws and guidelines existed, but how they were interpreted and implemented. Major disagreements arose between Mayor Nagin of New Orleans, Governor Blanco of Louisiana, President Bush, Michael Brown of FEMA, and Michael Chertoff, the head of Homeland Security, in regard to who was responsible for what action. Government officials at all levels bitterly blamed each other for the disastrous failure of government leaders to provide a speedy, efficient response. In particular, FEMA director Michael Brown was singled out and berated for his cavalier behavior.

Some residents engaged in looting immediately after the flooding; however, the stories of mass murder, rape, beatings, and general anarchy were more fiction than reality. For example, on Sep-

tember 5, 2005, Mayor Nagin stated on national television that people were being murdered at the Superdome and that babies were dying there. According to the Louisiana National Guard, however, no one was murdered inside the stadium and no babies were known to have died there.

Other assertions of a breakdown in law and order included contentions that hurricane victims were eating corpses to survive, bodies were stuffed inside a freezer at the convention center, bodies were stacked in the basement of the Superdome, people were shooting at helicopters, foreigners perished, and the levees were blown up to destroy the black part of town.

The National Guard reported that six people died at the Superdome, four from natural causes, one from a drug overdose, and one by suicide. Investigations later discredited stories of armed bands of looters trying to shoot down rescue helicopters. Although there were confirmed incidents of gunfire in New Orleans, investigators could not confirm a case of an airborne rescue team taking fire. Some of the gunfire may have been attributed to people trying to identify their position in hopes of rescue. The deputy police superintendent of New Orleans reported that one-third of the roughly 1,600 members of the city's police force deserted in the days following the hurricane. Later analysis concluded that only about 15 percent of the force was absent without permission. Some of these officers may have been searching for family members. Finally, it was reported that Louisiana's Governor Blanco did not formally declare a state of emergency until many days after the hurricane struck. In reality, she declared a state of emergency three days before Katrina made landfall (Gateway Pundit 2005; *Time* 2005, 55).

Some degree of lawlessness and looting occurred following the hurricane. For example, Brinkley reports that all sense of law was expunged from New Orleans within hours of the hurricane's passing. Looters saw the hurricane as a "shopping" opportunity and a couple of thousand people were seen wandering around with bags of stolen merchandise over their shoulders. One Wal-Mart opened its doors for local emergency personnel and police to collect needed items. Before long people were taking food, drinks, and toiletries. Eventually they stormed the electronics and jewelry departments. Some claimed that the police joined in the looting and even got "all the best stuff" (Brinkley 2006, 361–362).

A difference of opinion emerged in regard to how the looters should be treated. Governor Blanco, at one extreme, suggested that hotels and stores put an IOU pad at the checkout so people could sign their names alongside a list of items taken. At the other extreme, Mississippi's Governor Barbour made it clear that looters would be shot. In New Orleans a decision was made to arrest looters and bring them to the Greyhound Bus Terminal, the makeshift jail. If they tried to escape, they would be shot (Brinkley 2006, 209). On August 31, a lieutenant general arrived in the region to lead a military relief effort. On that day, Mayor Nagin ordered almost all the city's police officers off search-and-rescue duty in order to control looting and arson. On September 3, the Department of Defense announced that 10,000 more National Guard troops were being sent to the region, in addition to the 30,000 already there or en route (*Time* 2005).

Questions for Student Group Discussion

1. Were the deaths and devastation caused by Hurricane Katrina avoidable?
2. What could government officials have done to reduce the human suffering caused by the storm?
3. Who deserves the most blame for the government's poor performance in responding to the hurricane?
4. Do you think America is better prepared for the next big hurricane?
5. What do you think political leaders learned from Hurricane Katrina?
6. What were the political implications of Katrina?
7. What does Katrina imply in regard to responsible governance? What acts were most irresponsible?
8. What role did the practice of patronage play in the Katrina debacle?
9. What does Katrina suggest about the role of government in America?

Chapter 5

Responsibility and International Law

This chapter discusses the concept of international law and presents two high-profile cases that address in detail apparent violations of international convention. The chapter contends that since ancient times adversaries have endeavored to establish guidelines for permissible conduct, especially during times of war. It has been argued that in times of war the only rule is that there are no rules, however, an alternative position posits that the rule of law separates civilized humanity from barbarity. Adherence to minimum standards of permissible behavior is based on principles such as respect for others, order, and basic humanity.

The two case studies of the massacre of civilians by U.S. soldiers at My Lai in Vietnam and the treatment of prisoners at the Abu Ghraib prison complex in Iraq describe in detail incidences of questionable behavior on the part of U.S. military and paramilitary personnel. The first case study identifies questionable conduct of U.S. soldiers during the Vietnam War—specifically, the "wasting" of Vietnamese women, children, and old men who were slowing down a fast-moving U.S. military operation in hostile territory. My Lai aroused strong disagreement among U.S. military personnel. Many American soldiers viewed the conduct at My Lai as a disgrace to their uniform. Other critics considered My Lai indicative of American barbarity and disdain for international treaties, such

as the Geneva Convention relating to treatment of prisoners of war. Still others, including Lieutenant William Calley, justified My Lai as a legitimate action that took place during the "fog" of war.

Critics view My Lai as an egregious violation of basic understandings of human dignity. The incident suggested that American soldiers might be no better than the enemies that the United States fought against throughout the twentieth century. U.S. violations of international rules and norms of civilized behavior have the potential effect of isolating the United States from the international community and deepening the resolve of adversaries, who can claim a moral advantage. The conduct of American personnel in incidents such as My Lai cedes the moral superiority that Americans like to think they possess.

Alternatively, some argue that the fact that My Lai was uncovered and its participants prosecuted indicates that it represents an extreme exception to the norm of U.S. military behavior. From this perspective, the United States has self-correcting mechanisms in place that monitor transgressions, assign punishment, and guard against future recurrences. Considered as an anomaly, My Lai shows that norms of acceptable behavior are usually followed and that violations are punished.

The second case study of Abu Ghraib presents a contemporary example of international law and the treatment of prisoners. It raises the question of whether the United States was in breach of international law, specifically in breach of the Geneva and United Nations (UN) Conventions. The issues of classification of detainees and prisoner interrogation are addressed in detail in this case.

This case has many parallels to My Lai. Abu Ghraib represents a different war from Vietnam but involves similar illegal and disgraceful conduct, with similar damage to the U.S. image and similar, potentially harmful effects on enemy resolve. Jarring news photos from Abu Ghraib depicted naked prisoners piled on top of each other and electrical wires attached to a hooded detainee standing on a box. Reason and common sense aroused ordinary American citizens to question what was going on in the Iraq prison. The Abu Ghraib case reveals how simple it can be to abandon commitments to international treaties when it becomes convenient. The slippery slope of legalistic interpretation and internal memos illustrates that justification for questionable actions is always available if it is desired.

On the other hand, as in the My Lai case, Abu Ghraib shows that when laws were broken, the violators were identified and punished; that is, the system worked. Institutions such as the U.S. Supreme Court became involved in defining the rights of prisoners. Policy positions regarding treatment of detainees were reexamined and altered. From this perspective, the exposure of prisoner abuses at Abu Ghraib helped to check executive branch abuses of power and restore a more prudent balance with the judicial and legislative branches of government.

This chapter emphasizes that the concept of responsible governance transcends a purely domestic setting. Responsibility also applies to the international arena and to the image that other nations acquire of the United States. In its codification of behavior, international law has attempted to go beyond the simplistic notion that "might makes right." Wanton disregard for basic human rights and for conceptions of law and order should be viewed with alarm. The two cases discussed here suggest that custodians of the law, protectors of basic rights, and guardians of freedoms must be especially vigilant during times of war.

The Concept of International Law: Guiding Documents

From the mythical times of King Arthur and the Knights of the Round Table, people have longed for some all-wise, all-powerful body of individuals that distilled truth and dispensed justice to everyone in creation. In a less idealized conceptualization of the world, representatives of nations or tribes gathered at various times to create understandings of what rules they would abide by in regard to distributions of land, reparations, economic sanctions, and punishments for war crimes.

A basic precept of international law is that signatories to various agreements abide by the regulations, that punishment for noncompliance is clear, and that there is a body that has the power to enforce sanctions against violators. The Geneva Convention accords are probably the best known of all international attempts to regulate rules of conduct pertaining to civilians in times of war, prisoners of war, torture, and other issues. It is apparent, however, from the two case studies discussed in this chapter (My Lai and Abu Ghraib) that the honorable goals established in various international agreements are often not achieved. The requirements of treaties are sometimes haphazardly and at times knowingly ignored.

Numerous documents have attempted to provide appropriate rules of conduct in times of war. These documents include the Lieber Code (1863), the Charter of the United Nations (1945), the United Nations Universal Declaration of Human Rights

(1948), the International Covenant on Civil and Political Rights (1966), and the United Nations Convention Against Torture and Other Cruel, Inhuman or Degrading Treatment or Punishment (1985). All these documents foster the ideal of establishing international standards of just, humane behavior. These agreements, however, have sometimes been selectively enforced, leading to the cynical conclusion that the strong can do what they want, when they want, without fear of retaliation. As a corollary, it appears that treaties are only enforced against weaker parties when the stronger party provides the enforcement capacity. Despite these limitations, international treaties, rules, and guidelines do have some benefit in that they establish rough parameters of accepted behavior for civilized, humane, law-abiding societies.

The Theory of International Law

Limitations of the Concept of International Law

International law theorists recognize that humans seek order, welfare, and justice not only within the state in which they live, but also within the international system (Shaw 1997, 12). Recognizing these needs, international law sets out a series of principles that identify how states should behave. International law, with its emphasis on guiding principles of correct action, stands in sharp contrast to power politics, which emphasizes competition, conflict, supremacy, and the struggle for survival. Might or power determines what is right in power politics, not an overriding image of what is good. International law strives to achieve harmony and peaceful regulation of disputes. While striving to graft a measure of humanity onto environments often conducive to barbarity, international law sets a high standard—which, unfortunately, is often ignored.

A primary structural weakness of international law relates to the issue of enforcement. While sovereign states have legislative branches to pass laws, judicial branches that try violators of the law, and executive branches that enforce the law, sovereign states might not accept rulings of international organizations and might not even agree to appear before an international tribunal. There is no centralized executive body that is consistently capable of enforcing determinations of international organizations (Malanczuk 1997, 3). Without an effective structure for enforcement, international law is toothless and can be wantonly ignored or selectively applied. As noted by the sixteenth-century Italian political philosopher Niccolò Machiavelli (1469–1527), order requires both good laws and the ability to enforce the laws—that is, good arms (Burgstaller 2005, 2).

Previous international organizations such as the League of Nations failed because of their inability to rein in the belligerence of sovereign states. The successor to the League of Nations was the United Nations. The UN has intervened militarily in various international conflicts, but as the 1991 Gulf War illustrates, large-scale intervention is likely to be selective and rarely very successful unless it is backed thoroughly by major military powers. Violations of UN agreements have often gone unpunished because of the UN's unwillingness or inability to commit the military forces necessary to enforce compliance. These weaknesses have led to various unflattering images of international law, including the following:

- The orphan theory—the idea that international law is so weak and unable to assert itself that it can be, and is, consistently disregarded. At best, only dreamers put any reliance on international law.
- The harlot theory—the idea that international law is so vague and ill defined that with some

legalistic gymnastics it can be made to serve virtually every policy.

- The jailer theory—the idea that the central feature of every legal system is the threat of punishment. If there are no means to enforce the law by punishing violators, international law lacks the essential characteristics of law.
- The never-never theory—the idea that until international law is universally enforceable, there can be little reliance on it. (Ku and Diehl 1998, 5–6)

These theories of international law might suggest that international law is hopelessly flawed: either a depository of empty rhetoric or a rationalization for the strong to impose their will on others. This view, however, is too negative, since international law serves some useful functions. Primarily, international law provides a framework for accepted rules of behavior. It sets parameters for interaction and establishes forums for resolving disputes. Furthermore, international law identifies the values and goals that are honored by the international community. It promotes decent behavior in regard to regulating the use of force and protecting human rights, the environment, prisoners of war, and civilians in war zones.

Primary among the differences between international law and laws that apply within sovereign nations is the concept of vertical versus horizontal jurisdiction. Under vertical jurisdiction, a legislature has the power to enact and enforce legislation. Horizontal jurisdiction denotes a condition in which all states are sovereign and theoretically equal. Under horizontal jurisdiction, therefore, implementation of law is dependent upon the voluntary participation of sovereign states.

International law strives to attain justice and order throughout the world. Two main schools of thought have evolved in mainstream Western conceptions of international law: the naturalist view and the positivist view (Malanczuk 1997, 15). The naturalist view was promoted in the seventeenth century by the Dutch writer Hugo Grotius (1583–1645). Due to the popularity of his writings, Grotius is often regarded as the founder of modern international law. According to Grotius, the basic principles of all law (national as well as international) were derived from principles of justice that had a universal and eternal validity. This universal validity could be discovered by pure reason. Law was therefore to be found in nature, not manmade. The intellectual position advanced by Grotius borrowed heavily from earlier natural law philosophers.

Grotius contended that the existence of natural law was the automatic consequence of the fact that men lived together in society and were capable of understanding that certain rules were necessary for the preservation of their society. For example, according to this line of argument, the prohibition against murder was a rule of natural law that was independent of any government legislation because every intelligent person would realize that such a rule was just and necessary for the preservation of human society.

In contrast to the natural law discussed by Grotius, the positivist perspective holds that law is manmade and varies from time to time and from place to place. Positivism regarded the actual behavior of states as the basis of international law. It recognized that law and justice are not identical since some manmade laws in a given time and place may not be just (Malanczuk 1997, 17). The early positivist school emphasized the importance of custom and treaties as sources of international law.

In the eighteenth century, the popularity of legal positivism increased and natural law theories were ridiculed. A leading figure among eighteenth-century legal positivists was the Dutch jurist Cornelius van Bynkershoek (1673–1746). Bynkershoek asserted that the bases of international law were customs and treaties commonly consented to by sovereign states. Positivists such as Bynkershoek contended that laws and rules were made by human beings; therefore there was no necessary connection between morality and the validity of law. According to the positivist perspective, a law is valid if it is formulated in the proper manner, by a recognized authority, regardless of its moral implications.

The Historical Development of the Concept of International Law

International laws can be traced to the beginnings of recorded history. In 3000 BC, the rulers of ancient Egypt and Mesopotamia signed treaties that were mutually beneficial. A modern conception of international law emerged at the conclusion of the Thirty Years War and the signing of the Peace of Westphalia in 1648 (Wright 1961, 21; Malanczuk 1997, 11). Recognizing that nations or states could be independent of the church, this peace treaty allowed individual princes to decide the religion for their area. The Peace of Westphalia also established a mechanism for disputes to be peacefully settled by a third party. If no settlement could be found in three years, others were allowed to come to the aid of the injured party and the use of force was permitted. This system lasted until the French Revolution of 1789.

The French Revolution challenged the established order and international rules with its ideas of freedom and self-determination. The philosophies underlying the French Revolution denied the rights of monarchs to dispose of territory and populations according to their own discretion. After the defeat of Napoleon in 1815, however, the Congress of Vienna reestablished the previous order. The Holy Alliance of Christian nations was created to intervene against nationalist uprisings that threatened the status quo. This cooperation between nations established continuity in Europe and strengthened the concept of international law (Malanczuk 1997, 12).

During the nineteenth century, efforts were made to conclude various international agreements that humanized and codified the law of warfare. Although not an international agreement, the Lieber Code of 1863 was formulated by the United States government during the Civil War to provide instructions regarding the rules of warfare. The Geneva Convention of 1864 established international guidelines aimed at assisting the wounded and created the International Committee of the Red Cross (ICRC) to oversee treatment of the wounded and sick. The Hague Peace Conferences of 1899 and 1907 produced agreements dealing with the law of land warfare, the law of sea warfare, and peaceful settlement of disputes.

At the conclusion of World War I, the League of Nations was created in a futile effort to achieve everlasting peace. Seeking to regulate the behavior of states, the League established the Permanent Court of International Justice in The Hague as a judicial body to arbitrate disputes. This court was the forerunner of the present International Court of Justice. After World War II, international law was established through the efforts of the UN. The UN Charter was originally signed by fifty-one nations with the aim of fostering law and order in the international community. The UN gave considerable recognition to rights of individuals in the world community in contrast to classical (pre–World War II) international law, which merely considered the individual as an object of regulations. After World War II, international organizations developed specific guidelines that protected the rights of all human beings regardless of where they resided (Malanczuk 1997, 31). For example, in 1948 the General Assembly of the

United Nations adopted the Universal Declaration of Human Rights.

The preamble to this declaration asserts the inherent dignity, equality, and inalienable rights of all members of the human family as the foundation of freedom, justice, and peace in the world. It also contends that disregard and contempt for human rights have resulted in barbarous acts that have outraged the conscience of mankind. Human rights are to be protected by the rule of law. The declaration further contends that member states, in cooperation with the UN, have pledged themselves to promote universal respect for and observance of human rights and fundamental freedoms. The Universal Declaration of Human Rights is viewed as a common standard for all peoples and all nations. It advocates that every nation should strive by teaching and education to promote respect for specified rights and freedoms and to secure their universal and effective recognition.

The values of human rights come under particular pressure in times of war, when the drive for military success leads signatories to international agreements to suddenly forget or ignore important provisions. International law carefully formulates extensive rules and regulations, but they exist as empty phrases unless they are followed. The absence of international police with the means and desire to enforce broad rules of behavior prevents a more faithful execution of international laws. These problems have been identified in the American war against terrorism. The high demands of war seem to be correlated with abuses of civilians and prisoners. This has been true in Iraq, Afghanistan, Vietnam, and wars throughout history. While warfare has not been prevented, despite the best intentions of the League of Nations and the UN, for well over 100 years concerted efforts have been made to regulate war. The Geneva Conventions represent the most well known of these efforts, particularly in regard to the treatment of civilians and torture.

International Agreements Relating to Torture and Treatment of Civilians

The Geneva Conventions and International Humanitarian Law

The Geneva Conventions laid the foundation for what is referred to as international humanitarian law. The first Geneva Convention was the result of the carnage of the Battle of Solferino in northern Italy in 1859. More than 41,000 troops from the French and Austrian armies died in the battle, and it is estimated that another 40,000 soldiers who took part in the battle later died of their wounds. In 1862, a spectator to the battle, Henri Dunant, published the book *A Memory of Solferino*, in which he appealed for volunteers to care for those who are wounded in the course of warfare. Dunant urged that these volunteers, who would assist the military medical services, should be recognized and protected through an international agreement. As a result of Dunant's efforts, an international conference was held in Geneva in 1863 and ultimately an agreement was signed that led to the founding of the International Committee of the Red Cross.

In 1864, the Swiss government hosted the Convention for the Amelioration of the Conditions of the Wounded in Armies in the Field, which endorsed the ideals of the Red Cross. The aim of the gathering was to come up with an agreement that could save lives, alleviate the suffering of the wounded, and protect civilians who were in the act of rendering aid. The conference established the flag of the Red Cross—a red cross on a white background, the reverse of the Swiss flag. The Red Cross would protect those serving the wounded.

The ten articles that came out of the Convention for the Amelioration of the Conditions of the Wounded in Armies in the Field are considered to represent the first treaty of international humanitarian law (International Red Cross n.d.). The articles established basic principles of behavior for Europeans in the mid-nineteenth century. The essential rules of international humanitarian law that were derived from the articles are as follows:

- Persons who do not or can no longer take part in the hostilities are entitled to respect for their life and for their physical and mental integrity.
- It is forbidden to kill or wound an adversary who surrenders or who can no longer take part in the fighting.
- Captured combatants and civilians who find themselves under the authority of the adverse party are entitled to respect for their life, their dignity, their personal rights, and their political, religious, and other convictions. They must be protected against all acts of violence or reprisal.
- No one may be denied basic judicial guarantees.
- No one may be subjected to physical or mental torture or to cruel or degrading corporal punishment or other treatment.
- The parties to a conflict must at all times distinguish between civilian populations and combatants. Neither the civilian population nor individual civilians may be attacked. Attacks may be made solely against military objectives. (International Red Cross n.d.)

A second Geneva conference in 1906 extended the principles of the Geneva Convention of 1864. A third conference met in Geneva in 1949 and addressed the issue of the treatment of prisoners of war. This treaty, the Third Geneva Convention (GCIII), established criteria for who should and who should not be considered a prisoner of war. It also specified permissible and improper treatment of prisoners. Relevant sections of the Third Geneva Convention are described in Table 5.1.

The objective of the Third Geneva Convention was to ensure humane treatment of prisoners. It consisted of 143 articles addressing topics such as the general protection of prisoners of war, captivity, internment, food and clothing, medical attention, treatment of captured chaplains, religious rights of prisoners, discipline, transfers, work, financial resources of prisoners, and complaints. The 1949 GCIII agreement replaced the Prisoners of War Convention of 1929, an earlier Geneva treaty relating to the treatment of prisoners. The 1929 agreement was shorter, consisting of only ninety-seven articles, and less specific. The 1949 agreement was more explicit, broadening categories of persons entitled to prisoner of war status and more precisely defining conditions of captivity and work responsibilities of prisoners.

The Third Geneva Convention treaty laid out clear guidelines for proper treatment of prisoners. For example, Article 13 of GCIII states, "prisoners of war must at all times be humanely treated." Article 87 bars "corporal punishment, imprisonment in premises without daylight and, in general, any form of torture or cruelty." Article 89 states, "In no case shall disciplinary punishments be inhuman, brutal or dangerous to the health of prisoners of war." GCIII further stipulates that no physical or moral coercion should be exercised to obtain information from civilians in times of war. Support for GCIII placed the United States at the forefront of support for human rights in the 1940s (McCoy 2006, 15).

The determination of prisoner of war (POW) status has assumed particular importance in America's war against terrorism. Since the beginning of U.S. military operations in Afghanistan in October 2001, both Taliban and al-Qaeda fighters have been detained. These detainees were categorized as "unlawful combatants" and denied POW status as well as the privileges of POWs described in the Third Geneva Convention agreement.

Table 5.1

Provisions of Third Geneva Convention

Article 3: Violence to life and person, in particular murder of all kinds, mutilation, cruel treatment and torture, taking of hostages, outrages upon personal dignity, humiliating and degrading treatment prohibited.

Article 4: Prisoner of war identified as persons belonging, or having belonged, to the armed forces of the occupied country, if the occupying power considers it necessary by reason of such allegiance to intern them.

Article 5: Should any doubt arise as to prisoner of war status such persons should enjoy the protections of the present agreement until such time as their status has been determined by a competent tribunal.

Article 13: Prisoners of war must at all times be humanely treated, prisoners of war must at all times be protected, particularly against acts of violence or intimidation and against insults.

Article 14: Prisoners of war are entitled in all circumstances to respect for their persons and their honor. Women shall be treated as favorably as men.

Article 17: No physical or mental torture, nor any other form of coercion, may be inflicted on prisoners of war to secure from them information.

Article 19: Prisoners of war shall be evacuated, as soon as possible after capture, to camps situated in an area far enough from the combat zone for them to be out of danger.

Article 25: Prisoners of war shall be housed under similar conditions as those of the forces of the detaining power that are housed in the same area. Conditions should make allowances for the habits and customs of the prisoners.

Article 39: Every prisoner of war camp shall be put under the immediate authority of a responsible commissioned officer belonging to the regular armed forces of the detaining power. Such officer shall have in his possession a copy of the present Convention; he shall ensure that its provisions are known to the camp staff and the guard and shall be responsible, under the direction of his government, for its application.

Article 41: In every camp the text of the present Geneva Convention shall be posted, in the prisoners' own language, at places where all may read them.

Article 87: Collective punishment for individual acts, corporal punishments, imprisonment in premises without daylight and, in general, any form of torture or cruelty prohibited.

Article 89: In no case shall disciplinary punishments be inhuman, brutal or dangerous to the health of prisoners of war.

Source: Geneva Convention relative to the Treatment of Prisoners of War, 1949.

Many critics disagree with the U.S. government regarding the proper classification of these detainees, specifically whether they should be afforded the status of prisoners of war. Some organizations, such as Human Rights Watch, claim that the issue is moot because persons not entitled to POW status under the Third Geneva Convention (including those classified as "unlawful combatants") would still be entitled to protections under the Fourth Geneva Convention. The Fourth Geneva Convention agreement was published in 1949 and stipulates that noncombatants or members of armed forces who have laid down their arms shall in all circumstances be treated humanely. Human Rights Watch, an organization based in the United States that investigates human rights abuses, notes that the International Committee of the Red Cross, in an authoritative commentary, states, "nobody in enemy hands can fall outside the law." Under international law, every person in enemy hands would be either a prisoner of war covered by the Third Geneva Convention, medical personnel covered by the First Geneva Convention, or a civilian covered by the Fourth Geneva Convention (Human Rights Watch 2004).

According to Human Rights Watch, an organization of more than 150 professionals (lawyers, journalists, academics, and country experts) working for human rights around the world, U.S. policies do not conform to Geneva Convention accords, particularly in regard to classifying captured individuals as "unlawful combatants," "illegal combatants," or "battlefield detainees." Human Rights Watch states that the U.S. position (exemplified in the January 11, 2001, assertion by Secretary of Defense Donald Rumsfeld that those held as "unlawful combatants" do not have any rights under the Geneva Convention) is out of alignment with the Geneva Convention accords on three counts. First, all detainees from a conflict (such as that in Afghanistan) may not be categorized as exempt from POW status, since such determinations must be made on an individual basis by a competent tribunal. Second, there is a presumption that the captured combatant is a POW until determined otherwise. Third, all persons apprehended in the context of international armed conflict receive some level of protection under Geneva Convention accords (Human Rights Watch 2004). This position that all people should be given some level of protection has also been endorsed by the International Red Cross.

The Fourth Geneva Convention (GCIV) specifically addressed the issue of protecting civilians during times of war. Adopted in 1949 and partly based on the 1907 Hague Convention, it makes explicit the protections that should be given to civilians during times of war. The Fourth Convention covers the treatment of diplomats, spies, and

bystanders; mandates humane treatment for "protected persons" (such as civilians, the wounded, and POWs); and requires respect for the religion of protected persons. In addition, no physical or moral coercion can be used against protected persons in order to obtain information. These prescriptions, in general, lay out rough guidelines for how civilians in war zones should be treated. Specific provisions of the GCIV are identified in Table 5.2.

Article 3, prohibiting the use of specific acts of violence against persons taking no active part in the hostilities, is of particular importance. This article applies to all four Geneva Conventions and is often referred to as Common Article 3. It clearly prohibits acts of violence against life and person and outrages upon personal dignity, including humiliating and degrading treatment. Articles 4 and 5 define the category "protected persons." This definition is of importance since it identifies the scope of Geneva Convention protections. Article 4 is particularly relevant since it states that in all cases persons shall be treated with humanity even if they are viewed as a threat to state security.

Other Geneva Convention articles set minimum protections of due process for those detained and minimum rights such as protections against transfer to a county where detainees fear persecution. During the war on terrorism, the United States was involved in transferring individuals to places that had a reputation for torturing detainees. Common destinations for transferring terrorist suspects included Egypt, Morocco, Syria, and Jordan. All of these countries have been cited for human-rights violations by the State Department, and are known for torturing suspects (Mayer 2005). The *Washington Post* also reported that the CIA was interrogating terror suspects at undisclosed locations in Eastern Europe. The existence and location of such prison facilities, referred to as "black sites," were not widely publicized but at various times included sites in Thailand, Afghanistan, and several

Table 5.2

Provisions of Fourth Geneva Convention

Article 3: Violence to life and person, in particular murder of all kinds, mutilation, cruel treatment and torture, taking of hostages, outrages upon personal dignity, humiliating and degrading treatment prohibited.

Article 4: Protected persons are those who in case of a conflict find themselves in the hands of a party to the conflict of which they are not nationals.

Article 5: If protected persons are suspected of hostile activities such individuals shall not be entitled to rights under the Geneva Convention if such exercise would harm state security. In all cases persons shall be treated with humanity.

Article 27: Protected persons are entitled to respect for their persons, their honor, their family rights, their religious convictions and their customs. They shall be protected against all acts of violence or threats. Women shall be protected against acts on their honor, in particular against rape, enforced prostitution, or any form of indecent assault.

Article 31: No physical or moral coercion shall be exercised against protected persons, in particular to obtain information from them or from third persons.

Article 32: A protected person shall not have anything done to them as to cause physical suffering or extermination. The prohibition applies not only to murder, torture, corporal punishments, mutilation and medical experiments but also to any other measures of brutality.

Article 33: Pillage as well as reprisals against protected persons are prohibited.

Article 34: The taking of hostages is prohibited.

Article 37: Protected persons who are confined pending proceedings or serving a sentence involving loss of liberty, shall be humanely treated.

Article 43: Any protected person who has been interned shall be entitled to have the action reconsidered as soon as possible by an appropriate court or administrative board.

Article 45: In no circumstances shall a protected person be transferred to a county where he or she may have reason to fear persecution for political opinions or religious beliefs.

Article 72: Accused persons shall have the right to present evidence necessary to their defense and may call witnesses. They shall have the right to be assisted by a qualified counsel of their choice.

Source: Geneva Convention relative to the Protection of Civilian Persons in Time of War, 1949.

countries in Eastern Europe (Priest 2005). Terrorist suspects were denied Geneva protections because they were not classified as prisoners of war.

Other Understandings Concerning Prisoners, Torture, and Treatment of Civilians

While the four Geneva Conventions are the best-known treaties dealing with rules of war, a number of other treaties and agreements have helped to

define acceptable treatment of prisoners or civilians in war zones. An early American attempt to codify rules of war was the Lieber Code of 1863. The Lieber Code (also referred to as the Lieber Instructions or Instructions for the Government of Armies of the United States in the Field, General Order No. 100), instructed soldiers how to conduct themselves during the American Civil War. Its 157 articles and 10 sections provided specific guidelines for the treatment of civilians, partisans, spies, and prisoners of war. It also covered such diverse topics as retaliation, exchange of prisoners, and parole. Although the Lieber Code was binding only on U.S. forces, it exerted a strong influence on later international agreements. In particular, it influenced later international conferences on the laws of war, such as the conference at Brussels in 1874 and the two conferences at The Hague in 1899 and 1907. It is widely considered as a precursor to the Geneva Convention accords.

Important provisions of the Lieber Code addressing treatment of civilians and prisoners include the following:

- Article 16—Military necessity does not admit to cruelty; that is, the infliction of suffering for the sake of suffering or for revenge, nor of maiming or wounding except in fight, nor of torture to extort confessions.
- Article 19—Commanders, whenever admissible, inform the enemy of their intention to bombard a place, so that the non-combatants, and especially the women and children, may be removed before the bombardment commences.
- Article 22—The unarmed citizen is to be spared in person, property, and honor as much as the exigencies of war will admit.
- Article 23—Private citizens are no longer murdered, enslaved, or carried off to distant parts, and the inoffensive individual is as little disturbed in his private relations as the commander of the hostile troops can afford to grant.
- Article 28—Retaliation will never be resorted to as a measure of mere revenge, but only as a means of retribution, cautiously and unavoidably used. Unjust or inconsiderate retaliation moves the belligerents farther from the mitigating rules of regular war, and leads them nearer to the internecine wars of savages.
- Article 37—The United States acknowledges and protect, in hostile countries occupied by them, religion and morality.

- Article 44—All wanton violence committed against persons in the invaded country, all destruction of property not commanded by the authorized officer, all robbery, all pillage or sacking, all rape, wounding, maiming, or killing of inhabitants, are prohibited under the penalty of death, or such other severe punishment as may seem adequate for the gravity of the offense.
- Article 56—A prisoner of war is subject to no punishment for being a public enemy, nor is any revenge wreaked upon him by the intentional infliction of any suffering, or disgrace, by cruel imprisonment, want of food, by mutilation, death, or any other barbarity.
- Article 71—Whoever intentionally inflicts additional wounds on an enemy already wholly disabled, or kills such an enemy, or who orders or encourages soldiers to do so, shall suffer death, if duly convicted, whether he belongs to the Army of the United States, or is an enemy captured after having committed his misdeed. (International Red Cross n.d; www.civilwarhome.com/liebercode.htm n.d.)

Two other international agreements that define the parameters of acceptable and unacceptable conduct in regard to civilians and prisoners are the 1966 International Covenant on Civil and Political Rights and the 1984 Convention Against Torture and Other Cruel, Inhuman or Degrading Treatment or Punishment. Both these agreements were promulgated by representatives to the UN.

On December 16, 1966, the General Assembly of the United Nations adopted the International Covenant on Civil and Political Rights. The preamble to this agreement explicitly commits signatories to recognize the inalienable rights of all members of the human family, rights derived from the inherent dignity of the human person. Articles

6 and 7 of the covenant are relevant to the issues of torture and treatment of civilians discussed in the case studies. For example, Article 6 states that every human being has the inherent right to life. This right is protected by law. No one should be arbitrarily deprived of life. Article 7 states that no one should be subjected to torture or to cruel, inhuman, or degrading treatment or punishment, while Article 9 provides for due process protections and rule of law. Article 9 specifically states that no one should be subjected to arbitrary arrest or detention or deprived of liberty except in accordance with procedure established by law. Anyone arrested or detained on a criminal charge should be brought promptly before a judge or other officer authorized by law to exercise judicial power and is entitled to trial within a reasonable time or to release (UN Office of the High Commissioner for Human Rights 2007a).

The UN General Assembly adopted the Convention Against Torture and Other Cruel, Inhuman or Degrading Treatment or Punishment on December 10, 1984. The Convention Against Torture defines the practice of torture as any act by which severe physical or mental pain or suffering is intentionally inflicted on a person for such purposes as obtaining information or a confession. The agreement is complete and explicit in its prohibitions against torture, declaring that no exceptional circumstances, including a state of war or a threat of war, internal political instability, or other public emergency, and no order from a superior officer or public authority can be invoked as a justification of torture (McCoy 2006, 100).

The Convention Against Torture unambiguously defines the UN's position. For example, Article 2 notes that signatory states should take effective legislative, administrative, judicial, or other action to prevent acts of torture in any territory under their jurisdiction. Article 3 orders that no government can expel, return, or extradite a person to another state where there are substantial grounds for believing that he or she would be in danger of being tortured. Article 10 declares that education regarding the prohibition against torture must be included in the training of all law enforcement personnel, medical personnel, public officials, and others involved in the custody, interrogation, or treatment of any individual who is subjected to any form of arrest, detention, or imprisonment.

Other provisions of the UN Convention Against Torture refer to prevention and investigation. For example, Article 12 mandates prompt and impartial investigation by competent authorities whenever a signatory state has reasonable ground to believe that an act of torture has been committed in any territory under its jurisdiction. Article 13 declares that all individuals who allege that they have been subjected to torture have the right to complain to, and to have their case promptly and impartially examined by, competent authorities. Article 16 requires that each signatory state should attempt to prevent other types of cruel, inhuman, or degrading treatment even if not classified as torture (UN Office of the High Commissioner for Human Rights 2007b).

The 1984 Convention Against Torture was unanimously approved by UN vote and endorsed by U.S. president Ronald Reagan. Reagan sent it to Congress for approval in 1988. The Reagan administration, however, proposed an array of reservations that stalled ratification in the U.S. Senate until 1994. One of the reservations related to the use of psychological torture. The State and Justice Departments of the Reagan administration declared that the UN agreement contained "unacceptable levels of vagueness" in the definition of mental pain. In order to remedy this problem, the State Department drafted an exception to U.S. approval that defined psychological torture to mean prolonged mental harm by (1) the intentional infliction or threatened infliction of severe physical pain or suffering, (2) the administration of mind-altering substances, (3) the threat of imminent death, or (4) the threat that another person will imminently be subject to death. Notably, the State Department's view of mental harm excluded techniques that the Central Intelligence Agency had used over several decades, including sensory deprivation (such as the placing hoods over someone's head in order to cut off sight and hearing), self-inflicted pain (such as making someone stand on a box with arms extended for long periods of time), and disorientation caused by isolation and denial of sleep (McCoy 2006, 100).

Court decisions in other countries have also further defined the parameters of acceptable actions. For example, in 1999, the Israeli Supreme Court considered the legality of the use of specific types of force used by the Israeli General Security Service (GSS) in interrogating Palestinians suspected of terrorist activity. GSS (later known as the Israel Security Agency or Shin Bet) was responsible for Israeli counterintelligence and internal security. The Israeli Supreme Court ruled that the extreme methods used by GSS in interrogating suspects were illegal. The court determined that the agency's power to interrogate people suspected of terrorism was similar to the power of the ordinary police force and that interrogations used by the GSS should be "fair" and "reasonable."

The Israeli court based its findings on international law. The court stated that a reasonable investigation is "free of torture, free of cruel, inhuman treatment of the subject and free of any degrading handling whatsoever. . . . This conclusion is in perfect accord with (various) International Law treaties—to which Israel is a signatory—which prohibit the use of torture, 'cruel inhuman treatment' and 'degrading treatment'" (Gurr-Ayre 2004, 186). The court further declared that the legislative branch of the Israeli government should provide authorization if force was to be used in interroga-

tions. This position was consistent with the principle of separation of powers, the rule of law, and democracy. The perception of the "necessity" of preventing danger to legitimate interests did not, in the eyes of the court, allow GSS interrogators to use physical means during interrogations. Although the Israeli court did not impose a general ban on the use of force during interrogations, it concluded that it was the role of the legislative branch of the government, not security forces, to decide whether extreme coercion techniques were appropriate. The legislators could consider the security needs of the nation in their deliberations on the legality of various means of interrogation.

Conclusions

Many people in modern nations have condemned the use of torture and murder of innocent civilians, even in times of war. Despite a wide array of international treaties and humanitarian law, however, the use of torture persists. More than thirty years ago, in fact, Amnesty International (1975, 114–242) noted the widespread use of torture throughout Africa, Asia, Western Europe, Eastern Europe and the Soviet Union, the Americas, and the Middle East. Greece, Algeria, Chile, Cambodia, Israel, Argentina, Northern Ireland, and South Africa are just a few of the countries cited for torture in modern times.

Torture and abuse of civilians has once again become a high-priority subject in the United States. Alleged abuses in Afghanistan, at Abu Ghraib, and at the U.S. naval base at Guantanamo as well as alleged murder and rape of civilians in Iraq, have brought these subjects to the nation's attention. These subjects are addressed here in Case No. 5, which addresses the My Lai massacre in Vietnam in 1968, and Case No. 6, which looks at abuse in the Abu Ghraib prison complex of Iraq.

If history is any guide, it seems to infer that

trends are not linear. Abuses occur, horror is expressed, some people (usually low-ranking officials) are punished, rhetorical statements proclaim the triumph of justice, abuses recur, and the cycle repeats itself. Both case studies in this chapter indicate that representatives of the United States have engaged in behavior deemed to be illegal by international law and international agreements. At My Lai, U.S. military personnel killed unarmed women and children in an assault on a defenseless village. Rules of engagement were at best ambiguous. It remains unclear whether the assault at My Lai was an aberration of a few disgruntled soldiers or encouraged and approved by individuals higher up in the chain of command. This "rotten apple" hypothesis of wrongdoing by a few aberrant individuals, which effectively absolves higher-ups of any guilt, was revisited in the Abu Ghraib trials.

At Abu Ghraib, shocking photographs of piles of naked prison detainees jarred the sensitivities of American citizens. As at My Lai, abusive behavior was attributed to a few low-ranking soldiers who allegedly acted counter to official guidelines. Seven enlisted personnel—no officers—were tried before a military tribunal and punished, some by fairly lengthy prison sentences. The question that remains is how, after purportedly vigorously championing human rights and individual rights since World War II, the United States became linked to such questionable behavior at both Abu Ghraib and My Lai. How does the concept of responsibility equate with torture and massacre? Are government representatives in violation of international or higher laws? What guideposts should responsible administrators follow?

In both the cases of My Lai and Abu Ghraib, a few scapegoats were identified and punished. This action, however, avoided the more fundamental questions of policy and accountability. If one accepts the possibility of international law and the rule of law, then responsible governance is defined by ad

herence to rules. An objective of international agreements such as the Geneva Convention accords was to prevent egregious abuses to civilized sensibilities. Such agreements were forged not out of idealized constructs of what a nice world should look like, but from realistic views of people's capacity for inhuman treatment of other humans. The question to ask about both My Lai and Abu Ghraib is whether the spirit as well as the letter of international rules were followed. Both Abu Ghraib and My Lai serve as reality checks on how well the high-minded human rights rhetoric expounded in the United States correlates with actions on the ground. Responsible governance seeks to narrow the wide divide between the rhetoric, the law, and the reality.

CASE NO. 5: My Lai

An Overview

The My Lai incident became synonymous with everything that was wrong with the American engagement in Vietnam. It illustrated illegal behavior, cover-up, and the pursuit of justice through rule of law. The case exemplified both responsible and irresponsible governance during a critical period of American history. From the dual perspectives of ethics and responsible governance, My Lai reflected a severe breakdown in behavior that violated natural law, international humanitarian law, and military rules of engagement.

The truth about My Lai was revealed only after ex-GIs came forward to question behavior they had witnessed. This open airing helped to establish parameters of acceptable and unacceptable conduct. This case should provide a guide to assess responsible actions in present and future military engagements. Ethical treatment of civilian noncombatants remains an issue whether the fighting occurs in Vietnam, Iraq, Afghanistan, or other regions of the world.

The basic facts of the My Lai case are relatively clear. There was an assault on a Vietnamese village in 1968; women and children were killed; the incident was investigated; and one of the perpetrators involved in the incident was convicted and sentenced to life in prison. He was later pardoned. The implications of My Lai, however, remain clouded. My Lai helped to turn Americans against the war in Vietnam and opened their eyes to American abuses. My Lai also suggested that a workable system was still in place to punish violations of international law. The following chronology identifies important dates relating to the My Lai incident itself as well the actions taken to identify and punish wrongdoers.

- February 1968—Discipline begins to break down in Charlie Company of the 11th Brigade in the Americal Division.
- March 15, 1968—During a company level briefing, Charlie Company's commanding officer, Ernest Medina, urges his soldiers to take more aggressive action against the enemy.
- March 16, 1968—Charlie Company destroys the village of My Lai, demolishing every house and killing many Vietnamese women and children.
- Around March 19, 1968—Helicopter doorman, Ron Ridenhour, flies over My Lai and notices the body of a woman spread out as if on display.
- Early May 1968—Ridenhour meets up with friends he knew from training and they begin telling him about My Lai. He begins collecting information.
- Early December 1968—Ridenhour discharged from Army.
- March 29, 1969—Ridenhour sends thirty copies of a letter describing behavior of American GIs at My Lai to prominent leaders.

- April 23, 1969—Political leaders take note of Ridenhour's letter and begin asking questions. Chief of Staff William Westmoreland turns My Lai questions over to the Office of Inspector General, the army's main investigatory agency. Colonel William Wilson is assigned to head an investigation.
- August 4, 1969—Wilson's report is submitted to Chief of Staff Westmoreland, the findings are turned over to the Army's criminal investigation division (CID).
- September 5, 1969—Lieutenant William Calley is charged with premeditated murder for the death of 109 Oriental human beings near the village of My Lai.
- November 17, 1970—Court-martial trial of Calley begins.
- March 29, 1971—Calley found guilty of premeditated murder of at least twenty-two Vietnamese civilians.
- March 31, 1971—Calley sentenced to life in prison with hard labor.
- April 1, 1971—President Nixon announces that Calley is to be released from the Fort Benning stockade and assigned house arrest.
- September 10, 1975—Calley granted parole, after serving about three and a half years.

A variety of inferences can be made from the chronology described above. It is clear that U.S. army personnel engaged in unlawful behavior at My Lai on March 16, 1968. Only one member of the armed forces, however, was convicted of a crime and sentenced. Lieutenant William Calley was sentenced to life in prison, yet he was placed under house arrest rather than in the stockade. In 1975, Calley was paroled after serving about three and a half years of his sentence. The mission that precipitated the illegal behavior and criminal conviction of Calley is described below.

Assault at My Lai

The assault at My Lai was conducted by soldiers of Charlie Company who were part of a task force consisting of three rifle companies and an artillery battery. The task force had reason to believe that they were going to conduct an important operation. The army brought in a photographer and reporter on the day of the assault to document the attack. GIs in the units comprising the task force believed they were finally getting the attention they deserved.

The assault plan included attacks by a platoon of Charlie Company (headed by Lieutenant Calley) and another platoon of Charlie Company. These two platoons were assigned the mission to sweep into the village of My Lai; a third platoon was held in reserve. Above the ground, the action would be monitored at the 2,500-foot level by Colonel Oran Henderson, commander of the 11th Brigade. My Lai had about 700 residents. By 8 A.M. on March 16 Calley's platoon entered the village. They encountered families cooking rice in front of their homes. The men began their usual search-and-destroy task of pulling people from homes, interrogating them, and searching for Vietcong.

On this day, however, the men of Calley's platoon went far beyond usual search and destroy practices. A man was stabbed in the back with a bayonet; another man was picked up, thrown down a well, and a grenade was lobbed in the well. A group of fifteen to twenty mostly older women were gathered around a temple, kneeling and praying. They were all executed with shots to the back of their heads. Eighty or so villagers were taken from their homes and herded together. Calley ordered one of his soldiers to "waste them," then joined the soldier in firing into the group from a distance of ten to fifteen feet.

The assault at My Lai was followed by an army photographer, Ron Haeberle, who was assigned to document what was supposed to be a significant encounter with the enemy. Haeberle later stated that he saw about thirty different GIs kill about 100 civilians. Calley was at a drainage ditch where about seventy to eighty old men, women, and children had been brought. Calley ordered members of his platoon to push the civilians into the ditch, then ordered his men to shoot into the ditch. By noon, all the buildings at My Lai were destroyed and its people dead or dying. Soldiers later said they did not remember seeing one military-age male in the entire place. Twenty months later, army investigators discovered three mass graves containing the bodies of about 500 villagers (Linder n.d.)

Not unexpectedly, diverging accounts of the action of March 16, 1968, are available. One Saigon-based report, which was sent to the Pentagon on the night of March 16, indicated that the final body count for the entire task force (My Lai was a small part of the larger task force operation) was 128. Three enemy weapons were reported captured.

Charlie Company was given credit for fifteen of the 128 enemy kills. None of the company's claimed kills was reported as inside the village of My Lai. The head of the Task Force, Lieutenant Colonel Frank Barker, is quoted as stating that "the combat assault went like clockwork. We had two entire companies [that] were put on the ground in less than an hour" (Hersh 1970, 79). Accounts of the March 16 operation appeared in the *Trident,* the weekly newspaper of the Americal Division, and in military publications such as the *Pacific Stars and Stripes.* A story of the engagement was published on the front page of the *New York Times* and in other news outlets on March 17 noting that two Americal Division companies had caught the North Vietnamese in a pincer movement, killing 128 enemy soldiers. Newspaper accounts explained: "The operation is another American offensive to clear enemy pockets still threatening the cities. While the two companies of United States soldiers moved in on the enemy force from opposite sides, heavy artillery barrages and armed helicopters were called in to pound the North Vietnamese soldiers." Two American GIs were reported killed and ten wounded during the operation. There was no mention of civilian casualties (Hersh 1970, 79).

The assault at My Lai would become synonymous with the irresponsible use of American power in Vietnam, and became a moral embarrassment. At a minimum, My Lai violated basic instructions that GIs received upon arriving in Vietnam—respecting the traditions of the native people, protecting civilians who resided in Vietcong areas, and not harming unarmed civilians who were acting in a non-threatening manner (Hammer 1970, 110). My Lai did more than violate these instructions. It cast a pall on the entire U.S. military, destroyed any positive images of American combat troops, and discredited the sacrifices of U.S. soldiers who not participate in war crimes. My Lai undermined any moral superiority that Americans were hoping to claim and weakened the legitimacy of the entire U.S. operation. Some Americans, however, sought to defend the assault at My Lai on the basis of combat stress, the need to defend America, the breakdown of leadership at the brigade and company level, and confusion about the proper rules of engagement.

Psychological State of Soldiers and Understanding of Rules of Engagement Prior to Assault at My Lai

My Lai did not occur in a vacuum but was influenced by the general milieu prevalent in Lieutenant Calley's unit. Charlie Company was operating near a Vietcong stronghold and U.S. soldiers termed the surrounding area "Indian Country" for its perceived danger and lawlessness (Hammer 1970, 88). Calley's company was responsible to search and destroy Vietcong throughout the region. Much of

the area was considered a free-fire zone, defined as any area ostensibly cleared of all civilian noncombatants, leaving only enemy troops (Olson 1999, 176). The men of Charlie Company were told that the Vietcong had had free rein in the region for twenty or twenty-five years.

The danger of the area had an impact on the GIs in Calley's platoon. Casualties suffered prior to the My Lai incident fueled a desire for revenge. It was understood that GIs were tired of fighting an enemy they could not see. The psychological environment was conducive to questionable conduct: the assault on My Lai represented an opportunity to unleash pent-up frustrations (Gershen 1971, 89). Events preceding the attack on March 16 suggested that control was breaking down within the ranks. For example, interviews of GIs revealed that in February 1968, members of Charlie Company broke the jaw and ribs of an old Vietnamese "papa-san," fired on a person who was walking across a field carrying something that turned out to be a written document in a tube, and shot an old man who was in a well (Hersh 1970, 33).

It was also reported that GIs of Charlie Company were beginning to abuse Vietnamese women, behavior that troubled some members of the company. According to sworn testimony, on one occasion a few GIs accosted a woman working in a field in a friendly area; they took away her baby and then "they raped her and killed her." It was assumed that the soldiers killed the baby also, but this was not verified (Hersh 1970, 34). Two days before the March 16 mission, a small squad from Charlie Company walked into a booby trap. One soldier was killed and others were injured (Hersh 1970, 36).

The unraveling of discipline and the increasingly lawless environment upset a number of the GIs of Charlie Company. One of the soldiers (one of two GIs who did not fire his weapon at My Lai) wrote home to his father, describing the actions of his platoon and asking why seemingly normal guys should act like wild animals (Hersh 1970, 38).

The officers in Charlie Company seemed to have few concerns about the behavior of their unit. This indifference appeared to condone and legitimate the action of the soldiers. Over time, abuse of women as well as abuse of prisoners escalated. According to one GI, prisoners were shot and forced to serve as human mine detectors (Belknap 2002, 56). For at least one member of Charlie Company, My Lai was the logical outcome of a vicious escalation that had begun months earlier: "it was like going from one step to another, worse one. First you'd stop the people, question them, and let them go. Second, you'd stop the people, beat up an old man, and let them go. Third you'd stop the people, beat up an old man, and then shoot him. Fourth, you go in and wipe out a village" (Hersh 1970, 43).

In addition to the desire to avenge the deaths of their buddies, there was pressure on officers in Charlie Company to make their reputation. Those who aspired to careers in the military viewed the war in Vietnam as possibly a once-in-a-lifetime opportunity to achieve both renown and occupational advancement. All these factors—revenge, poor discipline, career reputation, and loss of a moral compass—motivated the troops and precipitated the abuses of My Lai.

The night before the assault on My Lai, the Charlie Company commander, Captain Ernest Medina, reminded his troops of the casualties that their unit had suffered. He urged them to be extremely aggressive. Members of Charlie Company recalled Medina telling them that there were no innocent civilians in the village and that they were all Vietcong. One member of Charlie Company remembered that "Captain Medina told us we might get a chance to revenge the deaths of our fellow GIs" (Hammer 1970, 111). Medina, informed his men that the objective of the mission was to engage and destroy the Vietcong, burn the houses in

the village, blow up bunkers and tunnels, kill the livestock, destroy the crops if possible, and move any civilians out of the area (Hammer 1970, 11).

According to an Episcopal priest who attended a brigade level briefing, the general mood was very hostile and upper level officers said nothing about resettlement of the civilians (Hersh 1972, 75). Officers reportedly demanded more aggressive action in closing with the enemy. Intelligence reports had incorrectly asserted that there would be no civilians in the area at the time of the attack (Hersh 1972, 77). The precise orders that Charlie Company's commander Medina gave to his men at a company level briefing are unclear. One GI testified that Captain Medina ordered the company "to kill everything in the village." The GI stated that members of the company believed that the intent of Medina's directives was for them "to kill every man, woman and child in the village." Another soldier of Charlie Company thought he remembered Medina saying, "When we go into My Lai, it's open season. When we leave nothing will be living." One member of the company was sure that Medina did not order the killing of women and children but to "shoot the enemy" (Hersh 1970, 42). Medina said that Charlie Company would stay in the area "till we clean it up." After the briefing, GIs started drinking beer, smoking pot, and watching a pornographic movie. Because of the parties that, according to testimony, "lasted all night long," there were said to be "a lot of hangovers in the morning" (Gershen 1971, 295).

Lieutenant William Calley was singled out for committing the most egregious of the abuses during the assault at My Lai. Soldiers at the scene reported that Calley was responsible for killing the most Vietnamese in the village (Belknap 2002, 69). Calley did not deny that he killed Vietnamese, but he claimed that he was following the directives of his immediate supervisor, Captain Medina. Calley testified that Medina told him to "get rid" of Vietnamese who were slowing down the operation (Belknap 2002, 111). At his trial, Calley was charged with premeditated murder (Belknap 2002, 71). Throughout the trial, Calley showed no remorse, yet other GIs experienced profound misgivings.

GI Misgivings

The true events of My Lai eventually came out due to the actions of U.S. Army personnel. Various soldiers of Charlie Company were deeply troubled by what they did and what they witnessed on March 16, 1968. They recognized that what they did was wrong even though they were not immediately condemned or punished. On March 17, the day after the My Lai operation, a soldier from the first platoon (Calley's platoon) of Charlie Company stepped on a mine, blowing off his right foot. As he was waiting to be evacuated for medical treatment, he cursed and yelled at Calley, "God will punish you. If you don't get out of the mine field the same thing will happen to you." It was reported that the GI also stated, "God will punish you for what you made me do" (Hersh 1970, 84). The soldier later testified that Calley shot Vietnamese men, women, and children, and ordered him to shove people into a ditch and shoot them (Belknap 2002, 165).

Army investigations revealed that after the operation at My Lai the soldiers of Charlie Company were sent to the field for the next sixty days. Some of the GIs thought that the army was trying to get rid of the company, hoping that its members would be wiped out in an ambush. There was speculation that the army tried to keep the company out of contact with the rest of the world for fear that the killings of civilians would be reported (Gershen 1971, 304). If this was the intent of the army, it did not succeed; the account of My Lai eventually leaked out, aided by the efforts of a young GI who did not participate in the assault at My Lai but had trained with the men who conducted the operation.

While still in Vietnam, around May of 1968, Ron Ridenhour ran into one of his old friends who, over a beer, described what Charlie Company had done at My Lai. Over the next few months, Ridenhour tracked down other members of Charlie Company who confirmed the story and added details of their own. One fellow GI, Michael Bernhardt, was wrestling with an ethical dilemma: he wanted to report what he knew about shooting so many unarmed men, women, and children, yet was reluctant to be labeled a "rat" for reporting the actions of his former buddies. Upon talking to Ridenhour, however, Bernhardt promised that he would support Ridenhour's account of the incident if and when Ridenhour chose to reveal what he had heard.

Ridenhour returned home to Phoenix, Arizona, after his discharge from the army in December 1968. Encouraged by one of his high school teachers, who noted that his own experience with army and school bureaucracy had taught him that one must be very persistent in order to be heard (Hersh 1970, 106), Ridenhour drafted a letter describing the behavior of the GIs at My Lai and sent thirty copies to prominent American leaders on March 29, 1969.

One advantage that Ridenhour possessed is that he could not be easily dismissed as an antiwar crazy, having served honorably as a helicopter door gunner and a team leader of long-range reconnaissance patrols and earned "the usual medals" (Hersh 1970, 105). With a legitimate source and too much detail to seem fabricated, the letters began to gain attention and produce results. Two members of the U.S. House of Representatives, Morris Udall and L. Mendel Rivers, took a special interest in Ridenhour's letter. Udall wrote to Secretary of Defense Melvin Laird about the charges and sent a copy of Ridenhour's letter to the chair of the House Armed Services Committee. By April 10, the army had received six congressional referrals concerning My Lai. Udall received a visit by a Pentagon officer who promised that an investigation would take place. Ridenhour received a letter from the army thanking him for bringing the matter to its attention. On April 23 Army Chief of Staff William Westmoreland officially turned the case over to the office of the inspector general (IG), the army's main investigatory agency for administrative and procedural complaints. General Westmoreland directed the IG to conduct a full-scale inquiry, with Colonel William Wilson assigned chief responsibility (Hersh 1970, 112).

The Ridenhour letter ultimately led to two separate army investigations that produced an array of charges. In the end, however, only Lieutenant Calley, was tried before a military tribunal. Calley, as leader of the second platoon, Charlie Company, of the 11th Infantry Brigade, American Division, was sentenced to life imprisonment on March 31, 1971 (Belknap 2002, 264). After the conviction, he spent about three and a half years in his base camp apartment (house arrest at Fort Benning) until he was paroled on September 10, 1975. Various reasons were given for the leniency of Calley's treatment—sympathy for Calley among a large segment of the American population, perceived ambiguity in orders received from Calley's commanding officer, Ernest Median, and the lawless environment that permeated Charlie Company around the time of the My Lai incident.

Army Investigations: Bringing My Lai to Light

The incident at My Lai initially received little attention. Although a helicopter pilot on the scene, Warrant Officer Hugh Thompson, immediately reported to his superiors that at My Lai civilians were being rounded up, placed in ditches, and shot, no disciplinary actions were taken against members of Charlie Company. Accurate accounts

of the behavior at My Lai were not sent up the chain of command; there was no immediate pressure to identify illegal behavior and punish the wrongdoers. Not surprisingly, many of the high-ranking army personnel seemed more interested in advancing their careers and hiding embarrassments than in exposing transgressions. Careers were more likely to be tied to accomplishing missions and generating body counts than to documenting and punishing improper behavior. One of the groups that later investigated the My Lai incident, the Peers Commission, concluded, "Within the Americal Division, at every command level from company to division, actions were taken or omitted which together effectively concealed from higher headquarters the events which transpired in [Task Force Barker's] operation" (Belknap 2002, 79).

Real action to identify violations in protocol began only after General Westmoreland charged Colonel Wilson of the IG office with investigating the incident. Operating under official secrecy, Wilson traveled across the United States to interview ex-GIs who were at My Lai. Calley was pulled out of Vietnam in June 1969, brought to the States, placed in a lineup, and picked out by Hugh Thompson (helicopter pilot who was at the scene) as the officer who shot civilians at My Lai. By the end of July, Wilson had interrogated thirty-six witnesses. His report was submitted to General Westmoreland on August 4, and Westmoreland then ordered the IG to turn over the results of the investigation to the provost marshal's office of the army and its criminal investigation division (CID). This unit was then given the responsibility to determine if there was enough evidence to file criminal charges against Calley and others in Charlie Company (Hersh 1970, 120).

Following the CID report, the Pentagon notified officials at Fort Benning that William Calley should be tried at a general court-martial. The charges included six specifications of premeditated murder.

The official charge accused the lieutenant of killing 109 "Oriental human beings, occupants of the village of My Lai 4, whose names and sexes are unknown, by means of shooting them with a rifle" (Hersh 1970, 125).

In addition to the Wilson inquiry, the army conducted a second inquiry under the direction of Lieutenant General William R. Peers, who addressed the issue of whether high-ranking officers covered up the events at My Lai. This inquiry was motivated by recognition that the army could not hide the My Lai story any longer from an inquisitive press. In late 1969 investigative reporter Seymour Hersh met with senior Pentagon officials and requested information about the unfolding story of civilian killings at My Lai. Shortly after an explosive CBS report, Westmoreland instructed Peers to conduct a formal investigation. General Peers was instructed to explore the scope of the original U.S. Army investigation under Colonel Wilson and to determine the possible suppression or withholding of information by persons involved in the incident (Belknap 2002, 122).

The Peers Commission interviewed 398 individuals in the United States and in Vietnam and accumulated over 20,000 pages of testimony. In mid-February 1970 a preliminary report was sent to Westmoreland and Secretary of the Army Stanley Resor. The Peers report concluded that troops from Task Force Barker "had massacred a large number of noncombatants." The commission was unable to determine precisely how many Vietnamese had been killed, but stated that the number was "at least 175 and may exceed 400." In regard to the cover-up or nonreporting of the incident, the commission concluded, "At every command level within the Americal Division, actions were taken, both wittingly and unwittingly, which effectively suppressed information concerning the war crimes committed at Son My village [which included the hamlet of My Lai]." The commission

identified thirty individuals who had deliberately suppressed relevant information, including brigade commander, Colonel Oran Henderson and commander of the task force, Lieutenant Colonel Frank Barker (Belknap 2002, 128). The Peers report concluded that knowledge of the extent of the incident existed at Company level, at the Task Force Barker level, and at the 11th Brigade level. The report noted that efforts at the Americal Division level to conceal information about what was believed to be the killing of twenty to twenty-eight civilians resulted in the suppression of a war crime of far greater magnitude. The report also stated that efforts to suppress information were assisted by U.S. officers serving in advisory positions with Vietnamese agencies.

As a consequence of the Peers report, army lawyers decided that fourteen officers including Charlie company commander Ernest Medina, task force commander Frank Barker, brigade commander Oran Henderson, assistant commander for the Americal Division George Young, and Americal Division leader Major General Samuel Koster should be charged. Eventually only Lieutenant Calley was convicted of any crime. The Peers inquiry, however, did have an impact on the careers of some of the military personnel. For example, Major General Samuel Koster received a one-grade reduction in rank, and Brigadier General George Young received an official censure (Belknap 2002, 216). Overall, the penalties leveled against those engaged in concealing facts about My Lai were not severe.

The Press and Conflicting Perspectives on My Lai

The press eventually played an important role in publicizing the events of March 16, 1968. On November 29, 1969, the *Cleveland Plain Dealer* published an account, along with pictures, of the massacre at My Lai. The story had an immediate effect in England, where accounts of My Lai pushed news of the second U.S. landing on the moon off the front pages. British headlines included "The Story That Stunned America" and "War Crime. If This Can Happen, America Has Lost" (Hersh 1970, 138).

In addition to the print media, television also began to capitalize on My Lai's sensational story. A GI interviewed on the CBS evening news stated that at My Lai, "I went in a village and killed everybody" (Hersh 1972, 120). My Lai became an open and much discussed topic for the print media. Many newspapers were highly critical. For example, the *Philadelphia Inquirer* described My Lai as "the kind of atrocity generally associated with the worst days of Hitler and Stalin and other cruel despotisms." Other newspapers, however, were more guarded. The *Chicago Tribune* stated, "Americans should not be deceived by the contemptible lamentations that we are all guilty and that our troops in Viet Nam have been brutalized by the war and are just as inhuman as the Communists" (Hersh 1970, 142).

It should be no surprise that there were differing perspectives on My Lai. Journalist Richard Hammer observed that the punishment given to the U.S. troops involved in My Lai was too lenient. He found it ironic that we act with brutality toward civilians at My Lai and "let loose those who killed the innocent [members of Charlie Company]" (Hammer 1971, 373).

While some Americans felt that the army should lock up Calley and throw away the key for his behavior at My Lai, a large segment of the American population stood solidly behind the second lieutenant. Governor George Wallace of Alabama made the exoneration of Calley a theme of his presidential bid in 1968. Lester Maddox, lieutenant governor of Georgia, urged President Richard Nixon to free Calley, while the Louisiana

legislature and the Texas senate passed resolutions urging Nixon to grant Calley a pardon. A telephone survey conducted by the Nixon administration not long after Calley was convicted found that 78 percent of those interviewed disagreed with Calley's conviction. A Gallup poll commissioned by *Newsweek* showed that 79 percent disapproved of the court-martial's findings while only 9 percent of Americans approved. A Harris poll found 65 percent disapproving of the guilty verdict versus 24 percent agreeing (Belknap 2002, 192).

Some of those reporting on My Lai portrayed the soldiers who shot the Vietnamese civilians as the real victims since society had "abused their bodies" and "confused their minds." One reporter concluded that there was no massacre at My Lai, only an error in judgment due to bad intelligence, faulty leadership, inadequate indoctrination, and a questionable counterguerrilla policy. According to this reporter, what happened was less serious than the human error of an artilleryman firing a round that mistakenly kills American troops from "friendly fire" (Gershen 1971, 302).

Application of Case No. 5 to Ethics and Responsible Governance

Breaches of Responsibility: The Public Interest

On a number of dimensions, the My Lai incident poorly served the public. Arguably, national safety and the war effort were ill served. In the eyes of the world, the United States was sullied by the actions of its GIs at My Lai—the killing of unarmed women and children, rape, and general mistreatment of civilians—leading people to believe that America had lost its moral advantage in the war and therefore was no better than the Vietcong. In addition, My Lai may have stiffened the resolve of America's enemies, inspiring hatred of the United

States and generating sympathy for the underdog North Vietnamese and Vietcong. The legitimacy of American institutions, such as the military, appears to have eroded as a result of My Lai.

While My Lai seems to have sullied America's reputation, the incident also demonstrated that, even in cases of unethical and irresponsible conduct, a few individuals will responsibly and honorably serve the public. Such was the case with Ron Ridenhour when he decided to seek out the truth of what happened at My Lai. Ridenhour was not alone in his efforts to see that the public was fully informed about the events at My Lai. GIs testified about the shootings; both print and television journalists vigorously sought out the truth about March 16.

A former Army photographer, Ron Haeberle, promoted the public interest by showing slides of the My Lai killings, shortly after his discharge from the army in 1968. Haeberle began to show his slides to clubs such as the Optimists, Kiwanis, and Jaycees (Belknap 2002, 111). Haeberle served the public interest by exposing questionable behavior and facilitating debate about right and wrong, ethical and unethical types of behavior.

The army CID investigators became aware of Haeberle's photos in August 1969, which became the first hard evidence about the killings that could be used in court. On November 20, 1969, eight of the pictures were printed on the front page of the *Cleveland Plain Dealer* and the world press scrambled to reproduce them. One magazine editor characterized the My Lai pictures as the hottest property since the Zapruder film of President John F. Kennedy's assassination (Belknap 2002, 120).

Another GI who helped expose the massacre at My Lai was helicopter pilot Hugh Thompson who landed his helicopter between the American troops and Vietnamese civilians in order to protect them from probable death. Personally affronted by what he was witnessing from the air, Thompson

saved civilian lives, demonstrating that there were "good guys" as well as "bad guys" in the American military. Thompson's actions suggest that the ideal of responsible governance is a possibility and that people low down in the chain of command can also work to prevent future injustices.

Thompson would later testify before Congress, a military inquiry, and the court-martial of William Calley. He acted to prevent behavior that was later determined to be illegal and in doing the right thing he supported the integrity of the military and good governance in general. The Peers Commission investigators stated that Thompson was a soldier who "had maintained his basic integrity . . . who knew right from wrong and acted accordingly." The report noted that such soldiers were bright spots in a "generally bleak and depressing picture" (Belknap 2002, 124).

Breaches of Responsibility: Natural Law

According to natural law, reason is used to discover the correct application of universal principles. Applying this framework, one could argue that the shooting of unarmed civilians at My Lai violated basic principles or universal rules of conduct. The application of reason, however, often is not straightforward. What is reasonable to one person or group at one time may seem totally unreasonable to others at another time. Although the facts of the Calley case violated universal principles according to many reasonable Americans living in the late 1960s, in Lieutenant Calley's mind his acts were justified.

Calley showed little remorse after his sentence was handed down. He stated, "I've never known a soldier, nor did I myself ever wantonly kill a human being in my entire life. If I have committed a crime, the only crime I've committed is in judgment of my values. Apparently I valued my troops' lives more than I did that of the enemy" (Hammer 1971, 367). For Calley, his actions were reasonable since he was only protecting his troops from potential danger. In Calley's mind, the villagers were either the communist enemy or communist sympathizers who were aiding the enemy or, given the chance, would aid the enemy in the future. For Calley, war called for total elimination of the enemy, not strict adherence to rules and regulations defining permissible action.

Calley also noted that killing a person during a time of war was nothing new. He noted that in Vietnam the people adopted guerrilla tactics. He cited a letter sent to him by a man in Missouri that discussed the actions of Civil War general William T. Sherman, who ordered his troops to burn, kill, rape, pillage, and plunder their enemies in the South. Rather than being condemned as a war criminal, Sherman became a hero of the war (Sack 1971, 92).

According to the army prosecutor, Captain Aubrey Daniel, some basic parameters of humanity were nevertheless violated at My Lai. Daniel concluded that Calley was not compelled to mindlessly carry out orders, but had an obligation to make moral decisions. The army prosecutor observed, "When he [Calley] put on the American uniform he still had the obligation to think and act like a reasonable person and have proper respect for life" (Hammer 1971, 332).

Applying the principle of natural law to the concept of reason, Captain Daniel concluded that shooting unarmed women and children even in times of war violates parameters of humanity. No clear directives for identifying violations of natural law, however, are evident. Signals of what are or are not violations of natural law may be time- and culture-bound. Viewed today, and viewed in 1971 at the time of the Calley trial, the acts of My Lai are jarring and in clear violation of norms of acceptable behavior. Large numbers of Americans,

nevertheless, supported Calley, exerting pressure on President Nixon to grant leniency to Calley and others associated with My Lai.

Breaches of Responsibility: The Rule of Law

Responsible government faithfully executes the laws of the land. America is said to be a nation ruled by law, not by men. Justice is often depicted as blindfolded to signify neutral, impartial, even-handed treatment. In theory, the law is above the individual and applies to all in the same manner. In light of the rule of law mandates, responsible governance therefore must not only administer the law, but should strive to uphold principles of justice on which the law is based.

The legality of the behavior at My Lai was addressed in a military court of law. Many of the individuals assigned to the My Lai case displayed a deep respect for the law and a strong desire that justice should prevail. Indicative of this respect for the law, four young army captains at Fort Benning tossed coins to see which of them would assume the unenviable task of opposing the army's inclination for a possible cover-up. The loser of the coin toss, Captain William Hill, then signed the charges against Calley (Belknap 2002, 112). Hill, as well as the other officers, recognized that the position they took in all likelihood would harm their careers in the military. However, their sense of justice prevailed over their short-term material interests.

Another example of responsible governance involved Captain Daniel, the army prosecutor, who would eventually come to see himself as upholding human morality. Daniel effectively laid out the case against Calley, and on March 29, 1971, the military jury found Calley guilty of the premeditated murder of at least twenty-two Vietnamese civilians. On March 31 (after a forty-five-day trial),

Calley was sentenced to life in prison with hard labor, ending one of the longest courts-martial in American history.

The sentencing of Calley, however, did not end Daniel's involvement in defending the law. In an action that deeply disturbed him, on April 3, 1971, President Richard Nixon promised the public that he would personally review Calley's case after all appeals within the military's legal system were exhausted. The White House, Fort Benning, and congressional offices had been flooded with telegrams, phone calls, letters, and petitions demanding that Calley's sentence should be reduced or commuted. Some letters requested that Calley should be declared innocent and decorated. The military jurors who delivered the verdict were vilified and received obscene phone calls. Instead of viewing the verdict as an opportunity for reflection, many Americans saw the sentence as an attack on themselves and their nation (Hammer 1971, 386).

Captain Daniel expressed his concerns to the commander in chief, President Nixon, in a letter that rebuked the president for Nixon's failure in his duty to justice, his duty to morality, his duty to his office, and his duty to the nation. Daniel contended that the Calley trial was conducted in the finest tradition of the American legal system, that it was in every respect a fair trial, and that the selection of the jury was impartial. He expressed dismay at the president's decision to intervene and interject politics into the legal system. According to Daniel, Nixon weakened respect for the judicial system as well as respect for the principle of the rule of law. From Daniel's point of view, it was quite clear that punishment should be unambiguously delivered to a man convicted of at least twenty-two premeditated murder. It made no sense to him to try to elevate such a person to the status of a national hero. Captain Daniel concluded that if the United States as a nation condoned the acts of Lieutenant Calley, it would be no better than its enemies, making any

plea for the humane treatment of Americans who are held prisoner by others meaningless (Hammer 1971, 382–386).

George Latimer, the defense attorney for Lieutenant Calley, sought to exonerate Calley on the grounds that he was merely following orders. Under questioning, Calley testified that he had been informed that all orders were assumed to be legal, that the soldier's job was to comply with orders, that a soldier could be court-martialed for refusing an order, and that if a soldier refused an order in the face of the enemy he could be put to death. In response to a question about what to do if he had doubts about an order, Calley stated that the order should be carried out and then a complaint could be filed (Hammer 1971, 240–241).

Calley contended that his actions at My Lai were justified because he was operating in a free-fire zone, his operation had clearance to destroy everything, and the job of his company was to neutralize the hamlet. Furthermore, he asserted that he had been given a direct order to "waste the Vietnamese" who were slowing the platoon down. For Calley, there was no premeditation to kill old men, women, and children, only a desire to comply with orders and destroy the enemy.

The rule of law was a major feature of the prosecution against Calley. As Captain Daniel stressed in his summary before the jury, the rule of law mandates that "summary execution is forbidden" and that even if the people at My Lai had aided the Vietcong they were still entitled to protection under the law. Daniel instructed the jury that the Vietnamese civilians posed no immediate threat; therefore, "if any of them were killed and any order to kill them was given, it was an illegal order" (Hammer 1971, 332). A requirement of the rule of law holds that offenders should be apprehended, tried before a jury of their peers, and punished if found guilty. Any attempt to circumvent these procedures violates due process and the ability to demonstrate innocence. Soldiers who anoint themselves as judge, jury, and executioner violate legal traditions that bolster governance.

Captain Daniel reinforced the concept of the rule of law in his actions and therefore supported the concept of responsible governance. The captain claimed that nothing would justify the execution of the children and infants killed at My Lai (Hammer 1971, 346). According to Daniel, by taking the law into their own hands, Calley and his fellow soldiers had acted irresponsibly and illegally. Calley's actions showed disrespect for the rule of law, the American system of justice, due process, and the rights of the accused.

Questions for Student Group Discussion

1. To what degree was My Lai an aberration?
2. To what degree was My Lai inconsistent with or consistent with American culture?
3. Were Calley's penalties too lenient or too harsh?
4. Did My Lai damage the image of the U.S. military?
5. What recommendation would you offer for rebuilding the ethical posture of the army after My Lai?
6. Should people other than Calley have been convicted of crimes?
7. Some people argue that incidents like My Lai occur in every war and that therefore the GI's behavior at My Lai was acceptable. Do you agree?
8. In the investigations of My Lai and the Calley trial, did the system work?
9. What are the lessons of My Lai?
10. How can incidents like My Lai be prevented in future wars?

Case No. 6: Abu Ghraib

An Overview

In April of 2004 following the release of photographs taken at the large Abu Ghraib prison complex, twenty miles west of Bagdad, Iraq, it became obvious to growing numbers of Americans that something had gone terribly wrong at the prison camp. The piles of naked bodies, as well as leashed detainees surrounded by grinning GIs, were not images that comforted typical Americans. Some action was necessary in order to restore a sense of responsibility to the country's military, specifically to the military personnel who had oversight over the prison detainees. The action that followed was initiation of investigations, identification of wrongdoers, military trials, convictions, and prison sentences. The military appears to have followed the usual precedent of identifying a few low-ranking wrongdoers, convicting them of illegal behavior, attributing the objectionable behavior only to the few soldiers who participated, and finally congratulating itself that the shocking situation had been rectified.

A more careful review of the investigations conducted after the release of the Abu Ghraib photographs suggests that the behavior of U.S. soldiers at the prison may have been less the result of aberrant behavior by a few misfits and more the consequence of standard operating procedures that were approved at high levels within the Bush administration. Investigation of internal government memos reveals that interrogation policies such as those found at Abu Ghraib were advocated by Bush administration officials. The need for good intelligence in order to save lives was given as a justification for the questionable behavior at Abu Ghraib. This need was the driving force that negated compliance with humanitarian and international law.

The road to Abu Ghraib was paved with legal interpretations and semantic parsing at high levels within the Bush administration. The case study illustrates how White House lawyers, officials at the attorney general's office and the Department of Defense, military officers, and ordinary soldiers at the prison complex were all directly or indirectly implicated in the conduct uncovered at Abu Ghraib. The case study also describes the history of the use of torture, including the abandoning of the practice in the late eighteenth century in Europe. Both practical and philosophical reasons discredited torture as a useful means of extracting information. Public opinion in America labeled torture as fundamentally "un-American" and helped to alter policies regarding the treatment of prisoners in America's war on terror. World opinion also has been highly critical of American treatment of prisoners in Iraq, Cuba, and other nations. Finally, the Supreme Court also played a role in setting parameters of permissible and impermissible behavior regarding people held in American-run prisons.

After the release of the damaging photographs, conduct at Abu Ghraib became a profound embarrassment for the Bush administration. Many Americans expressed their outrage in the bumper sticker, "Torture is un-American." Like first lady Nancy Reagan's "Just Say No" slogan to combat drug abuse, this bumper sticker was able to compartmentalize feelings in a few short words. The slogan encapsulated the gut reaction of many Americans about the behavior photographed at Abu Ghraib. The saying "A picture is worth a thousand words" seems to apply to Abu Ghraib since it concisely summarized the state of affairs at the prison complex. Boss Tweed recognized the potential danger of cartoons since most of his constituents could not read. Similarly, officials of the Bush administration recognized that their image of the "good guy" in Iraq, helping the Iraqi people achieve democracy, was significantly damaged.

The pictures of prisoners at Abu Ghraib grated on American consciousness as many Americans intuitively felt that this was not what they were about. The pictures also did considerable damage in the public relations war for the support of average Iraqi citizens.

The Facts of the Case

The conditions at Abu Ghraib came to light largely as a result of a military police whistle-blower, Specialist Joseph Darby, who on January 13, 2004, slipped a compact disc (CD) with the incriminating photographs under the door of the Criminal Investigation Division (CID) at the Abu Ghraib prison. Darby had received the CD from Corporal Charles Graner and was upset by what the disc revealed. Some of the photos on the CD eventually were broadcast on CBS's *60 Minutes 2* television show, opening up a Pandora's box of problems for the GIs in the photos (McCoy 2006, 142). In one photograph, Private Lynndie England stands arm in arm with Graner, both grinning and giving the thumbs-up sign behind a cluster of naked Iraqis piled in a pyramid. In another photograph, a kneeling, naked male prisoner appears to be performing oral sex on another male prisoner. The second prisoner is naked and hooded (Hersh 2004a). Other photographs display dogs barking at naked men and Iraqis writhing in pain.

A photo of an Iraqi standing on a box with wires connected to his body and a photo of an Iraqi on a leash were widely circulated over the Internet. This publicity, which was certainly unwanted by the military, immediately got the attention of high-ranking U.S. officials. In response to the release of the photos, General Ricardo Sanchez, the U.S. commander for Iraq, immediately placed the blame for the illegal conduct at Abu Ghraib on Brigadier General Janis Karpinski the military police commander for Iraq. Karpinski, however, claimed that personnel from military intelligence (MI) or the Central Intelligence Agency (CIA) had usurped her authority at Abu Ghraib and that there was an ambiguous chain of command. Soldiers who testified at various court-martial proceedings stated that they were not sure who was in charge. Some thought that the intelligence officer Colonel Thomas Pappas was in charge of the prison, while others believed that another intelligence officer, Lieutenant Colonel Steven Jordan, was in charge (Mestrovic 2007, 58). This confusion fostered the breakdown in accountability and authority found at the prison complex.

When General Karpinski inspected Abu Ghraib's 280-acre prison complex in July 2003, she found only twenty-five prisoners, yet three months later the prison housed about 14,000 "security detainees." The prison was surrounded by twenty-foot concrete walls and consisted of three distinct areas: (1) a cluster of minimum-security tents, (2) ordinary lockups, and (3) maximum-security cellblocks. One problem Karpinski faced was the presence of Special Access Program (SAP) operatives within the prison. These operatives included CIA officials and others engaged in interrogating "ghost" detainees, identified as individuals who were never registered as prisoners. These individuals were detained and interrogated over Karpinski's objections.

In addition to the SAP interrogators, who were essentially beyond Karpinski's control, after August 2003 military intelligence and the CIA also began to undertake questionable and perhaps illegal types of interrogations at Abu Ghraib. These interrogations used physical and psychological techniques that previously had been used during the conflict in Afghanistan and at the Guantanamo naval base in Cuba but that, according to U.S. interpretations of the Geneva Convention, should not apply to Iraq. These interrogation techniques were used at Abu Ghraib despite President George

W. Bush's assurances that the Geneva Convention applied to Iraq, even if it was not being applied in other countries such as Cuba and Afghanistan.

Secretary of Defense Donald Rumsfeld also played a role in subverting Karpinski's influence and creating the confusing lines of authority at the prison complex. Confusion legitimated abuse since there was a general belief at the lower levels of the chain of command that someone at higher levels had to approve of the behavior. There was also pressure from upper levels to start generating better information about terrorist activities even if this required "getting tough" with detainees. At one briefing, Rumsfeld complained about poor intelligence from Iraq, contrasting it with the better information elicited by "extreme" interrogation practices that were being used at the prison in Guantanamo. Rumsfeld expressed frustration that the Geneva Convention rules applied to Iraq. In order to remedy the situation, Rumsfeld gave oral orders for the commander at Guantanamo, Major General Geoffrey Miller, to "Gitmoize" (apply the same interrogation techniques at Abu Ghraib as those used at Guantanamo) Iraqi intelligence (McCoy 2006, 133).

In September 2003, General Miller and others paid an inspection visit to the Abu Ghraib prison. After their inspection, they urged a radical restructuring of existing detainee policy. According to the *New York Times*, Miller began dictating the new procedures to Karpinski, noting that the U.S. commander for Iraq, General Ricardo Sanchez, had given him permission to use whatever prison facility he wanted in order to train military police (MPs). Following training in the procedures used at Guantanamo, the MPs would serve as interrogators in Iraq. General Miller left an interrogation manual and compact disk with "training information" that could instruct MPs at Abu Ghraib about the new procedures. Just five days after Miller left Iraq, General Sanchez signed a memo authorizing a dozen interrogation techniques beyond those listed in the [Army] "Field Manual 34-52" and five beyond those applied at Guantanamo (McCoy 2006, 134).

General Sanchez moved quickly to implement the new Guantanamo-style techniques and provided copies of his instructions to personnel in MI. General Karpinski and MP officers at Abu Ghraib, however, were out of Sanchez's information loop and were denied knowledge of the new guidelines. Sanchez ordered psychological torture, derived from techniques developed by the CIA and previously put into practice. Techniques approved by Sanchez included changing the diet of a detainee; altering the environment to create moderate discomfort (e.g., adjusting temperatures or introducing an unpleasant smell); adjusting the sleeping times of detainees; isolating the detainee from other detainees; using falsified documents and reports; using military work dogs to exploit Arab fear of dogs, playing loud music to create fear and disorient detainees; and use of physical posturing (sitting, standing, kneeling, prone) for up to one hour (McCoy 2006, 135). Eventually the maximum-security areas at Abu Ghraib (where the photos were taken) were totally removed from Karpinski's command and put under the jurisdiction of two intelligence officers, Colonel Thomas Pappas and Lieutenant Colonel Steven Jordan, who reported directly to General Sanchez. On November 19, 2003, Sanchez removed the entire Abu Ghraib prison from Karpinski's command and assigned it to the 205th Military Intelligence Brigade under Pappas (McCoy 2006, 137).

Pappas immediately began to implement techniques approved by Sanchez. The intent of these techniques was to "soften up" detainees. Under Pappas's command, the military police at Abu Ghraib were assigned responsibility for "preparing" detainees who later would be interrogated by the CIA, military intelligence, and private contractors. Forced nudity became a standard procedure

that was used to humiliate prisoners. Karpinski denied knowledge of the new techniques that were being used inside the prison. She stated that she was "shocked" and "sick to her stomach" when she saw the Abu Ghraib pictures. She noted that within the Arab culture what occurred at the prison was "equivalent of castrating them [detainees] in public" (McCoy 2006, 142).

Sociologist S.G. Mestrovic (2007, 3) states that the whole truth about what happened at Abu Ghraib might never be known; however, it is possible to state clearly what is not true about the abuse that occurred there. These observations are delineated in Table 5.3.

From Table 5.3 a number of misconceptions can be debunked. Mestrovic contends that wayward individuals ("rotten apples") were not architects of the abuse that occurred at Abu Ghraib. Mestrovic observes that the International Committee of the Red Cross (ICRC) had informed U.S. Army officials of abuse in American military prisons prior to the release of the damaging Abu Ghraib photographs. It was further reported by Mestrovic that when some army officers questioned the legitimacy of the interrogation tactics, their superiors told them that the tactics were approved by MI. Mestrovic concludes that rather than Abu Ghraib being the case of a few bad apples within the military, "the orchard [the U.S. military prison system] is contaminated, and the orchard keepers have escaped the sort of scrutiny that was leveled at low-ranking soldiers" (2007, 4).

The legal endgame for Abu Ghraib was witnessed in the prosecution of seven enlisted MPs and two additional individuals from MI. The harshest sentences were given to soldiers who were associated with the pictures of a simulated electrocution of an Iraqi standing on a box and the picture of an Iraqi being held on a leash. Corporal Charles Graner and Private First Class Lynndie England were both shown in the leash picture. Both the leash and

---

Table 5.3

Misconceptions About Prisoner Treatment at Abu Ghraib

1. It is not true that abuses were confined to a small cohort of rotten apples, they were not the architects of the abuse.

2. It is not true that abuses were limited to incidents prosecuted, others were not prosecuted.

3. It is not true that abuses were confined to Abu Ghraib. Abuses happened elsewhere.

4. It is not true that the government did not know about the abuses at Abu Ghraib prior to publication of the incriminating photographs.

5. It is not true that officers were ignorant of abuses; officers questioned abusive tactics but were told by superiors that they were approved by military intelligence.

6. It is not true that abuses stemmed exclusively from improper understanding of interrogation techniques.

7. It is not true that soldiers thought up the abuses on their own.

8. It is not true that all or most of the blame for the abuse can be placed on a few bad apples. The orchard was contaminated and the orchard keepers escaped the scrutiny leveled at low-ranking soldiers.

Source: Mestrovic 2007.

---

electrocution pictures were widely circulated in the media and over the Internet. After military trials, Graner was sentenced to ten years and England was sentenced to three years in prison. Staff Sergeant Ivan Frederick, who was linked to the simulated electrocution, received a sentence of eight and a half years in prison (Mestrovic 2007, 9).

Perhaps the most enduring legacy of Abu Ghraib was its impact on America's reputation for fair play and its impact on America's war on terror. There was general condemnation of Abu Ghraib throughout the world. For example, in February 2005, acting Assistant Secretary of State Michael Kozak stated that the events of Abu Ghraib "were

a stain on the honor of the U.S." Army interrogator Chris Mackey felt that the images from Abu Ghraib would "inflame anti-American sentiment in the Muslim world for a generation, driving who knows how many would-be jihadists into the ranks of Al Qaeda." A British intelligence agent noted that the U.S. was doing what the British did in their fight against the IRA in the 1970s, detaining people and violating their civil liberties. The *New York Times* editorialized on the second anniversary of the war that when the average Egyptian, Palestinian, or Saudi thinks about the Americans in Iraq "the image is not voters' purple-stained fingers but the naked Iraqi prisoners at the other end of Pfc. Lynndie England's leash" (McCoy 2006, 201).

When Egypt's democratic reformers marched down the streets of Cairo in April 2005, they chanted, "Down Down with Mubarak! Guantanamo! Enough! Abu Ghraib! Enough!" In November of 2003, an American reporter interviewed a young Iraqi man from Falluja about the reasons for resistance to the U.S. presence. The man stated, "It is a shame for the foreigners to put a bag over their [detainees] heads, to make a man lie on the ground with your shoe on his neck. . . . This is a great shame for the whole tribe. It is the duty of that man, and of that tribe, to get revenge on this soldier [whose shoe was on the Iraqi neck], to kill that man. Their [the tribe's] duty is to attack them [the foreigners], to wash the shame . . . we cannot sleep until we have revenge" (McCoy 2006, 200–201). It should be noted, however, that torture was not invented by Americans but rather has a long history.

Precedent for Torture

Early Times

Torture dates back to the beginning of recorded history. In ancient Greece, it was accepted that slaves and foreigners could be tortured in order to provide testimony in legal disputes. Free citizens of Greece, however, were exempt from torture. The Greek courts believed that slaves, if tortured, would tell the truth in order to end their ordeal but, if questioned openly, would lie to protect their masters. The Greek legal orator Demosthenes even argued that juries should not use the statements of free witnesses, but should apply torture to slaves in order to discover the truth. He concluded, "witnesses have sometimes been found not to have given true evidence, whereas no statements made as a result of torture have ever been proven untrue" (Ross 2005, 5).

All Greeks, however, did not accept the idea that statements made by tortured slaves were infallible. For example, Aristotle contended that torture produced a kind of evidence that appeared trustworthy; however, "those under compulsion are as likely to give false evidence as true, some being ready to endure everything rather than tell the truth, while others are really ready to make false charges against others, in the hope of being sooner released from torture" (Ross 2005, 5).

Initially, the Roman republic followed the Greek precedent of subjecting only slaves to torture. As the Roman Empire expanded, however, a class of freed slaves and non-Romans with partial rights of citizenship developed. Eventually, in the latter days of the empire, torture was extended to this large group of "second-class citizens." The legal basis for torture under the Roman Empire is identified in the Justinian Code and the Digest of Justinian. The Justinian Code was a synthesis and clarification of existing laws that was formulated by Justinian, the Roman emperor between AD 527 and 565. The Digest of Justinian (AD 533) is an organized compilation of quotations from earlier Roman law decisions, legal principles and commentaries from both Christian and pre-Christian times.

Among the hundreds of sections of the Digest, only one (part 48, section 18) addresses the issue of torture. This section quotes dozens of norms from previous centuries and acts as a guide of accepted jurisprudence. The section details under what conditions torture may be used, for what sorts of crimes and for which classes of persons. For example, the Digest clearly states that slaves of a condemned man can be tortured because they have ceased being his property, slaves were liable to torture to give evidence in cases of incest, slaves could be tortured when there was an investigation of a forged will. Bishops were exempt from torture even under strong presumption of guilt; noblemen, doctors and lawyers had a general immunity from torture; a free person was not subject to interrogation as a slave; and privilege from torture was a valid defense against confessions, except in cases of high treason.

The practical value of torture was broadly questioned in Roman times. For example, prior to Jusitinian's compilation of the Digest, the Roman jurist Ulpian (d. 228) stated that torture should not always be trusted because "many persons have such strength of body and soul that they heed pain very little, so that there is no means of obtaining the truth from them; while others are so susceptible to pain that they tell any lie rather than suffer it" (Ross 2005, 6). Justinian placed reservations about the use of torture in the Digest. In what appears to be his own personal view he noted that, "torture should be considered neither as always trustworthy, nor as always untrustworthy. And as a matter of fact it is a fickle and dangerous business that ill serves the cause of truth" (Harrison 2005). Over time, more individuals began to doubt the quality of information received through torture.

During the rise of Christianity, the practice of torturing traitors was extended to include any individual who rejected the emperor's power, either in heaven or on earth. Suspected Christians would be tortured first to make them reveal the crime of being a Christian and next tortured to force them to renounce their faith. With the triumph of Christianity, however, the official church opposed torture and its practice fell into relative disuse. Pope Nicholas I officially banned the practice of torture in 866.

In the thirteenth century, European civil courts revived old Roman laws that relied upon torture in order to obtain confessions. Torture was meticulously regulated and codified; it was administered in a special chamber by a civil servant who also served as the public executioner. Magistrates recorded the confessions. Paralleling this use by the civil courts, church interrogators also used torture under the rules of the Inquisition. Torture for both confessions and punishment was approved and formalized under Pope Innocent IV in 1252. The Catholic Church justified torture by alleging that mobs were already burning and torturing heretics and that if the church assumed responsibility for torture it could control and minimize it. The church reasoned that if the state could torture common criminals, those charged with the more serious crime of heresy should suffer similar punishment (Amnesty International 1975, 28). The papal bull of Innocent VIII in 1484, and the *Malleus Malefi- carum* of 1490 justified witch-hunts in Europe that would claim from 200,000 to 1 million lives over the next two centuries. Most of those killed and tortured for the crime of witchcraft were women (Ross 2005, 11).

Legalized torture came under attack with the rise of the Enlightenment. Many eighteenth-century authors, such as Montesquieu, Voltaire, and Beccaria, argued that torture was a relic of barbarism, superstition, and tyranny. The Italian marquis Cesare Beccaria (1738–1794) excoriated torture and other judicial practices of the day in his 1764 pamphlet *On Crimes and Punishments*. Following the logic of Ulpian and Justinian, Beccaria observed

that torture was a sure route to acquittal for robust ruffians and conviction for weak innocents. His book became a best seller throughout Europe, and by the end of the eighteenth century most nations in Europe had banned judicial torture, defined as tortures that were lawfully used to compel confessions and testimony (Ross 2005, 4).

After his coronation in 1740, Frederick II of Prussia barred the use of torture, calling it cruel as well as useless. In 1770, Saxony and Denmark abolished torture. The practice was abolished in Poland and Austria-Bohemia in 1776, in Tuscany in 1780, in the Austrian Netherlands (Belgium) in 1787, and in Sicily in 1789. Much of the credit for the abolition of torture was given to the writings of Beccaria and Voltaire. By the nineteenth century European states had revised their laws of criminal procedure. The revised laws condemned accused criminals on the basis of standards of proof (defined as unrestricted evaluation of evidence), rather than on the basis of confessions obtained through torture (Langbein 2005, 97). Over time, the symbols of torture, such as the Bastille prison in France, gave way to the science of criminology. In 1874, French novelist Victor Hugo declared, "torture has ceased to exist" (McCoy 2006, 16).

Modern Times

Despite the prohibitions against torture issued in the eighteenth century, it still prevailed against those who were considered a threat to the government. Torture was used against revolutionaries (in Italy and Austria) after the revolutions of 1848; against opponents of the Russian czarist regime throughout time; in India when it was ruled by the British; in the Congo when it was governed by Belgian colonial officials; by the French during the Algerian War of Independence (1954–1962); and by the Americans in Vietnam (1959–1975). In the 1920s and 1930s, torture was used in Soviet Russia,

Fascist Italy, and Nazi Germany against perceived traitors to the state. Torture in the name of state security was also a hallmark of the Khmer Rouge in Cambodia in the 1970s (Ross 2005, 15).

Perhaps most relevant of the modern incidents of torture are the cases of Algeria and Vietnam. Historian Alfred McCoy (2006, 18–20) reports that in an effort to crush a nationalistic uprising in Algeria between 1954 and 1962, France launched a massive "pacification" program. This program resulted in the forcible relocation of 2 million Algerians, the death of 300,000 Algerians, and the torture of several hundred thousand suspects. During the Algerian uprising, guerrillas were branded "outlaws" and denied the protections of lawful combatants as specified in the Geneva Conventions. Similarities between this policy and America's actions in Iraq are evident.

The French excused their conduct in Algeria in the Wuillaume Report, in which they argued that they were not in violation of the Geneva Convention. The report stated that the use of water and electricity in interrogation was within the bounds of the law because the shocks they produce are more psychological than physical and therefore "do not constitute excessive cruelty." The report further contended that forcing water down a victim's throat to simulate drowning was perfectly acceptable since it "involves no risk to the health of the victim" (McCoy 2006, 19).

The torture techniques employed by the French, however, appear to have stiffened the resistance of the Algerians. Between 1956 and 1957, violence on the part of the anti-French Front de Libération Nationale (FLN) intensified, as did the aggressive use of torture in order to break the resistance. During the Algerian War, rebel suspects were taken to safe houses for torture during the night and by dawn their bodies were dumped into shallow graves outside the city. McCoy (2006, 19) notes that these "summary executions" were identified by a senior French officer as "an inseparable part of the task associated with keeping law and order." These actions resulted in 3,024 of those arrested in Algiers going "missing."

Although the French army subdued the rebels in the battle for the city of Algiers (1954–1960), the revolt spread and the French were eventually forced to withdraw as more and more Algerians turned against them. With an angry introduction by French novelist Jean-Paul Sartre, the book *The Question* was published in 1958 by Henri Alleg. Alleg, editor of an Algiers newspaper who was tortured during the battle of Algiers, offered a highly controversial view of French military action, including the use of torture. Although the book was banned in France, it became an underground bestseller in Paris and was translated into both English and German. Spurred by Alleg's account of events, public criticism of French military abuses increased. The French press condemned the army's use of torture, and support for the war slowly eroded. In 1962, after 130 years, France finally abandoned Algeria (McCoy 2006, 20).

In retrospect, it appears that the French made a number of mistakes, including clear violations of the Geneva accords. The government clearly lost the support of the French population in the war just as the United States lost the support of the American people during its war in Vietnam. The use of torture was common to both wars, shaping perceptions of the occupying power. Torture induced fear and resentment in the colonial populations, yet appears to have been counterproductive. Violence did not subside and stability was not attained through the use of torture in either Algeria or Vietnam.

The history of the war in Vietnam indicates that suspected guerrillas were regularly tortured in an attempt to break their resistance. From 1962 to 1974, the CIA, working through the Office of Public Safety (OPS), a division of the U.S. Agency for International Development, posted police advisors to developing nations. By 1971, the OPS had trained over 1 million police officers in forty-seven nations, including 85,000 in South Vietnam. In South Vietnam, OPS trained Vietnamese police in the use of "stringent wartime measures to assist in defeating the enemy" (McCoy 2006, 61). At the provincial level, the Vietnamese police then worked with CIA mercenaries in apprehending suspected Communists for interrogation.

By 1964, each of South Vietnam's forty-plus provinces had its own concrete prison compound called Provincial Interrogation Centers. These provincial centers were established to supplement the police operation in the capital of Saigon. "Sophisticated" interrogation techniques were taught by the CIA and used in addition to older methods like electric shock, beatings, and rape (McCoy 2006, 63).

By 1965, the CIA was engaged in counterterror programs in which teams of interrogators were recruited, supplied, and paid by the United States. Counterterror teams used intimidation, kidnapping, torture, and assassination against Vietcong leaders and suspects. In 1966, the CIA, in a public relations effort, changed the name of the counterterror teams to provincial reconnaissance units. Vietnamese nationals usually carried out the torture against the Vietcong suspects (McCoy 2006, 63).

By 1967, CIA activities were consolidated into what was known as the Phoenix program. The aim of this program was to destroy the Vietcong as a viable force. The Phoenix project used sophisticated computer banks to centralize data on the Vietcong, identifying key people for interrogation or elimination. The project soon became associated with extreme brutality that produced many casualties. Prisoners were tortured and many were summarily executed without trial or due process. According to a 1970 *New York Times* report, many of the South Vietnamese who participated in the Phoenix project were local hoodlums, soldiers of fortune, draft dodgers, or defectors (McCoy 2006, 64–65).

In 1970, Congress began to investigate abuses associated with the Phoenix project. William Colby, the chief of "pacification" for Vietnam, testified before the Senate Foreign Relations Committee that in 1969 alone the Phoenix project killed more than 6,000 Vietcong. Colby noted that between 1968 and 1970, the Phoenix program had killed more than 20,000 Vietcong suspects. A subcommittee of the House of Representatives conducted its own investigation and found that Phoenix killed almost 10,000 suspects in a period of fourteen months. In contrast, the Saigon government assigned almost 41,000 deaths to the Phoenix program. A military intelligence operative stated that in his eighteen months with the Phoenix program between 1967 and 1968, not a single Vietcong suspect survived interrogation. In addition, the operative testified that an intelligence manual issued to him during his training included illegal procedures (McCoy 2006, 68). It is unclear if useful information was obtained through these interrogations or whether the reservations on the application of torture (expressed by Justinian and Ulpian) were supported. More explicit are the distasteful (for the United States) end results of the war and the failure of the overall American strategy in Vietnam.

Amnesty International reported that torture was common in interrogation centers at provincial prisons in Vietnam, as well as at the national police headquarters in Saigon. The respected international organization noted that torture was used partly to suppress prisoner rioting and partly to "rehabilitate" suspected communists. Amnesty International reported particularly appalling prisoner conditions on the island of Con Song off the coast of South Vietnam—beatings, other forms of torture, and prisoners who were permanently shackled in cages (Amnesty International 1975, 164).

Amnesty International identified various forms of torture used in South Vietnam. Some prisoners were immersed in tanks of water that were beaten with sticks from the outside. Reverberations caused internal injury, but left no marks. Another form of torture involved placing a water-soaked cloth over the nose and mouth of a tied-up prisoner, removing it at the last minute before the victim choked to death, and then reapplying the cloth—a procedure known as taking the submarine. In another procedure known as the plane ride, victims were hung by rope or wire attached to their toes or feet and beaten. Allegedly, electricity and sexual torture were also often used, especially on women. Amnesty International concluded that "the brutalizing effects of the Vietnam war have become so entrenched that some of the time the use of torture during interrogation is no longer even motivated by a desire to gain 'intelligence.' An administration defending itself against what it or its major ally construes to be an insurrectionary movement may regrettably find it hard to resist the expedient of torture in efforts to crush its elusive opponent" (1975, 168).

Uncovering Torture at Abu Ghraib and Other Prisons

Role of the Media and Public Opinion

Both the electronic and print media were highly instrumental in publicizing conditions at the Abu Ghraib prison complex. On April 28, 2004, the television program *60 Minutes II* displayed photos showing Iraqis stripped naked and subject to humiliation by American soldiers. Harvard law professor Alan Dershowitz, interviewed on *60 Minutes*, argued that torture is sometimes justified. In advancing what has been called the ticking bomb case, Dershowitz stated that if there was a ticking time bomb and a terrorist who knew exactly where and when the bomb would go off, and if torture was the only way to get the terrorist to talk, thereby saving 500 or 1,000 lives, every

democratic society would use torture. In a *Los Angeles Times* article, Dershowitz elaborated on his position, stating that judges should be allowed to issue "torture warrants" for "non-lethal pressure" in a "ticking bomb" case when a captured terrorist knows about an "imminent large-scale threat" and "refuses to disclose it." Countering this perspective in a *Boston Globe* article, Dershowitz's Harvard University colleague Phillip Heymann challenged the notion of limited, judicially controlled torture, claiming that "torture will spread" and ultimately compromise international "support for our beliefs" (Dershowitz 2001; Heymann 2002; McCoy 2006, 111–112).

The *Washington Post* and *New York Times* both were engaged in keeping the story of torture at Abu Ghraib before the American people. These newspapers conducted independent investigations and sought out government documents that were featured in front-page headlines. The newspapers tried to uncover the original sources of the abuses rather than blame low-level scapegoats. In addition, editorial comments by the *New York Times* roundly condemned American behavior at Abu Ghraib. The *Times* noted at the second anniversary of the Iraq war that atrocities in prisons like Abu Ghraib were "the product of decisions that began at the very top, when the Bush administration decided that Sept. 11 had wiped out its responsibility to abide by the rules, including the Geneva Conventions and the American Constitution" (*New York Times* 2005).

Seymour Hersh, the journalist who helped uncover the My Lai massacre in Vietnam, also spread the Abu Ghraib story with a series of articles for the *New Yorker* magazine (Hersh 2004a, 2004b, 2004c). In the articles, Hersh publicized the findings of a report written by Major General Antonio Taguba. Hersh described the humiliation of Iraqi detainees and the confusion of authority at the prison complex. He also noted that the officer in charge of the prison, General Janis Karpinski, lacked training in handling prisoners. Based on numerous interviews, Hersh described general unease with the situation at Abu Ghraib expressed by leaders of the CIA and military legal officers. The CIA's unhappiness was attributed to the spread of "rough interrogation" operations that initially began with high-value terrorists in Afghanistan. Eventually rough interrogation techniques were applied to lower value individuals in Iraq such as "cabdrivers, brothers-in-law, and people pulled off the streets" (Hersh 2004c). Senior legal officers in the office of the judge advocate general (JAG) were concerned about the apparent disregard for international law shown by Secretary of Defense Donald Rumsfeld.

In 2003 a group of JAG officers paid two visits to Scott Horton, the chair of the New York City Bar Association's Committee on International Human Rights. Hersh reported that the legal officers told Horton "there was an atmosphere of legal ambiguity being created as a result of a policy decision at the highest levels in the Pentagon." The JAG officers further emphasized to Horton that with the war on terror, a fifty-year history of exemplary application of the Geneva Conventions had come to an end. The officers urged Horton "to get involved and speak in a very loud voice" (Hersh 2004c).

Public support for the war in Iraq eroded as American casualties mounted and as the prison abuses at Abu Ghraib and elsewhere became more widely known. The release of the damaging photographs and the widespread news stories still left one question unanswered: whether American GIs at Abu Ghraib were going wild, exhibiting a complete lack of discipline, or whether their superiors had approved of the horrific abuse of Iraqi prisoners. Either way, the objectionable conduct demanded investigation, punishment, and alteration of American military policy. As with the My Lai massacre, the military and the Bush administration were forced to investigate.

Investigations of Abu Ghraib Abuses

McCoy (2006, 154–157) and Mestrovic (2007, 49–86) describe in detail the various reports that uncovered a widespread pattern of abuse throughout Iraq. These abuses were linked to behavior that was previously initiated at Guantanamo and in Afghanistan. A sampling of the findings from various reports is provided below.

The Herrington Report

This report was issued on December 12, 2003, by retired colonel Stuart Herrington. The main conclusions of the report were as follows:

- Overpopulation was a serious problem at Abu Ghraib.
- It was only a matter of time before prisoners staged an uprising.
- Violations of the Geneva Convention stemmed from the fact that senior Iraqi detainees were not treated with regard to their rank and age.
- Detainees showed signs of being beaten by their captors.
- Family members of targets were detained if the target was not found; this created a "hostage feel."
- There was a low number of military police guards for the number of detainees.
- Sweep operations resulted in many people being detained who should not have been detained. This was viewed as counterproductive to efforts to win the cooperation of Iraqi citizens.

The Taguba Report

Major General Antonio Taguba released his report in the spring of 2004. This was the first official report to be released after the disclosure of the infamous photographs at the prison complex. Major findings of the report included the following:

- Numerous sadistic, blatant, and wanton abuses were inflicted on several detainees.
- Systemic and illegal abuse of detainees was evident.
- Military intelligence and other government agency interrogators requested conditions to facilitate "favorable interrogations."
- Little instruction or training was provided to Military Police about the application of the Geneva Convention relative to treatment of prisoners of war.
- Prison conditions included overcrowding, lack of standardization, confusion, lack of discipline, poor accountability, lack of training, and lack of standard operating procedures.
- Camp rules and the provisions of the Geneva Convention were not posted.
- An ambiguous command relationship existed at the prison, with friction and a lack of effective communication between military intelligence and Military Police brigades.

The Fay Report

The report issued by Major General George Fay in August 2004 included a number of damaging revelations:

- Leaders in key positions failed to properly supervise interrogations at Abu Ghraib.
- What started out as undressing and humiliation carried over into sexual and physical assaults by a small group of morally corrupt, unsupervised soldiers and civilians.
- There was confusion about who was in charge and responsible at Abu Ghraib.
- Interrogation and counterresistance policies were poorly defined and changed several

times. Interrogation sometimes crossed the line into abuse.
- Approaches to interrogation used in Afghanistan and Guantanamo were implemented at Abu Ghraib without proper authority or safeguards.
- Dogs were used to "fear up" detainees without proper authorization.
- There were indications that Military Police and Military Intelligence were aware that the use of dog teams in interrogation was abusive.
- Individuals at Abu Ghraib lacked sufficient training in operating a detainment and interrogation facility.
- About 35 percent of contract interrogators lacked formal military training as interrogators.
- Soldiers at Abu Ghraib did not train together and the personnel at the prison were from disparate military units or were civilians.
- There was intense pressure to get good intelligence from detainees.
- Soldiers were confused about whether they had a duty to report violations of the Geneva Convention.
- CIA interrogation practices led to a loss of accountability, abuse, and an unhealthy atmosphere that poisoned the environment at Abu Ghraib.
- Supervisors ignored objections to the abuses at the prison.
- Forced nudity contributed to an escalating "dehumanization" of detainees and set the stage for additional and more severe abuses.
- It is probable that the use of nudity was approved at some level within the chain of command.

The Schlesinger Report

On August 24, 2004, an independent Department of Defense panel headed by former Secretary of

Defense James Schlesinger issued its report. Prominent among its findings were the following:

- Interrogation techniques intended only for Guantanamo, where the Geneva Convention did not apply (because Guantanamo housed al-Qaeda and Taliban who were considered illegal enemy combatants, not prisoners of war), came to be used in the larger war in Iraq, where the Geneva Convention was accepted in principle by President George W. Bush.
- A lack of information about the role of the CIA warranted further review.
- The most egregious abuses, as shown in the photographs taken at Abu Ghraib, were freelance activities.
- No approved procedures called for or allowed the kinds of abuses that in fact occurred.
- The working relationship between the Military Police and Military Intelligence was not understood and could not be implemented.
- Abuses derived from the failure to enforce proper discipline. Institutional and personal responsibility for the abuses lay with individuals at high levels of command.

International Committee of the Red Cross Report

In February 2004, after making twenty-nine visits to U.S. detention facilities throughout Iraq, members of the International Committee of the Red Cross supplied explicit details about interrogation techniques. Their report stated that conditions for most detainees were satisfactory; however, those "under supervision of Military Intelligence were at high risk of being subjected to a variety of harsh treatments ranging from insults, threats and humiliation to both physical and psychological coercion, which in some cases was tantamount to torture" (McCoy 2006, 140). The Red Cross also reported

that it had been informed by various sources that between 70 and 90 percent of detainees in Iraq had been arrested by mistake. The report detailed the following forms of treatment that Military Intelligence used to extract information from detainees:

- Hooding, used to prevent people from seeing, to disorient them, and to prevent them from breathing freely.
- Beatings with hard objects, including pistols and rifles.
- Threats of ill treatment, reprisals against family members, and imminent execution.
- Being stripped naked for several days while held in solitary confinement.
- Being paraded naked outside cells in front of other prisoners.
- Being attacked repeatedly over several days.
- Being handcuffed to cell door bars in humiliating (naked or in underwear) and/or uncomfortable positions.
- Being forced to remain for prolonged periods in stress positions, such as squatting or standing with arms lifted. (McCoy 2006, 141)

During a visit to Abu Ghraib in 2003, Red Cross inspectors discovered detainees completely naked, in totally empty cells and in total darkness. Red Cross medical staff members observed that prisoners treated in this manner exhibited memory loss, difficulties in verbal expression, incoherent speech, and suicidal tendencies. The Red Cross report ultimately concluded that U.S. Military Intelligence at Abu Ghraib was engaged in practices that are prohibited under international humanitarian law.

The Human Rights Watch Report

The organization Human Rights Watch issued a report in April 2005 that supplemented the official U.S. government reports and came to many of the same conclusions. In the report, titled "Getting Away with Torture? Command Responsibilities for the U.S. Abuse of Detainees," the human rights organization asserted the following:

- Abu Ghraib represented only one of many illicit operations.
- Torture and abuse took place not only at Abu Ghraib, but also at dozens of U.S. detention facilities worldwide.
- Many detainees were civilians with no connection to terrorism.
- The only wrongdoers brought to justice were those at the bottom of the chain of command, even though people at the top of the chain of command knew or should have known that violations took place.
- Coercive methods approved by senior U.S. officials included tactics that the United States has repeatedly condemned as barbarity and torture when practiced by other countries.
- Detainees were "rendered" by the United States for interrogation by governments that, according to the U.S. State Department, practice torture routinely. Such rendition violates U.S. and international law.
- The United States "changed the paradigm" of what constitutes violations of the Geneva Conventions and what violates U.S. Army standards for the treatment of detainees.
- White House counsel Alberto Gonzales and Secretary of Defense Donald Rumsfeld both contributed to the paradigm shift by encouraging "flexibility" in the war on terrorism. Language found in a memo written by Gonzales and techniques for interrogation approved by Rumsfeld both violated Geneva Convention provisions.

Application of Case No. 6 to Ethics and Responsible Governance

Breaches of Responsibility: The Public Interest

Upholding the public interest in the United States is consistent with protecting both the safety of citizens and the values held dear by its people. The values of decency, respect for life, honor, fairness, integrity, kindness, empathy, and compassion sometimes may be viewed as "soft" and incompatible with the mandate of ensuring safety. This assertion, however, is subject to question. Arguably, the cost of sacrificing moral integrity by directly or indirectly promoting torture as a legitimate component of the military's capacity to create fear among adversaries is simply too high. The cost is too high for two primary reasons: (1) torture does not produce good intelligence and (2) torture can deepen the resolve of those sympathetic to the tortured. These two pragmatic concerns ignore the moral question of the universal right or wrong of the action itself.

On the one hand, the assertion that instilling fear is always counterproductive flies in the face of a venerated body of literature. In the sixteenth century, the political philosopher Niccolò Machiavelli stated that it was best for rulers to be both feared and loved but, if a ruler could not be both, it was better to be feared than loved. According to Machiavelli, moral principles must be subordinate to necessity: a ruler must be willing to do anything necessary in order to maintain power. On the other hand, the experiences of the French in Algeria (1954–1962) and the United States in Vietnam (1959–1975) provide some empirical evidence that wanton abuse of human rights is dysfunctional to long-term objectives.

From the perspective of the public interest, one needs to ask whether policies that promote torture actually help or harm American security and whether they are justified by Machiavelli's view that moral principles must be subordinated to necessity. To the extent that policies do not help to achieve a desired objective (such as enhanced safety), they should be rejected for the practical reason that they fail to serve the public. On a different level, however, one must also ask whether policies are compatible with the sensibilities and values of the people who empowered the policy makers. One can also question the legitimacy of public policy being made by nonelected representatives of the government (for example, the CIA, Military Police, Military Intelligence, and the U.S. Justice Department). The public interest is ill served if nonelected officials consistently use their discretionary power to foster behavior that is antagonistic to the precepts of the U.S. Constitution and core values of the population.

The ambiguity of interpreting exactly what is in the public interest presents both elected and unelected officials with the opportunity for great discretion in formulating policies that they think will promote the well being of the populace. The ultimate check on policies that are out of synch with the sensibilities of the citizenry remains the ballot box. Abusing the public trust by implementing policies that damage the public interest should produce a reaction that throws out existing leaders and replaces them with others who are more in line with popular sentiment. These leaders in turn appoint officials who use their discretion to make policy that is consistent with the values and priorities of the newly elected leaders. In theory, government is responsive to the public interest as long as appointments are consistent with the values of the elected officials and a nonresponsive, permanent, autonomous, self-serving bureaucracy does not become entrenched. In essence, the ability to "throw the bums out" and replace them with new bums who should, at least initially, be more

responsive to majority beliefs is a hallmark of democracy and the government's responsiveness to the public interest.

From the perspective of the public interest, the overall principle of serving the many, not just the few, helps in evaluating public policy. Specifically, directives that ignore popular opinion, violate international laws, violate national laws, and are carried out in secret should be questioned. The activities at Abu Ghraib can be evaluated according to categorical principles of right and wrong or from the pragmatic perspective of whether they enhanced the safety of Americans. This evaluation of service to the people, however, can be highly subjective, turning on the weights assigned to outcomes such as the perceived benefit or cost to the nation of instilling fear in enemies, the benefit or cost of timely information obtained through extreme coercion, and the benefit or cost to the national interest of specific action in terms of image, reputation, regime legitimacy, and violation of universal moral values.

Breaches of Responsibility: Natural Law

Insights derived from natural law address whether or not certain actions must be rejected out of hand on the basis of "higher law" and human interpretation of that law. This subject is one of the three political influences described in Chapter 2. Natural law can be viewed as interpretation of the unseen, unwritten law that is identified on the gut level as instinctively right or wrong.

Holy war and unspeakable action justified in the name of God are a common theme throughout recorded history. Al-Qaeda is a modern example of a group of people who believe that they are infused with the spirit of God, striking blows against the evil enemies of God. Combatants in war often ask on whose side God is on and whether one is on God's side. Invariably, all participants in conflicts invoke God's name as the justification for their actions. From the time of the ancient Hebrews to the Crusades to the modern times of al-Qaeda, conflicts are framed as good versus evil, godly versus ungodly, moral versus immoral. The "Great Communicator," President Ronald Reagan, had the power of a higher authority in mind when he labeled communism as "ungodly" and an "evil empire."

Natural law suggests that humans can judge behavior based upon both reason and conscience (see Table 2.2). For example, former Secretary of State Colin Powell appears to have used both conscience and reason in expressing strong opposition to behavior at Abu Ghraib. On September 13, 2006, Powell wrote a letter to Senator John McCain where he stated, "the world is beginning to doubt the moral basis of our fight against terrorism." Powell asserted that redefining the Geneva Conventions would "put our own troops at risk" and that the United States should "remind our soldiers of our moral obligations with respect to those in custody" (Gonyea 2006). The UN Office of the High Commissioner for Human Rights condemned the "willful killing, torture and inhuman treatment" of prisoners in Iraq." In 2004, when President George W. Bush visited the Vatican, Pope John Paul II mentioned the "deplorable events" at Abu Ghraib that "troubled the civic and religious conscience of all" (McCoy 2006, 147).

In July 2005, Arizona senator John McCain, a prisoner of war and victim of torture for five years in Vietnam, implored the Senate to pass a clear position on the treatment of detainees. In three separate amendments to a 2006 Pentagon authorization bill, McCain proposed that: (1) the *Army Field Manual* be established as the standard of interrogation of all detainees held in the U.S. Department of Defense custody, (2) all nationals of a foreign country held by the U.S. be registered with the International Committee of the Red Cross, and (3) prohibitions on "cruel, inhuman, or degrading" treatment of anyone in U.S. custody. McCain claimed that Americans were fighting in Iraq not only to preserve lives and liberties, but also to preserve American values and morals. By December 2005, President George W. Bush accepted McCain's position on torture (Associated Press 2005). In his statement before the Senate, McCain asserted:

> The Army Field Manual authorizes interrogation techniques that have proven effective in extracting life-saving information from the most hardened enemy prisoners. It also recognizes that torture and cruel treatment are ineffective methods, because they induce prisoners to say what their interrogators want to hear, even if it is not true, while bringing discredit upon the United States. It is consistent with our laws and, most importantly, our values. Let us not forget that al-Qaeda sought not just to destroy American lives on September 11, but American values—our way of life and all we cherish. Now . . . preserving the common values we hold dear is more important than ever. We fight not just to preserve our lives and liberties but also our morals, and we will never allow the terrorists to take those away. In this war that we must win—that we will win—we must never simply fight evil with evil. (2005)

McCain further asserted that Americans hold themselves "to standards of treatment of people no matter how evil or terrible they may be." To do otherwise, according to the senator, would undermine both the nation's security and the nation's greatness. For McCain, the United States is qualitatively different from her enemies because "we're better than them, and we are stronger for our faith": "we stand for something more in the world—a moral mission, one of freedom and democracy and human rights at home and abroad. . . . The enemy we fight has no respect for human life or human rights. They don't deserve our sympathy. But this isn't about who they are. This is about who we are. These are the values that distinguish us from our enemies" (McCain 2005).

McCain's proposal to enforce the use of the military field manual received strong support from fellow senators Lindsey Graham, a former military lawyer, and John Warner, chair of the Armed Services Committee. These senators asserted that new standards were needed to clear up the kind of confusion among U.S. troops that had led to the abuse scandal at Abu Ghraib (Babington and Murray 2005). Retired military leaders also agreed that abuse of Iraqi prisoners could endanger U.S. service members. In arguing for adoption of his proposal, Senator McCain read a letter from Colin Powell that traced prison abuse to ambiguity in instructions and urged restricting interrogation methods to those clearly outlined in the *U.S. Field Manual on Intelligence Interrogation.*

Ultimately, the Senate agreed with McCain that torture was anathema to the values of Americans. On October 5, 2005, by a vote of 90–9, the Senate affirmed its commitment to establish uniform standards for the interrogation of people detained by U.S. military personnel.

The conservative magazine *Economist* noted as early as 2003 that there was "a line which democracies cross at their peril" and that "on one side of that line stand societies sure of their civilized values" (McCoy 2006, 125). The implication of the *Economist* was that acceptance of torture as a policy tool endangers civilized values and runs counter to beliefs long cherished in democracies such as the United States.

Breaches of Responsibility: The Rule of Law

The rule of law appears to have been ignored at the Abu Ghraib prison complex as well as at other prisons throughout the world. Numerous international treaties and domestic laws were eviscerated by events at Abu Ghraib in the name of "necessity." Law became an accepted casualty of the perceived

necessities of war. International agreements were skirted through legal loopholes that allowed the United States to do what it wanted to do by creating and following its own interpretations. Once loopholes were established, they served as rationales for wanton abuse and disregard of international agreements.

Abu Ghraib stands in contrast to human right advocacy that was previously associated with the United States. For example, after World War II, the United States became a leader in the pursuit of human rights. In 1948, former first lady Eleanor Roosevelt, the chair of the United Nations Commission on Human Rights, secured the adoption of the Universal Declaration of Human Rights. This agreement specified that no one should be subject to torture or to cruel, inhuman, or degrading treatment. In 1949, the United States ratified the Geneva Convention III treaty (also known as the Geneva Convention Relative to the Treatment of Prisoners of War) and accepted its strong prohibitions against torture.

During the war on terror, lawyers in the Bush administration as well as others such as Vice President Dick Cheney and Secretary of Defense Donald Rumsfeld advocated more aggressive treatment of detainees that would invalidate the spirit of the Geneva accords. Human Rights Watch reported that after the destruction of the World Trade Center on September 11, 2001, the Bush administration seemingly determined that winning the war on terrorism would require the United States to circumvent international law. A former director of the CIA's counterterrorism unit, Cofer Black, in testimony before Congress, stated simply, "there was a 'before 9/11' and there was an 'after 9/11.' After 9/11 the gloves came off" (McCoy 2006, 119).

According to Human Rights Watch, the first indication that the gloves were coming off occurred when the United States began sending suspects to its naval base at Guantanamo Bay, Cuba. The human rights organization claimed that Guantanamo was deliberately chosen in an attempt to put detainees beyond the jurisdiction of U.S. courts. Human Rights Watch declared that Secretary of Defense Donald Rumsfeld ignored the deeply rooted U.S. practice of applying the Geneva Convention broadly when the first detainees were designated "enemy combatants." This label denied the detainees the status of prisoners of war and overlooked abuses that later became synonymous with Abu Ghraib. Rumsfeld declared that "unlawful combatants do not have any rights under the Geneva Convention." Human Rights Watch, however, alleged that Rumsfeld overlooked the Geneva Conventions' provision of "explicit protections to all persons captured in an international armed conflict, even if they were not entitled to POW status" (Human Rights Watch 2004).

Human Rights Watch further declared that the Justice Department, in a series of legal memoranda written in late 2001 and early 2002, helped build a framework for circumventing international law. The Justice Department memos initially argued that the Geneva Convention did not apply to detainees from Afghanistan because they were not fighting for a legitimate government and were not prisoners of war but illegal combatants. A few memos and legal opinions in particular severed the link between the rule of law and interrogation procedures. For example, Vice President Richard Cheney's legal counsel, David S. Addington, drafted an order that permitted detaining suspects under "conditions as the Secretary of Defense may prescribe." This draft was accepted by the president on November 13, 2001, when Bush effectively denied al-Qaeda detainees access to any court and relegated these cases to U.S. military tribunals. Following this sweeping presidential order, John Yoo of the Department of Justice's Office of Legal Counsel coauthored a forty-two–page memo on January 9, 2002, concluding that

neither the Geneva Convention nor any of the laws of war applied to the conflict in Afghanistan. The Yoo memo argued that Afghanistan was a "failed state" and that both the Taliban and al-Qaeda were "illegal enemy combatants." By placing both the entire Taliban regime and al-Qaeda into this new category (neither soldier nor civilian), Yoo's memo excluded members of both entities from the Geneva Conventions (McCoy 2006, 113).

On January 18, 2002, White House counsel Alberto Gonzales endorsed Yoo's interpretation and recommended that the president declare Taliban and al-Qaeda forces outside the coverage of the Geneva Convention. When informed by Gonzales of the Justice Department's position as stated in the Yoo memo, Bush declared that since the war on terrorism was a new kind of war that placed a high premium on the ability to quickly obtain information from captured terrorists, the Geneva Convention would not apply to al-Qaeda or the Taliban. The next day Defense Secretary Donald Rumsfeld advised his combat commanders that al-Qaeda and Taliban individuals under the control of the Department of Defense were not entitled to prisoner-of-war status (McCoy 2006, 114–115).

On January 22, 2002, Assistant Attorney General Jay S. Bybee sent to Alberto Gonzales a thirty-seven–page memo arguing that the Geneva Convention would not apply to the detention conditions of al-Qaeda prisoners. In August 2002, Bybee, aided by his deputy John Yoo and the vice president's legal counsel David Addington, delivered to Alberto Gonzales a fifty-page memo that provided sweeping authority for harsh interrogation. This infamous "Bybee memo" interpreted torture as acts carried out with the intent to inflict severe pain or suffering. The memo, in essence, excused interrogation practices if the intent was to gain information rather than inflict pain. Furthermore, Bybee concluded that to constitute torture under U.S. statute the physical pain must "be equivalent in intensity to the pain accompanying serious physical injury, such as organ failure, impairment of bodily functions, or even death" (McCoy 2006, 121). The impact of the Bybee memo was profound. McCoy declares, "through this linguistic legerdemain, the Justice Department granted the CIA de facto authority to use torture techniques, excepting only 'the most heinous acts' that brought maiming or death. . . . By misinterpreting U.S. law Bybee issued a virtual license for torture that would remain in effect during two years of the most aggressive counterterror operation, August 2002 to June 2004" (2006, 122–123).

These legal opinions within the Bush administration helped to circumvent international law and shape U.S. interrogation policy in direct contradiction to the nation's strong human rights position advocated after World War II. A number of pressures, however, were able to arrest the drift away from the rule of law. By 2004 the White House issued apologies for the prisoner abuses yet insisted that Abu Ghraib was the result of abuse, not a systematic strategy of torture. The administration repudiated the August 2002 Bybee memo and in June 2004 the Supreme Court affirmed the right of enemy combatants to due process under the law. This decision rejected the White House's original contention that it had the right to impose unchecked, unlimited detention on prisoners in the war on terror. Speaking for the majority in the 6–3 decision, Justice Sandra Day O'Connor stated that "indefinite detention for the purpose of interrogation is not authorized" and "an unchecked system of detention carries the potential to become a means for oppression" (McCoy 2006, 148).

Questions for Student Group Discussion

1. Was the behavior at Abu Ghraib consistent with American values?
2. Is torture ever justified? When might it be justified?
3. Would you recommend trials for other individuals involved in Abu Ghraib? Which individuals do you think should have been tried?
4. Were the penalties associated with Abu Ghraib appropriate?
5. How did Abu Ghraib affect the image of the United States around the world?
6. What do you think the ultimate lessons of Abu Ghraib will be?
7. Is the propagation of fear among potential enemies an effective long-term strategy for the United States?
8. What dangers may flow from policies that sanction torture? Are these dangers acceptable?
9. Does the United States need to show potential adversaries that it will do whatever is necessary in order to survive in the world today?
10. Evaluate the costs and benefits of torture as an official policy.

Chapter 6
Conclusions

Ethics and Responsibility

"Morals," "ethics," "customs," and "mores" are largely interchangeable terms that explain acceptable or unacceptable forms of conduct. The word "ethical" is derived from the Greek *ethos*, which originally referred to the customs of a group and over time came to mean character. The word "moral" comes from the concept of mores, the accepted traditional customs of a particular social group. Mores and customs therefore define morality and attitudes toward acceptable behavior.

Responsibility, in contrast, has been defined as accepting and carrying out fairly well-defined roles, such as the roles of employee, parent, citizen, and group member. Sometimes these roles are in the process of changing, with little agreement about the parameters of acceptable behavior. Whether stable or in flux, responsibility implies some sort of obligation to law and common culture (Cooper 1998, xix). The morality or culture of the population is related to responsibility since adherence to obligation is shaped by culture.

Both ancient and recent history can serve as a guide to understand ethics, customs, and perceptions of responsibility. In ancient times the guardians of customs were old men or priests, medicine men or chiefs, or old women. These individuals would modify existing customs, add new cus-

toms, or explain the reasons for creating of new customs. The customs of the group included not only attitudes about living members of the group but also the views of the dead and ancestral gods. Customs were enforced by a combination of public approval, taboos, ritual, and physical force (Dewey and Tufts 1932, 54).

Ethics and morals are viewed within the context of politics. John Dewey (1859–1952) and his colleague James Tufts (1862–1942) were prominent American philosophers who taught at the University of Chicago around the time of its founding in 1890. These scholars argue that in a democracy political morals and ethics involve "safeguarding the democratic ideal against the influences which are always at work to undermine it." In addition, they advocate supporting the democratic ideal, a perspective that fosters "the development of all social capacities of every individual member of society" (1932, 474). Citizens, according to Dewey and Tufts, have a responsibility to safeguard, buttress, and defend the principles of democracy.

Responsible governance must advance democratic values through ethical behavior. This book has identified high-profile cases in order to illustrate the tension between democracy-enhancing and democracy-diminishing behavior. These cases should help students interpret right and wrong, moral and immoral, good and evil, and correct and erroneous actions. Once these assessments are made, corrective action can be taken. The framework of the public interest, natural law, and the rule of law has been used in order to explore the ethical or unethical nature of action. This framework provides a way to interpret public sector behavior. Each of the cases chosen for discussion dominated media coverage for an extensive period of time. Each case study identifies egregious forms of conduct and shows how the conduct interfaces with conceptions of ethical behavior.

Ethics typically is viewed from the perspectives of: (1) principles, (2) ends, (3) intuition, or (4) virtue. German philosopher Immanuel Kant (1724–1804) developed the idea of a "categorical imperative," or absolute moral law. From this perspective, individuals should act according to a universal code or an absolute moral command. This principle-based or deontological perspective contends that the ethics of an action depend not upon the consequences, but upon the features of the act itself. A categorical imperative denotes an absolute requirement that applies itself in all circumstances. For Kant, consistency was essential. People should not apply rules to others that they refuse to apply to themselves. The golden rule of "Do unto others as you would have them do unto you" is a commonsense application of Kant's notion of consistency (Geuras and Garofalo 2005, 53).

In contrast to the Kantian, deontological view of universal principles, the teleological view of ethics looks at ends, purposes, and goals. In a teleological view of the world, the morality of certain actions is justified on the basis of their consequences. Teleology is often equated with utilitarianism, the concept of promoting the greatest happiness. Action is justified when it promotes the greatest happiness for the greatest number.

Happiness is considered central to the idea of governance. The aims of public organizations include promoting health, education, safety, and economic prosperity. The pursuit of happiness is even identified in the Declaration of Independence as an "inalienable right." Utilitarian philosophers such as John Stuart Mill and Jeremy Bentham conceived of a world where the activities that made any individual happy would also promote the happiness of everyone. Utilitarian philosophers, however, did not provide a clear method for assessing happiness or determining what constituted the greatest happiness.

The intuitionist-based approach to ethics focuses upon gut-level moral feelings. Intuitionism reflects the belief that human beings have a moral sense that recognizes the moral character of an act. According to Professor of Philosophy Dean Geuras and Professor of Political Science Charles Garofalo (2005, 58), people's moral sense, not an esoteric theory, instructs them. For example, their moral sensitivities can tell them that helping other people is better than torturing them. Nevertheless, there are controversial ethical issues on which people's moral sense differs, and the intuitionist approach provides little help in deciding among different intuitions.

Finally, virtue theory considers an act to be good on the basis of the character trait or virtue that the act denotes. For example, saving children in the middle of a battle would be considered a good act on the basis of the character trait of courage or compassion. Giving money to the poor would be an example of the positive character trait of generosity. In contrast to these acts, unethical actions such as cruelty or cheating on income taxes are evidences of poor character traits (Geuras and Garofalo 2005, 59).

The case studies explored in this book refer to behavior that has consequences for either promoting or impairing governance. The case studies also refer to universal principles that appear to be either followed or violated, intuitive feelings of doing the right thing, and instances when acts displayed both positive and negative character traits.

Ethics can be viewed from either a holistic or an individualistic perspective. These perspectives are related to each other in the sense that individuals make up organizations and societies while at the same time the large groupings exert influence on individuals. The individual or microlevel view of ethics and the macrolevel (organization and society) view are described below.

The Individual View of Ethics

At the individual level, people possess different sets of values, norms, and habits. These are often inculcated into them at a young age and last their lifetime. From this individualistic perspective, ethical behavior emanates from ethical individuals who learned ethical values from parents, teachers, peers, political leaders, or religious leaders. Individuals may also be shaped by their broader environment and society or by their workplace organization. The ideal of free will implies that individuals can exercise control over their actions and decisions. It also suggests that individuals can be held morally accountable for their actions. The microlevel perspective of ethics implies that individual character can be developed and that common virtues can be fostered. Lists of positive character traits have been advanced as guides for living and examples for individuals to emulate. For example, the Boy Scout Law states that a scout is trustworthy (tells the truth, keeps promises), loyal (true to family, friends, nation), helpful (concerned with other people), friendly (seeks to understand others), courteous (polite to all regardless of position), kind (treats others as he wants to be treated), obedient (follows rules and obeys laws), cheerful (tries to make others happy), thrifty (saves for unforeseen needs), brave (has the courage to stand for what he thinks is right), clean (keeps his body and mind

fit), and reverent (faithful in his religious duties and respectful of the beliefs of others) (Boy Scouts of America 2008). The Girl Scout Law is another example of a character-based approach to building better and more ethical societies: "I will do my best to be honest and fair, friendly and helpful, considerate and caring, courageous and strong, and responsible for what I say and do, and to respect myself and others, respect authority, use resources wisely, make the world a better place, and be a sister to every Girl Scout" (Girl Scouts 2008).

Character and virtue are not recently discovered values. Moderation or the "golden mean" is discussed by Aristotle as one of the great individual virtues. His doctrine of the mean consists of three pillars. First, the "good person" is in possession of equilibrium. This is related to the idea that a healthy person is in a balanced state. Equilibrium is the right feelings at the right time about the right things, toward the right people, for the right end, and in the right way. The second pillar states that a person should strive to achieve a mean or equilibrium that is relative to the individual. Aristotle's conception therefore is not a one-size-fits-all system of ethics, but requires discovery of what is good for a particular person. The third pillar of Aristotle's golden mean refers to the idea that each virtue falls between two vices. Virtue is the intermediate between alternative vices such as excess or deficiency. If one's character is too near either vice, then the person will incur blame. For example, according to Aristotle, a person who seeks pleasure through drinking must find the mean between becoming a drunkard and not drinking at all. Aristotle's idea of virtue is reflected in the inscription at the temple of the oracle at Delphi, "Nothing in Excess."

Character-based as well as virtue-based ethics have attracted great attention in recent years (Dobel 1990; Cooper 1991; Denhardt 1994; Hart 1994; Svara 2007). Numerous traits have been identified that describe an ethical person. The following core values and principles represent one popular list of values: trustworthiness, integrity, reliability, loyalty, respect, responsibility, fairness, and caring (Josephson 2006). This laundry list also advocates honesty, truthfulness, sincerity, and candor. Enemies to integrity include self-interest, self-protection, self-deception, and self-righteousness. The character trait of fairness includes impartiality, equity, and fair process. The value of respect includes civility, autonomy, and tolerance. Responsibility includes accountability, pursuit of excellence, and self-restraint. To this list Terry Cooper, Maria B. Crutcher Professor in Citizenship and Democratic Values at the University of Southern California (1987, 324), adds the values of rationality, prudence, respect for law, self-discipline, and independence.

Virtue is linked to government action because a connection exists between the virtuous individual and the honorable government representative (Hart 1994). To be a virtuous citizen, David Hart, J. Fish Smith Professor of Free Enterprise Studies at Brigham Young University, believes people are required to find out about the moral character of others, believe in American core values, act as moral and independent agents, and treat others with respect and tolerance. Hart contends that government workers can become honorable bureaucrats through the possession of superior prudence, which includes traits such as commitment to American values, having the interests of citizens at heart, willingness to take moral risks, and the idea that the more one benefits from society, the more one has an obligation to reciprocate.

Patrick Dobel, professor of public affairs at the University of Washington, focuses on the concept of personal integrity as a means to ensure correct public sector behavior. He contends that personal integrity arises from the ability of people to organize their activities around core commitments that they view as central to their lives. Dobel lists seven commitments that embody public integrity: (1) being truthfully accountable to relevant authorities and the public, (2) addressing the public values of the regime, (3) respecting and building institutions to achieve goals, (4) ensuring fair and adequate participation of relevant stakeholders, (5) seeking competent performance in the execution of policy, (6) working for efficiency in government, and (7) connecting policy with the self-interest of the public in such a way that the basic purposes of the policy are not subverted (1990, 355).

Contemporary writers such as Stuart Hampshire and Alasdair MacIntyre also discuss the link between environmental influences and individual character traits. They contend that individual character traits are not innate, but are capable of being cultivated (Garofalo and Geuras 1999, 89). Hampshire and MacIntyre maintain that since character traits are malleable organizational or cultural setting can have at least some influence on the attitudes, values, and character traits of its members.

In theory, organizations should be able to promote certain types of values and discourage others. Organizations may discourage ethical behavior by adopting Machiavelli's view that one "must learn how not to be virtuous" and that "the man who wants to act virtuously in every way necessarily comes to grief among so many who are not virtuous" (Dobel 2006, 55). Alternatively, organizations might adopt the logic of promoting ethical behavior. Organizational culture as well as leaders in organizations may foster or discourage ethical behavior of members.

The Organizational or Societal View of Ethics

The microlevel understanding of ethics focuses on character traits. This view reflects the perspective that people who exhibit good character traits are more likely to produce ethical organizations, good societies, and sustainable cultures. This individualistic character view, however, appears to be incomplete because it does not consider the role of organizations and society at large in shaping individual values. From the macro organizational and societal view, it is possible that virtuous people exist but that they then become corrupted by bad organizations and destructive societal values.

Individual values are shaped by experiences with major institutions. It is possible that unethical organizations corrupt people; ethical organizations may have the opposite effect. James Bowman, professor of public administration at Florida State University, states that organizations have an effect on behavior and that organizations should strive for positive ethical influence: "Public and private organizations should plant and cultivate standards by which a professional can measure his or her behavior, encourage correction of deficiencies, and minimize institutional conditions that lead to unethical behavior." Bowman recognizes that organizations and leadership figures always send some type of signal to employees, even if it is indifference. He notes, "The issue is not whether norms of conduct will develop in an organization, but rather what they are, how they are communicated, and whether all are fully conscious of the ethical dimensions of work. The idea is to nourish a transparent institutional culture by offering incentives for ethical behavior, reducing opportunities for corruption, and decreasing the risk of untoward conduct" (2006, 35).

A variety of other authors have also explored the relationship between organizations and ethics. Cooper (1998, 176) contends that the structure of organizations is important to maintaining the ethical conduct of public organizations and that there is too much concern placed on the individual administrator. He suspects that this tendency has its roots in American individualism. For Cooper,

there exists a "coequal reality" of organizations as shapers of character, values, and identities. He feels that organizational structure can exercise significant influence on the ethical conduct of individuals.

The importance of informal group values has long been recognized in organizational theory. This recognition can be found in the works of Chester Barnard, which were inspired by the Hawthorne studies that began in 1924. The Hawthorne Studies (1924–1933) involved a number of experiments and reports at the Hawthorne plant of the Chicago Western Electric Company. These studies are widely recognized by organizational theories as the most significant demonstration of the importance of social and psychological factors in the workplace up to that time. They contributed to a major shift in research on organizations. This shift emphasized social influences, informal processes, and the motivational power of attention from others (Rainey 2003, 33).

Barnard's book *The Functions of the Executive* (1938) became one of the most influential books in the history of organizational theory. In this book, Barnard argues that any organization has both an informal and a formal component. These two aspects of organizations are interrelated and necessary for each other's success. Informal organizations establish general understandings, customs, and habits, creating conditions for the formal organization. The informal understandings within the organization assist communication, maintain cohesion, and foster a feeling of personal integrity (Fry 1989, 164). Barnard's writings on informal organizations have been viewed as an early recognition of the importance of organizational culture (Rainey 2003, 34).

Cooper (1998, 184) notes that organizational culture can either discourage or encourage ethical behavior. For example, police organizations often adopt a "code of silence" whereby police officers are strongly advised not to report unethical conduct of fellow officers. Alternatively, an organization's leadership can shape the organization's culture by setting a positive ethical tone (Schein 1985, 317). Leaders help in defining ethical norms, values, and accepted behavior. Cooper states, "What leaders pay attention to, how they react to critical incidents and organizational crises, the deliberate role modeling they provide, their criteria for allocating rewards and status, and their criteria for recruitment, selection, promotion, retirement, and excommunication are the primary shapers of an organization's culture, including its ethical norms" (1998, 184).

The presence of organizations with different missions, orientations, values, and ideals is intuitively obvious. For example, former president of the American Political Science Association, James Q. Wilson (1989, 91) recognizes that every organization has a culture, a persistent, patterned way of thinking about tasks and relationships within the organization. Organizational cultures, in turn, define organizational responses to situations. Organizational culture has also been linked to individual personalities, with different people responding to their situations in different manners. For example, Wilson claims that, when faced with aggression, some people will retreat, some will fight back, and some will be paralyzed by fear. When faced with the opportunity to make money, some will seize it, some ignore it, some anguish over it.

Differences between the cultures of different organizations are seen in large public sector organizations such as the U.S. Marine Corps and the Peace Corps. Each culture is supportive of its organization's distinctive mission: one dedicated to the military defense of the country, the other to world peace and friendship. Differences also exist within large public sector organizations such as the Central Intelligence Agency (CIA) or the U.S. Navy. Wilson notes that within the CIA historically

there have been two dominant cultures: (1) analysis of intelligence on the intentions and capabilities of other nations and (2) the clandestine gathering of intelligence and the conduct of covert operations abroad. Wilson identifies rivalries in the CIA between the "white" (analytical) and "black" (clandestine) sides of the organization (1989, 101).

Wilson also identifies competition for resources and recognition within the U.S. Navy, where at least three organizational cultures are symbolized by the kind of shoe their officers wear. The "black shoe" navy represents battleships, cruisers, and destroyers built to protect sea-lanes. The "brown shoe" navy represents aircraft carriers. The submarine fleet is identified as the "felt shoe" navy since officers wear cloth shoes to reduce noise and avoid detection by the enemy. Since World War II, the "brown shoe" navy has been recognized as the dominant culture (Wilson 1989, 106).

James Svara (2007, 129) states that members of organizations at all levels have opportunities to shape the ethical climate. Those at the top have opportunities to set priorities. Mid-level managers shape conditions of work, guide how staff members interact with citizens, and supervise subordinates. Street-level administrators such as teachers, social services eligibility specialists, inspectors, and police officers shape the organization's openness, fairness, and public perceptions of integrity. Approaches to management that could elevate the ethical climate in public organizations include management by example, establishing clear expectations in codes of ethics, establishing means of control through inspections and audits, ethics training, establishing channels for complaints, and establishing fair procedures for access and outcomes.

Public organizations also function within broader society and dominant values of the broader society affect values of individual workers. Discussion of ethics within organizations therefore also includes critiques of the broader society. Societal morality either positively or negatively impacts organizational morality and organizational effectiveness. Critiques of moral conduct are readily found among religious figures, interest group leaders, and politicians.

Some religious leaders point to what they see as immorality of American society as a cause of great concern. They focus on large societal factors such as divorce, homosexuality, adultery, abortion, crime, pornography, sexual promiscuity, popular music, and uncivil discourse as indicators of the breakdown of American culture. Other religious figures choose to see immorality in factors such as personal greed, environmental destruction, dishonest business practices, racism, homophobia, and economic injustice.

It is difficult to discern the moral status of an entire society at one point in time. Throughout history, demagogues have railed against the immorality of some sinners living in their midst. The inquisition of the middle ages as well as the infamous Salem witch trials in seventeenth century Massachusetts should at least give pause for those anxious to root out evil and purify the community. A revival of "family values" have been stressed by politicians such as Ronald Reagan, George W. Bush, and Mike Huckabee as a cure for America's problems. Whether or not an embrace of these values will lead to greater ethical conduct in governance, however, remains an open question.

Case Studies and the Public Interest, Natural Law, and the Rule of Law

Ethical transgressions in American politics have traditionally involved sex and money. From the deontological perspective, American attitudes toward sex can be seen as an outcome of religious values that were held by early American settlers. For example, a condemnation of adultery can be traced to the strict Calvinist philosophy that dominated the Massachusetts Bay Colony. Nathaniel Hawthorne's popular nineteenth-century novel *The Scarlet Letter* describes such attitudes. The novel takes place in seventeenth-century Boston, then a Puritan settlement. While waiting for her husband to arrive in America, Hester Prynne gives birth to another man's child. Refusing to identify her child's father, she is ostracized by the town and forced to wear the scarlet letter "A" as punishment for her adultery.

Puritan beliefs also can be seen as influencing American attitudes toward money. As illustrated in Case No. 1, the behavior of machine politicians such as William Tweed sharply contrasted with the beliefs of good-government reformers. Lavish spending, plunder of public resources for private gain, indolence, and the perception of monetary reward unattached to hard work are diametrically at odds with the Protestant ethic that prioritizes saving, sacrifice, and work. Similarly, Case No. 2 and Case No. 4 investigate attitudes toward money in modern society. In Case No. 2, money was utilized in order to control elections, thereby robbing citizens of the right to freely and fairly elect their representatives. In Case No. 4, patronage was used to reward friends by placing them in responsible positions with high salaries even though they did not have relevant qualifications. From the perspective of the Protestant ethic, the appointment of FEMA director Michael Brown contradicted Puritan beliefs in hard work, reward for effort, and a society based on the concept of meritocracy.

The case studies can also be viewed from the perspectives of public interest and the rule of law. Arguably, plunder of the public treasury, appointment of incompetent officials, unfair electoral advantage, and dishonesty (even if it is about sex) are not in the public interest. These acts violate cherished principles such as merit, honesty, hard work, and fair elections. The rule of law appeared to be violated in regard to perjury (Case No. 3) and proper elections (Case No. 2).

Case No. 5 and Case No. 6 identify apparent violations of international law as well as apparent violations of natural law. Natural law remains shrouded in mystery; the presence of natural law is not provable to the skeptic. A body of literature, however, exists that refers to intuition and gut-level understandings of right and wrong. The cases discussed in this book raise a number of questions that readers can try to answer on the basis of their "gut" or intuition. One can ask whether in the context of the Vietnam War a reasonable person would justify the shooting of unarmed women and children when moving through a village on a military operation. One could ask within the context of the war in Iraq if a reasonable person would justify the interrogation tactics employed at Abu Ghraib. These questions relate to intuition based on some universal, "higher" law that is instinctively identified by individuals.

Each of the cases reviewed in this book provides insight into ethical behavior. Questions raised are not frivolous or esoteric but based on high-profile, real-life experiences in American history. They relate to our understanding and interpretation of behavior in the broad society. They relate to violations of ethical norms and reactions from others in society. Dewey and Tufts (1932, 451) argue that every public act brings the agent who performs the act into association with others. These others interpret public acts as just or unjust, serving public or private ends, intuitively wrong or intuitively right.

Interpretations of public actions are shaped in turn by a variety of forces. These forces include the personal, microlevel values of the people who make and implement laws as well as macrolevel organizational and societal forces. Individuals operate within large organizations that possess distinct cultures. Individuals must adapt to the organization culture or face ostracism. Organizations encourage or discourage certain types of behavior by the cues, rewards, and punishments they dole out. Numerous authors conclude that organizations can encourage or discourage ethical and responsible behavior.

Responsible and Ethical Behavior in Twenty-First–Century America

It is easy to say that responsible governance is an oxymoron: if one works or represents the government, how can he or she be responsible? Perhaps this is too cynical a position to take. There is evidence that those who work in the public sector are more idealistic, more concerned for the social good, and less concerned with making money than other citizens. At a minimum, however, there is little reason to instinctively believe that public sector managers, workers, and government leaders are more corrupt, more irresponsible, and more dishonest than other citizens of the nation.

The old aphorism that "we get the government we deserve" is attributed to H.L. Mencken, the twentieth-century journalist and social critic known as the Sage of Baltimore. To the extent that Mencken was correct, America's governance therefore reflects the character, personality, and nature of its people. There is, however, no universal agreement about how to characterize the American people. The United States has always been more varied, heterogeneous, pluralistic, and culturally diffuse than other societies, traits attributed to the multiethnic composition of the country, its relatively young age, and the variety of early settlements.

It has been inferred that American greatness is tied to the character of its people. The idea that America is great because it is good and that if America ever ceases to be good, it will also cease to be great is commonly attributed to Alexis de Tocqueville, the French aristocrat who traveled throughout America in the 1830s. Tocqueville never uttered this line; however, in a 1952 campaign speech; Dwight D. Eisenhower attributed it not directly to Tocqueville but to "a wise philosopher [who] came to this country" (Pitney 1995). President Ronald Reagan referred to the statement in a 1982 speech, attributing it to Eisenhower's quotation of Tocqueville. Two years later, Reagan declared that Tocqueville observed that "America is great because America is good." After this point, the phrase showed up with great frequency in political rhetoric. President Bill Clinton also made reference to this idea in 1994 when he observed, "Alexis de Tocqueville said a long time ago that America is great because America is good; and if America ever ceases to be good, she will no longer be great" (Pitney 1995).

The popularity of the aphorism about America and its people is a testament to the popularity of American nationalism (America is great) as well as the nation's grounding in the common virtues of the average citizen (Americans are good). Ethical, moral, and cultural deterioration (Americans are no longer good) therefore is inextricably linked to the idea of national power.

The cases studies in this book indicate that questionable behavior has occurred throughout American history. Public sector representatives have acted ethically as well as unethically. Public leaders have taken advantage of opportunities open to them. Sometimes unethical behavior has been severely punished; other times it has not. Some actions led to legal prosecution and public outrage; other actions were ignored. Perhaps the ethical norms of the day determined what types of public behavior were punished. In this regard, the cases serve as a prism to reflect ethical values at different points in U.S. history.

History is a guide for the future. History in-

dicates that people in government have been both ethical and unethical; they have acted both responsibly and irresponsibly. As James Madison declared in the *Federalist Papers*, men are not angels and if angels were to govern men, neither external nor internal controls on government would be necessary. Controls on behavior are therefore necessary since it is widely recognized that men are not angels. These controls must coexist with positive incentives for ethical behavior.

Public organizations should promote behavior that supports their ability to act in the public interest. "Right" behavior remains a difficult concept for all citizens in the United States to agree upon; however, guides to action (such as abiding by both man-made and "higher" law) do exist. These guides can serve public organizations by enabling them to behave responsibly.

The public sector has been assigned serious responsibilities. Public officials have been handed tasks such as providing for the nation's defense, keeping citizens safe from street crime, educating the children, driving buses, putting out fires, inspecting food, and carrying out a host of other functions essential for the well-being of America. The nation faces an array of challenges in the twenty-first century. It must compete economically in a global environment, protect its citizens from external enemies, secure its borders, promote justice, and inculcate a sense of opportunity for all. In order to accomplish these goals, a trustworthy, responsible, and dedicated public sector workforce is essential. Without such a basis for public policy, selfish, capricious, unfair, and irresponsible actions are inevitable.

Conclusions

This book develops a framework to explain how ideas of right and wrong have been formulated in the United States. It posits that political influences as well as human ecology influences have shaped American conceptualizations of ethics and responsible public sector behavior. Ecological influences refer to the early settlement patterns that placed different ethnic, racial, and religious groups within the borders of the present-day United States as well as the influence of later immigration. Puritan, Presbyterian, and Quaker settlements established footholds in the New World and would compete for cultural supremacy. Political influence included diverse conceptions of natural law, the public interest, and the rule of law.

These three political influences have been used in this book in order to assess the ethicality of specific behavior. Ethical actions are viewed as the core component of responsibility since an ethical government is also viewed as a responsible government. Questions of ethical or unethical, responsible or irresponsible, right or wrong behavior, however, are not easily assessed. Natural law, similar to what is known today as intuitionism, provides some justification for instinctive assessments. The public interest provides a useful frame of reference to judge whether the tenets of democracy are being violated or reinforced. The rule of law refers to the inviolability of the governing principles. All three political influences are essential components of responsible governance.

History tells us that responsible governance has not always occurred in the United States. The philosopher George Santayana said that those who cannot remember the past are condemned to repeat it. This statement can be applied to acts of public responsibility and irresponsibility. From the case studies reviewed in this book, it is evident that people in positions of power can abuse their power. They can gain personal riches, garner income security, or treat others in a manner that they would not want to be applied to them. Often the abuses of the past are simply repeated. My Lai begets Abu Ghraib; Boss Tweed begets Tom

DeLay and Michael Brown. Abu Ghraib and Tom DeLay may in turn become latter-day models for future replication.

It is easy to despair about the state of governance. However, the lessons of the past also tell us that self-correcting mechanisms are available. Some of those who participated in abuses at My Lai and Abu Ghraib were prosecuted and sentenced. Tweed went to prison, DeLay was rebuked, Michael Brown was replaced, Clinton was impeached, Calley was convicted. An argument therefore can be made that someone is paying attention and that the government system of checks and balances preserves cherished institutions. The courts, the media, public opinion, voters, and diligent public servants all help to expose violations of the public trust and to chastise the wrongdoers.

Responsibility is a vague construct that should be reinforced in individuals as well as government institutions. At the level of the individual, steps can be taken to enhance the ethos of citizenship. In theory, constitutional democracy is best protected when individual citizens are informed about issues, recognize their interests, vote according to their interests, write to legislators, and, in general, become involved in politics. Behavior that does not promote these ends should not be considered responsible.

At the organizational or societal level, proactive steps can be taken to develop more ethical and responsible organizations. Ideas for enhancing organizational and societal responsibility include posting codes of ethics in visible places, protecting whistle-blowers, enhancing individual autonomy, passing ethics legislation, and reversing trends of immorality in society. Developing an "inner check" to uphold standards can be a powerful means of ensuring responsible action. Alternatively, external controls can curb abuses. These external controls include legislation as well as organizational punishments or inducements. Organizations exert

influence through career advancement, pay raises, promotions, and nonmonetary recognition.

Inculcating values that support the public interest and constitutional democracy is possible. These values will support institutions that act as important checks on abuses of power. Abuses may be inevitable, but the fundamental question is the extent to which the built-in checks on egregious public sector misbehavior work. History is our guide for both optimistic and pessimistic sentiment.

Bibliography

Adams, Guy B., and Danny Balfour. 1999. *Unmasking Administrative Evil.* Thousand Oaks, CA: Sage.

Alexander, Herbert E. 1992. *Financing Politics: Money, Elections, and Political Reform.* 4th ed. Washington, DC: Congressional Quarterly.

Allswang, John M. 1977. *Bosses, Machines, and Urban Voters.* Rev. ed. Baltimore: Johns Hopkins University Press.

amarillo.com. 2007. "Chung's Admission Deserves Investigation," www.amarillo.com/stories/090297/deserve.html.

American National Election Studies. 2007. "The ANES Guide to Public Opinion and Electoral Behavior," www.electionstudies.org/nesguide/toptable/.

Amnesty International. 1975. *Report on Torture.* New York: Farrar, Straus and Giroux.

Annenberg Political Fact Check. 2007. "Democratic Group's Ad Revives 'AWOL' Allegations Against Bush," www.factcheck.org.

Associated Press. 2005, December 15. "Bush Accepts Sen. McCain's Torture Policy," www.msnbc.msn.com.

Baba, Mary. 2004. "Irish Immigrant Families in Mid-Late 19th-Century America." Yale-New Haven Teachers Institute. www.yale.edu/ynhti/curriculum/units/1990/5/90.05.07.x.html.

Babington, Charles. 2004, October 7. "DeLay Draws Third Rebuke." *Washington Post.* www.washingtonpost.com.

Babington, Charles, and Shailagh Murray. 2005, October 6. "Senate Supports Interrogation Limits." *Washington Post.* www.washingtonpost.com.

Banfield, Edward, and James Wilson. 1967. *City Politics.* Cambridge, MA: Harvard University Press.

Barnard, Chester. 1938. *The Functions of the Executive.* Cambridge, MA: Harvard University Press.

Bartlett, John, and Justin Kaplan. 2002. *Bartlett's Familiar Quotations.* 17th ed. Boston: Little, Brown.

Becker, Jo. 2007, June 25. "Murdoch, Ruler of a Vast Empire, Reaches Out for Even More." *New York Times.* www.nytimes.com/2007/06/25.

Belknap, Michael. 2002. *The Vietnam War on Trial: The My Lai Massacre and the Court-Martial of Lieutenant Calley.* Lawrence: University Press of Kansas.

Bentley, Arthur F. [1909] 1949. *The Process of Government.* Bloomington, IN: Principia Press.

Bernstein, Jake. 2005, April 1. "TRMPAC in Its Own Words," www.texaobserver.org.

Birnbaum, Jeffrey, and Jim VandeHei. 2005, October 3. "DeLay's Influence Transcends His Title." *Washington Post.* www.washingtonpost.com.

Bloch, Ernst. 1986. *Natural Law and Human Dignity.* Cambridge, MA: MIT Press.

Bowman, James. 2006. "The Ethical Professional: Cultivating Scruples." In West and Berman 2006, 55–68.

Box, Richard, and Deborah Sagen. 1998. "Working With Citizens: Breaking Down Barriers to Citizen Self-Governance." In King and Stivers 1998, 158–174.

Boy Scouts of America. 2008. "Boy Scout Oath, Law, Mottom and Slogan," www.scouting.org/factsheets/.

Braithwaite, Valerie, and Margaret Levi, eds. 1998. *Trust and Governance.* New York: Russell Sage.

Bremer, Francis J. 1993. *Puritanism: Transatlantic Perspectives on a Seventeenth-Century Anglo-American Faith.* Boston: Massachusetts Historical Society.

Bremer, Francis J., and Lynn A. Botelho, eds. 2005. *The World of John Winthrop: Essays on England and New England, 1588–1649.* Boston: Massachusetts Historical Society.

Brennan, Michael, and Steven Koven. 2007. "Hurricane Katrina: Preparedness, Response and the Politics Administration Dichotomy." In *Handbook of Crisis and Emergency Management*, ed. Ali Farazmand. New York: Marcel Dekker.

Brimelow, Peter. 1995. *Alien Nation: Common Sense About America's Immigration Disaster.* New York: Random House.

Brinkley, Douglas. 2006. *The Great Deluge*. New York: HarperCollins.

Bryce, James. [1893] 1972. "Setting the Stereotype." In *Urban Bosses, Machines, and Progressive Reformers*, ed. Bruce Stave, 3–10. Lexington, MA: D.C. Heath.

Burgstaller, Markus. 2005. *Theories of Compliance with International Law*. Leiden: Martinus Nijhoff.

Busby, Robert. 2001. *Defending the American Presidency: Clinton and the Lewinsky Scandal*. New York: Palgrave.

Callow, Alexander. 1966. *The Tweed Ring*. New York: Oxford University Press.

Carnevale, David G. 1995. *Trustworthy Government: Leadership and Management Strategies for Building Trust and High Performance*. San Francisco: Jossey-Bass.

Carter, Stephen. 1999. "A Chance to Reset Our Moral Course." In Fackre 1999, 169–176.

Chambliss, William, and Robert Seidman. 1982. *Law, Order, and Power*. 2nd ed. Reading, MA: Addison-Wesley.

Cigler, Allan J. 2006. "Interest Groups and Financing the 2004 Election." In Maglby, Corrado, and Patterson 2006, 149–182.

CNN. 2005, November 4. "'Can I Quit Now?' FEMA Chief Wrote as Katrina Raged," www.cnn.com/2005/US/11/03/brown.fema.emails.

Cohen, Adam, and Elisabeth Taylor. 2000. *American Pharaoh: Mayor Richard J. Daley—His Battle for Chicago and the Nation*. New York: Little, Brown.

Colson, Charles. 1989. *Against the Night*. Ann Arbor, MI: Servant Publications.

Commager, Henry Steele. 1950. *The American Mind: An Interpretation of American Thought and Character Since the 1880s*. New Haven: Yale University Press.

Cook, Fred J. 1973. *American Political Bosses and Machines*. New York: Franklin Watts.

Cooper, Terry. 1987. "Hierarchy, Virtue, and the Practice of Public Administration: A Perspective for Normative Ethics." *Public Administration Review* 47, no. 4: 320–328.

_____. 1991. *An Ethic of Citizenship for Public Administration*. Englewood Cliffs, NJ: Prentice Hall.

_____. 1998. *The Responsible Administrator*. 4th ed. San Francisco: Jossey-Bass.

_____. 2004. "Big Questions in Administrative Ethics: A Need for Focused Collaborative Effort." *Public Administration Review* 64, no. 4: 395–407.

Corrado, Anthony. 2003. "The Legislative Odyssey of BCRA." In Malbin 1984b, 21–39.

CQ Transcripts Wire. 2006. "Representative Tom DeLay Delivers His Farewell Address," http://washingtonpost.com.

Crèvecoeur, J. Hector. 2004. *Letters from an American Farmer*, Letter III, http://xroads.virginia.edu~HYPER/CREV/letter03.html.

Crowe, Michael B. 1977. *The Changing Profile of the Natural Law*. The Hague, Netherlands: Martinus Nijhoff.

d'Entréves, Alessandro P. 1961. *Natural Law: An Introduction to Legal Philosophy*. London: Hutchinson University Library.

DeLay, Tom, and Stephen Mansfield. 2007. *No Retreat, No Surrender*. New York: Penguin.

deLeon, Peter. 1993. *Thinking About Political Corruption*. Armonk, NY: M.E. Sharpe.

Denhardt, Kathryn. 1994. "Character Ethics and the Transformation of Governance." *International Journal of Public Administration* 17, no. 12: 23–35.

Department of Homeland Security. 2006, March. *A Performance Review of FEMA's Disaster Management Activities in Response to Hurricane Katrina*. Report OIG-06-32.

Dershowitz, Alan. 1998. *Sexual McCarthyism: Clinton, Starr, and the Emerging Constitutional Crisis*. New York: Basic Books.

_____. 2001, November 8. "Is There a Torturous Road to Justice?" *Los Angeles Times*. www.latimes.com/news/opinion.

Dewey, John, and James Tufts. 1932. *Ethics*. New York: Henry Holt.

Dicey, A.V. 1885. Introduction to the Study of the Law of the Constitution. London: Macmillan. www.constitution.org/cmt/avd/law.

Dobbs, Michael. 2004, August 22. "Swift Boat Accounts Incomplete." *Washington Post*. www.washingtonpost.com/wp-dyn/articles/A21239-2004Aug21.html.

Dobel, Patrick. 1990. "Integrity in the Public Service," *Public Administration Review* 50, no. 3: 354–366.

_____. 1998. *Public Integrity*. Baltimore: Johns Hopkins University Press.

_____. 2006. "Political Prudence and the Ethics of Leadership." In West and Berman 2006, 55–68.

Dubose, Lou, and Jan Reid. 2006. *The Hammer Comes Down: The Nasty, Brutish and Shortened Political Life of Tom DeLay*. New York: Public Affairs.

Dunn, Richard. 1962. *Puritans and Yankees: The Winthrop Dynasty of New England 1630–1717*. Princeton, NJ: Princeton University Press.

Dworkin, Ronald. 1985. *A Matter of Principle*. Cambridge, MA: Harvard University Press.

Dyson, Michael. 2006. *Come Hell or High Water: Hurricane Katrina and the Color of Disaster*. New York: Basic Books.

Dyzenhaus, David. 2003. "The Justice of the Common Law: Judges, Democracy and the Limits of the Rule of Law." In

The Rule of Law, ed. Cheryl Saunders and Katherine Le Roy, 21–51. Sydney, Australia: Federation Press.

Ellis, Richard. 1993. *American Political Culture.* New York: Oxford University Press.

Elshtain, Jean B. 1999. "Politics and Forgiveness: The Clinton Case." In Facke 1999, 169–176.

Fackre, Gabriel, ed. 1999. *Judgment Day at the White House.* Grand Rapids, MI: William B. Eerdmans.

Fineman, Howard. 2005, September 19. "A Storm-Tossed Boss." *Newsweek.* www.msnbc.msn.com.

Finer, Herbert. 1936. "Better Government Personnel." *Political Science Quarterly* 51, no. 4: 569–599.

———. 1941. "Administrative Responsibility in Democratic Government." *Public Administration Review* 1: 335–350.

Fischer, David H. 1989. *Albion's Seed: Four British Folkways in America.* New York: Oxford University Press.

Fonda, Daren, and Rita Healy. 2005, September 5. "How Reliable Is Brown's Resume?" *Time.* www.time.com/time/nation/article.

Ford, Gerald. 1974, August 9. "Gerald R. Ford's Remarks on Taking the Oath of Office as President," www.ford.utexas.edu.

Fox Facts: Hurricane Katrina Damage. 2006. www.foxnews.com.

Friedrich, Carl. 1935. "Responsible Government Service under the American Constitution." In *Problems in the American Public Service*, ed. C.J. Friedrich, W. Beyer, S. Spero, J. Miller, and G. Graham, 3–74. New York: McGraw-Hill.

Fry, Brian R. 1989. *Mastering Public Administration: From Max Weber to Dwight Waldo.* Chatham, NJ: Chatham House.

Fukuyama, Francis. 1995. *Trust: The Social Virtues and the Creation of Prosperity.* New York: Free Press.

Galloway, John. 1970. *The Gulf of Tonkin Resolution.* Rutherford, NJ: Fairleigh Dickinson University Press.

Garofalo, Charles, and Dean Geuras. 1999. *Ethics in the Public Sector: The Moral Mind at Work.* Washington, DC: Georgetown University Press.

Gateway Pundit. 2005. http://gatewaypundit.blogspot.com.

Gaus, John M. 1936. "The Responsibility of Public Administrators." In *The Frontiers of Public Administration,* ed. John Gaus, Leonard White, and Marshall Dimock, 3–74. Chicago: University of Chicago Press.

Gawthrop, Louis C. 1998. *Public Service and Democracy: Ethical Imperatives for the 21st Century.* New York: Chatham House.

Genovese, Michael A. 1999. *The Watergate Crisis.* Westport, CT: Greenwood Press.

Gershen, Martin. 1971. *Destroy or Die: The True Story of My Lai.* New Rochelle, NY: Arlington House.

Geuras, Dean, and Charles Garofalo. 2005. *Practical Ethics in Public Administration.* 2nd ed. Vienna, VA: Management Concepts.

Gilderbloom, John. 2008. *Invisible City: Poverty, Housing, and New Urbanism.* Austin: University of Texas Press.

Girl Scouts. 2008. "Girl Scout Promise and Law," www.girlscouts.org/program/.

Gonyea, Don. 2006, September 14. "Powell Says Bush's Tribunal Plan Would Backfire," www.npr.org/templates/story.

Goodsell, Charles. 1990. "Public Administration and the Public Interest." In *Refounding Public Administration*, ed. Gary Wamsley et al., 96–113. Newbury Park, CA: Sage.

Gordon, Stacy B. 2005. *Campaign Contributions and Legislative Voting: A New Approach.* New York: Routledge.

Gore, Al. 1993. *From Red Tape to Results: Creating a Government That Works Better and Costs Less.* Report of the National Performance Review. New York: Random House.

Goulden, Joseph C. 1969. *Truth Is the First Casualty: The Gulf of Tonkin Affair.* Chicago: Rand McNally.

Green, Mark. 2002. *Selling Out: How Big Corporate Money Buys Elections, Rams Through Legislation, and Betrays Our Democracy.* New York: Regan Books.

Greenhouse, Linda, and David Kirkpatrick. 2007, June 25. "Justices Loosen Ad Restrictions in Campaign Finance Law." *New York Times.* www.nytimes.com.

Gurr-Ayre, Miriam. 2004. "Can the War Against Terror Justify the Use of Force in Interrogations?" In *Torture: A Collection*, ed. Sanford Levinson, 183–198. New York: Oxford University Press.

Hammer, Richard. 1970. *One Morning in the War: The Tragedy at Son My.* New York: Coward-McCann.

Hammond, Jeffrey. 2000. *The American Puritan Elegy: A Literary and Cultural Study.* New York: Cambridge University Press.

Harding, Russell. 1998. "Trust in Government." In Braithwaite and Levi 1998, 9–27.

Harrigan, John J., and Ronald K. Vogel. 2003. *Political Change in the Metropolis.* 7th ed. New York: Longman.

Harrison, Brian. 2005, September. "Torture and Corporal Punishment as a Problem in Catholic Theology," www.rtforum.org/lt.

Hart, David. 1994. "Administration and the Ethics of Virtue: In All Things, Choose First for Good Character and Then for Technical Expertise." In *Handbook of Administrative Ethics*, ed. Terry Cooper, 107–123. New York: Marcel Dekker.

Hayek, Friedrich. 1944. *Road to Serfdom.* Chicago: University of Chicago Press.

Herrnson, Paul S. 2006. "Financing the 2004 Congressional Elections." In Maglby, Corrado, and Patterson 2006, 149–182.

Hersh, Seymour. 1970. *My Lai 4: A Report on the Massacre and Its Aftermath.* New York: Random House.

———. 1972. *Coverup: The Army's Secret Investigation of the Massacre at My Lai 4.* New York: Random House.

———. 2004a, May 10. "Torture at Abu Ghraib." *New Yorker.* www.newyorker.com/archive/.

———. 2004b, May 17. "Chain of Command." *New Yorker.* www.newyorker.com/archive/.

———. 2004c, May 24. "The Gray Zone." *New Yorker.* www.newyorker.com/archive/.

Hershkowitz, Leo. 1977. *Tweed's New York: Another Look.* Garden City, NY: Anchor Press/Doubleday.

Heymann, Philip. 2002, February 16. "Torture Should Not Be Authorized." *Boston Globe*, A15.

Hofstadter, Richard. 1955. *The Age of Reform.* New York: Alfred A. Knopf.

Hsu, Spenser. 2005. "Brown Defends FEMA's Efforts." *Washington Post.* www.washingtonpost.com.

Human Rights Watch. 2004. "The Road to Abu Ghraib: A Policy to Evade International Law." www.hrw.org/reports/2004/.

Hunt, Albert R. 2007. "Sham Charges Against a War Hero." www.opinionjournal.com.

Huntington, Samuel P. 2004. *Who Are We? The Challenge to America's National Identity.* New York: Simon & Schuster.

Hyde, Henry. 1999. "The Impeachment Trial." www.pbs.org/newshour/impeachment/trial/hyde.

Ink, Dwight. 2006. "An Analysis of the House Select Committee and White House Reports on Hurricane Katrina." *Public Administration Review* 66, no. 6: 800–807.

International Red Cross. n.d. "Geneva Conventions," www.redcross.lv/en/conventions.htm.

Jeffersonian Cyclopedia. n.d. "Public Confidence." http://etext.lib.virginia.edu/jefferson/quotations/foley.

Johnson, Ronald, and Gary Libecap. 1994. *The Federal Civil Service System and the Problem of Bureaucracy: The Economics and Politics of Institutional Change.* Chicago: University of Chicago Press.

Josephson, Michael. 2006. "The Six Pillars of Character." In West and Berman 2006, 11–23.

Kaufman, Herbert. 1956. "Emerging Conflicts in the Doctrines of Public Administration." *American Political Science Review* 50, no. 4: 1057–1073.

Kilpatrick, Carroll. 1973, November 18. "Nixon Tells Editors, I'm Not a Crook." *Washington Post.*

King, Cheryl S., and Camilla Stivers, eds. 1998. *Government Is Us: Public Administration in an Anti-Government Era.* Thousand Oaks, CA: Sage.

Koven, Steven G. 1999. *Public Budgeting in the United States: The Cultural and Ideological Setting.* Washington, DC: Georgetown University Press.

———. 2003. "Trust in Government: Lessons from the Clinton Impeachment." *International Journal of Public Administration* 26, no. 2: 197–212.

———. 2007. "Patronage in the Commonwealth of Kentucky." *Public Integrity* 9, no. 3: 285–299.

Ku, Charlotte, and Paul F. Diehl. 1998. "International Law as Operating and Normative Systems: An Overview." In *International Law: Classic and Contemporary Readings*, ed. Charlotte Ku and Paul F. Diehl, 3–15. Boulder, CO: Lynne Rienner.

Lammers, Nancy, ed. 1982. *Dollar Politics.* 3rd ed. Washington, DC: Congressional Quarterly.

Langbein, John H. 2005. "The Legal History of Torture." In Roth and Worden 2005, 93–103.

Legal Theory Blog. 2006. http://lsolum.typepad.com/legaltheory/2006/12/legal_theory_le_1.html.

Levi, Margaret. 1998. "A State of Trust." In Braithwaite and Levi 1998, 9–27.

Linder, Doug. n.d. "An Introduction to the My Lai Courts-Martial," University of Missouri-Kansas City School of Law. www.law.umkc.edu/faculty/projects/ftrials.mylai/.

Lindsay, A.D. [1943] 1962. *The Modern Democratic State.* New York: Oxford University Press.

Lippmann, Walter. [1927] 1993. *The Phantom Public.* New Brunswick, NJ: Transaction.

Lowi, Theodore. 1981, September. "The Intelligent Person's Guide to Political Corruption," *Public Affairs*, Series 81, Bulletin 82.

Lyndon Baines Johnson Library and Museum. 1966. "President Lyndon B. Johnson's Annual Message to Congress on the State of the Union," www.lbjlib.utexas.edu/Johnson/archives.

Lynch, Denis. 1927. *"Boss Tweed": The Story of a Grim Generation.* New York: Boni & Liveright.

Maglby, David, Anthony Corrado, and Kelly Patterson, eds. 2006. *Financing the 2004 Election.* Washington, DC: Brookings Institution Press.

Malanczuk, Peter. 1997. *Akehurst's Modern Introduction to International Law.* 7th ed. London: George Allen and Unwin.

Malbin, Michael J. 1984a. "Introduction." In Malbin 1984b, 1–10.

———, ed. 1984b. *Money and Politics in the United States: Financing Elections in the 1980s.* Chatham, NJ: Chatham House.

———. 2003. "Thinking About Reform." In *Life After Reform: When the Bipartisan Campaign Reform Act Meets*

Politics, ed. Michael Malbin, 3–20. Lanham, MD: Rowman & Littlefield.

Mandelbaum, Seymour. 1965. *Boss Tweed's New York*. New York: J. Wiley.

Maritain, Jacques. 1947. *The Rights of Man and Natural Law*. Trans. by Doris C. Anson. New York: Charles Scribner's Sons.

Mayer, Jane. 2005, February 14. "Outsourcing Torture," *The New Yorker*. www.newyorker.com/archives/2005/02.

McCain, John. 2005. "Statement of Senator John McCain Amendment on Army Field Manual," http://mccain.senate.gov/press_office.

McCoy, Alfred W. 2006. *A Question of Torture: CIA Interrogation, From the Cold War to the War on Terror*. New York: Henry Holt.

McDonald, James J. 1907. *Life In Old Virginia*. Norfolk, VA: The Old Virginia Publishing Company.

McDougal, Walter A. 2004. *Freedom Just Around the Corner: A New American History, 1585–1828*. New York: HarperCollins.

McLaughlin, Mike. 2004 March. "Anatomy of a Crisis," *American Heritage Magazine*, 55, www.americanheritage.com/articles/magazine.

McNamara, Robert. 1995. *In Retrospect: The Tragedy and Lessons of Vietnam*. New York: Random House.

Merton, Robert. [1957] 1976. "The Latent Functions of the Machine: A Sociologist's View." In *The City Boss in America*, ed. Alexander Callow, 23–33. New York: Oxford University Press.

Mestrovic, S.G. 2007. *The Trials of Abu Ghraib: An Expert Witness Account of Shame and Honor*. Boulder, CO: Paradigm.

Moreno, Sylvia, and Jeffrey Smith. 2005, May 27. "Treasurer of DeLay Group Broke Texas Election Law." *Washington Post*. www.washingtonpost.com.

Mosher, Frederick C. 1974. *Watergate: Implications for Responsible Government*. New York: Basic Books.

National Security Archives. 2004. "The Gulf of Tonkin Incident 40 Years Later." www.gwu.edu.

———. 2005. "Tonkin Gulf Intelligence 'Skewed.'" www.gwu.edu.

Neumann, Michael. 2002. *The Rule of Law: Politicizing Ethics*. Burlington, VT: Ashgate.

New York Times. 2005, March 18. "Two Years Later," www.nytimes.com/2005/03/18/opinion.

Niskanen, William. 1971. *Bureaucracy and Representative Government*. Chicago: Aldine.

Olson, James S., ed. 1999. *Historical Dictionary of the 1960s*. Westport, CT: Greenwood Press.

Opensecrets.org. 2007. "Top PACs." www.opensecrets.org/pacs/topacs.asp?cycle=2008&Type=E.

Osborne, David, and Ted Gaebler. 1992. *Reinventing Government: How the Entrepreneurial Spirit Is Transforming the Public Sector*. Reading, MA: Addison-Wesley.

Pateman, Carole. 1970. *Participation and Democratic Theory*. Cambridge: Cambridge University Press.

Perl, Peter. 2001, May 13. "Absolute Truth." *Washington Post*. www.washingtonpost.com.

Pitney, John P. 1995, November 13. "The Tocqueville Fraud," *The Weekly Standard*, www.tocqueville.org/pitney.htm.

Priest, Dana. 2005, November 2. "CIA Holds Terror Suspects in Secret Prisons," *Washington Post*. www.washingtonpost.com.

Rainey, Hal. 2003. *Understanding and Managing Public Organizations*. 3rd ed. San Francisco: Jossey-Bass.

Rakove, Milton. 1975. *Don't Make No Waves, Don't Back No Losers*. Bloomington: Indiana University Press.

Rawls, John. 1993. *Political Liberalism*. New York: Columbia University Press.

———. 1999. *A Theory of Justice*. Rev. ed. Oxford UK: Oxford University Press.

Raz, Joseph. 1979. *The Authority of Law: Essays on Law and Morality*. Oxford: Oxford University Press.

Reid, John Phillip. 2004. *Rule of Law: The Jurisprudence of Liberty in the Seventeenth and Eighteenth Centuries*. DeKalb: Northern Illinois University Press.

Richman, Sheldon. 2001. "The Role of Law, R.I.P.," www.fff.org/freedom/0401d.asp.

Riordon, William L. 1948. *Plunkitt of Tammany Hall*. New York: Alfred A. Knopf.

Rohr, John. 1989. *Ethics for Bureaucrats*. 2nd ed. New York: Marcel Dekker.

Rommen, Heinrich A. 1948. *The Natural Law: A Study in Legal and Social History and Philosophy*. Trans. by Thomas R. Hanley. St. Louis: B. Herder.

Rosenthal, Harry F. 1997. "The Burglar That Brought Down a President."*Houston Chronicle Interactive*. www.chron.com/content.

Ross, James. 2005. "A History of Torture." In Roth and Worden 2005, 3–17.

Roth, Kenneth, and Minky Worden, eds. 2005. *Torture: Does It Make Us Safer? Is It Ever OK?* New York: New Press.

Rousseau, Jean-Jacques. [1762] 1994. *The Social Contract*. Trans. by Christopher Betts. Oxford: Oxford University Press.

Sack, John. 1971. *Lieutenant Calley: His Own Story*. New York: Viking Press.

Schattschneider, Elmer E. 1952. "Political Parties and the Public Interest." *Annals of the American Academy of Political and Social Science* 280: 18–26.

Schein, Edgar. 1985. *Organizational Culture and Leadership: A Dynamic View.* San Francisco: Jossey-Bass.

Schubert, Glendon. 1957. "The Public Interest in Administrative Decision-Making: Theorem, Theosophy, or Theory." *American Political Science Review* 51 (June): 114–115.

———. 1960. *The Public Interest.* Glencoe, IL: Free Press.

———. 1962. "Is There a Public Interest Theory?" In *Nomos V: The Public Interest,* ed. Carl Friedrich, 162–176. New York: Atherton Press.

Schumpeter, Joseph. [1943] 1981. *Capitalism, Socialism and Democracy.* London: George Allen & Unwin.

Shaw, Malcolm N. 1997. *International Law.* 4th ed. Cambridge: Cambridge University Press.

Simon, Yves R. 1965. *The Tradition of Natural Law: A Philosopher's Reflections,* ed. Vukan Kuic. New York: Fordham University Press.

Smith, Rogers M. 1988. "The 'American Creed' and American Identity: The Limits of Liberal Citizenship in the United States." *Western Political Quarterly* 41, no. 2: 225–251.

Sophocles. 1970. *The Theban Plays.* Translated by E.F. Whatling. Harmondsworth: Penguin.

Sowell, Thomas. 1981. *Ethnic America: A History.* New York: Basic Books.

Stein, Lana. 1991. *Holding Bureaucrats Accountable: Politicians and Professionals in St. Louis.* Tuscaloosa: University of Alabama Press.

Stern, Philip M. 1992. *Still the Best Congress Money Can Buy.* Washington, DC: Regnery Gateway.

Svara, James. 2007. *The Ethics Primer for Public Administrators in Government and Nonprofit Organizations.* Sudbury, MA: Jones and Bartlett.

Tamanaha, Brian Z. 2004. *On the Rule of Law: History, Politics, Theory.* Cambridge: Cambridge University Press.

Taylor, Frederick W. [1916] 1996. "The Principles of Scientific Management." In *Classics of Organization Theory,* ed. Jay Shafritz and J. Steven Ott, 66–77. Fort Worth, TX: Harcourt Brace.

Thayer, George. 1973. *Who Shakes the Money Tree? American Campaign Practices from 1789 to the Present.* New York: Simon and Schuster.

Thomas Jefferson on Politics & Government. n.d. "Majority Rule," http://etext.virginia.edu/jefferson/quotations/jeff0500,htm.

Thompson, Dennis. 1970. *The Democratic Citizen.* Cambridge: Cambridge University Press.

———. 2002. *Just Elections: Creating a Fair Electoral Process in the United States.* Chicago: University of Chicago Press.

Thompson, Nicholas. 2005, April 7. "The Tom Dellay Scandals." *Slate Magazine.* http://slate.msn.com.

Thompson, Victor. 1975. *Without Sympathy or Enthusiasm: The Problem of Administrative Compassion.* Tuscaloosa: University of Alabama Press.

Time. 1972. "More Fumes from the Watergate Affair," www.time.com/time/magazine/article.

Time Inc. 2005. *Hurricane Katrina: The Storm That Changed America.* New York: Time Inc. Home Entertainment.

Timney, Mary. 1998. "Overcoming Administrative Barriers to Citizen Participation: Citizens as Partners, Not Adversaries." In King and Stivers, 88–101.

Tocqueville, Alexis de. [1836] 1956. *Democracy in America.* New York: Mentor Books.

Townsend, Frances F. 2006, February. *The Federal Response to Hurricane Katrina: Lessons Learned.* Washington, DC: Government Printing Office.

Truman, David B. 1951. *The Governmental Process.* New York: Alfred A. Knopf.

UN Office of the High Commissioner for Human Rights. 2007a. "International Covenant on Civil and Political Rights." www.unhchr.ch/html.

———. 2007b. "Convention Against Torture and Other Cruel, Inhuman or Degrading Treatment or Punishment," www.unhchr.ch/html.

U.S. Department of Commerce, U.S. Census Bureau. 2004. "Ancestry: 2000," www.census.gov/prod/2004/pubs/c2kbr-35.pdf.

van Heerden, Ivor, and Mike Bryan. 2006. *The Storm.* New York: Viking Press.

Van Wart, Montgomery. 1998. *Changing Public Sector Values.* New York: Garland.

Waldo, Dwight. 1984. *The Administrative State.* 2nd ed. New York: Holmes & Meier.

Weber, Max. [1947] 1964. *The Theory of Social and Economic Organization,* ed. T.C. Parsons. New York: Free Press.

Wertheimer, Fred. 2007. "Unless We Ban Soft Money." *Washington Post.* www.washingtonpost.com.

West, Jonathan, and Evan Berman, eds. 2006. *The Ethics Edge.* 2nd ed. Washington, DC: ICMA Press.

Wikipedia. 2006a. "Stoicism," http://en.wikipedia.org/wiki/Stoicism.

———. 2006b. "Rule of Law," http://en.wikipedia.org/wiki/Rule_of_law.

———. 2007a. "Swift Vets and POWs for Truth," http://en.wikipedia.org/wiki/Swift_Boat_Veterans_for_Truth.

———. 2007b. "Swiftboating," http://en.wikipedia.org/wiki/Swiftboating.

———. 2007c. "Texans for Truth," http://enwikipedia.org/wiki/Texans_for_Truth.

_____. 2007d. "Tom DeLay," http://en.wikipedia.org/wiki/Tom_DeLay.

_____. 2007. "Canuck Letter," http://enwikipedia.org/wiki/Canuck_Letter.

Will, George. 2007, June 27. "Goodbye, McCain-Feingold?" *Louisville Courier Journal*.

Wilson, Andrew. 2006. "Oedipus: The Theban Story and Its Interpretation," www.users.globalnet.co.uk/~loxias/myth.htm.

Wilson, James Q. 1989. *Bureaucracy: What Government Agencies Do and Why They Do It*. New York: Basic Books.

Wilson, Woodrow. [1887] 1991. "The Study of Administration." In *Classics of Public Administration*, ed. Jay Shafritz and Albert Hyde, 11–24. Pacific Grove, CA: Brooks Cole.

Windchy, Eugene G. 1971. *Tonkin Gulf*. Garden City, NY: Doubleday.

Winship, Michael P. 2005. *The Times and Trials of Anne Hutchinson: Puritans Divided*. Lawrence: University of Kansas Press.

Wolf, Julie. 2007. "The Iran-Contra Affair," www.pbs.org/wgbh/amex/reagan.

Woodward, Bob, and Carl Bernstein. 1972a, June 10. "GOP Security Aide Among Five Arrested in Bugging Affair." *Washington Post*. www.washingtonpost.com.

———. 1972b, October 10. "FBI Finds Nixon Aides Sabotaged Democrats." *Washington Post*. www.washingtonpost.com.

Wright, Quincy. 1961. *The Role of International Law in the Elimination of War*. Manchester, UK: Manchester University Press.

www.civilwarhome.com/liebercode.htm. n.d. "The Lieber Code of 1863."

Zelinsky, Wilbur. 1973. *The Cultural Geography of the United States*. Englewood Cliffs, NJ: Prentice Hall.

Zernike, Kate, and Jim Rutenberg. 2004, August 20. "Friendly Fire: The Birth of an Anti-Kerry Ad." *New York Times*.

Index

Index

About the Author

Steven G. Koven is a graduate of City College of New York (BBA), Baruch College, City University of New York (MBA), and the University of Florida (PhD). In 1969 and 1970 he served as a mortorman in Vietnam, where he observed numerous acts of ethical, as well as unethical, behavior. He is currently a professor of urban and public affairs at the University of Louisville. He lives in Louisville, Kentucky, with his wife and daughter.